P9-EER-364

By Thomas R. Brooks

Clint: A Biography of a Labor Intellectual, Clinton S. Golden, 1978

Communications Workers of America 1977

Walls Come Tumbling Down 1974

Picket Lines and Bargaining Tables 1968

Toil and Trouble 1964

C L I N T

CLINT

A BIOGRAPHY OF A LABOR INTELLECTUAL Clinton S. Golden

BY THOMAS R. BROOKS

ATHENEUM
New York
1978

Library of Congress Cataloging in Publication Data

Brooks, Thomas R
Clint: a biography of a labor intellectual, Clinton S. Golden.
Bibliography: p.
Includes index.
1. Golden, Clinton Strong, 1888–1961. 2. Labor and laboring classes–United States–Biography. 3. Trade-unions–United States–Officials and employees–Biography. 4. Industrial relations–United States–History. I. Title.
HD8073.G58B76 1978 331.88'16'900924 [B] 78-3152
ISBN 0-689-10923-7

Published simultaneously in Canada by McClelland and Stewart Ltd.
Manufactured by American Book–Stratford Press, Inc.
Saddle Brook, New Jersey
Designed by Harry Ford
First Edition

TO

AUNT MARION,

MRS. RALPH E. BOOTHBY

For a lifetime of love and understanding

Introduction

Clinton S. Golden was a founder and vice-president of one of the country's largest unions, the United Steelworkers of America, who became a leading advocate of civil relations between labor and management, an accord based on the give-and-take of collective bargaining. Golden was among the first to recognize that industrial democracy begins when employers recognize the right of workers to organize. From that follows the right to bargain collectively through freely chosen representatives. These rights are now guaranteed by our government.

It was not always so. The United States has enjoyed remarkable industrial peace for nearly four decades. There have been strikes, angry confrontations between labor and management, but few, if any, can compare with the bitter outbreaks that marked the preceding seventy-five years of industrial strife. Golden, a veteran of those years, was a major figure in the development of constructive and, whenever possible, peaceable industrial relations in our country.

Collective bargaining gives laboring men and women some say about the conditions of their employment. It takes place on a constantly changing frontier as employers and employees, each in their own way, respond to changing economic and social conditions. Union-management contracts were once relatively simple documents, embodying recognition, a wage increase and a few rules governing seniority. Today, as a consequence of relentless pressures from the factory floor, bargainers discuss—and settle—an extraordinary range of questions having to do with vacations and sick leaves, shop rules and working conditions of all kinds, grievances, safety, maternity leaves, health benefits, severance pay and pensions. While workers recognize that management has its prerogatives, the nature and limits of those prerogatives are periodically questioned. There is an exchange of ideas, a give-and-take over material gains and a participation in decisions affecting all parties to the processes.

Today, there is a new interest in humanizing the workplace, in attaining job satisfaction and in securing worker participation in decision-making. There are experiments in work enhancement, self-discipline and group planning, and in improving the job environment. In part, this is due to rising expectations about life and work, but it also rises out of the character of modern production, distribution and service. The environmental crisis and a world-wide economic crisis give a biting edge to these concerns, a new awareness of productivity, the necessary coin for all other gains.

These are matters about which Clint Golden was imaginatively thinking, acting and writing over thirty years ago. He was, however, more than a theoretician. He conceived and directed early experimental programs developing concepts of worker participation still valid today. Productivity committees, accountability in the professions and among white-collar workers, whether in the private or public sector, are precisely what he urged as essential to cooperation between labor and management. He developed over the years a profound faith in the creative role that working people can play in almost every aspect of life. He also had an unwavering belief in the constructive role that the labor movement can play in resolving the problems of the larger community and the imperative necessity that it do so. He never once forgot, however, that the union—and much of the worker's life—is rooted in the workplace, and that it is there that industrial democracy contributes to a meaningful life for working men and women. Collective bargaining, he recognized had to concern itself not only with the cut of the pie, but also with increasing the size of the pie, lest it end in a frustrating stalemate, eventual chaos and the irreparable rupture of the fabric of our democracy.

Golden's career was unique. He was a self-educated worker as were most of his contemporaries in union leadership. However, he was much more an intellectual and, unlike most union leaders, he did not rise up through the ranks of a single union or craft. He started his working life as a mine-boy; his education as a follower of the Knights of Labor, that all-embracing holy order that dared dream of a cooperative commonwealth for industrial America. Golden became a craftsman, a Debsian railroad fireman and, later, a machinist. He got his graduate training in the pre-World War I socialist movement. During the 1920s he was agitator and educator for "amalgamation," or what later became the industrial unionism of the 1930s. He helped shape the philosophy and policies of Brookwood Labor College, a radical intellectual attempt at reshaping the character of American labor in the decade of "Normalcy." As the New Deal and our present form of labor relations took shape, Golden gained new experiences and insight as one of the new professionals—the third-party arbitrators, conciliators, fact-finders and mediators—provided by government to ensure collective bargaining. As one of the first regional directors of the National Labor Relations Board, he uncovered the facts that went into the Supreme Court case upholding the constitutionality of our industrial relations law. John L. Lewis called Golden back into the service of the labor movement as the northeastern regional director of the CIO's great effort to organize the steel industry. As a member of the Steel Workers Organizing Committee, he was the constitutional and bargaining architect of the United Steelworkers. Few union leaders have had so broad an experience, so great an education.

He drew upon this background to counsel the government during World War II on manpower problems. *The Dynamics of Industrial Democracy*, written with Harold J. Ruttenberg, became an industrial-relations bible for students crowding college labor-relations courses in the immediate postwar period. Golden was the chief labor advisor to the European Recovery Program, popularly known as the Marshall Plan. Russell W. Davenport, editor of *Fortune*, called him "the dean of the American labor movement." Golden became a crusader for peaceful and fruitful industrial relations, instigating, among other developments, the National Planning Association's monumental study, *The Causes of Industrial Peace*.

This book is the story of Golden's life. But it is not a full biography. Golden was a reticent man, and much of his private, inner life remains just that. Nonetheless, he was a labor intellectual who expressed his ideas in writing, and in action. So, what we get from his life is some insight into the transformation of a Debsian class-confronting, quasi-syndicalist industrial unionist into a highly sophisticated proponent of an industrial democracy based on a worker-management partnership. It is an individual development that parallels, indeed, is involved in, the corresponding change within our society from hostility toward and rejection of unions to acceptance and recognition. To the extent that individual experience can explain the whole of history, Golden's life explains the history of labor over some three-quarters of a century.

Acknowledgments

WHEN I became interested in the labor movement shortly after World War II, I heard much of Clint Golden though, unhappily, I never met him. For the present opportunity, therefore, I am grateful to Henry Fleisher, who suggested the subject of this biography; Earl Bourdon and Tom Breslin, old friends active in the steelworkers union who encouraged me to go ahead; and, especially, to Frank Fernbach, who chivied me on, helped to arrange the necessary financial assistance and without whom I doubt that there would be a Golden biography.

For financial aid I am indebted to the Ford Foundation, the Clinton S. Golden Lodge of the United Steelworkers of America, the United Steelworkers of America, the National Planning Association and the Harvard University Trade Union Program.

I want to thank, too, Olive H. Golden, who shared her memories of her mother and father; Mark and Helen Norton Starr, who revived Brookwood days for me; Katherine Ellickson and Mrs. David Saposs, who graciously shared their Brookwood Golden memories; P. Alston Waring, who served as my guide to Solebury; I. W. Abel, Meyer Bernstein, David J. McDonald, Tom Murray, Harold J. Ruttenberg and Gertrude

Ruttenberg, whose recollections enrich this book; and D. Allan Strachan, whose keen observations also helped.

Mae S. Smith, who deciphered Golden's crabbed handwriting and typed his diaries; Ronald L. Filippelli, who guided me through the excellent labor archives at the Pennsylvania State University library; Alice M. Hoffman, who opened the Oral History Project; Dr. Benjamin Barkas; John Franklin Correll; Seymour Martin Lipset; John Miller; Raymond W. Pasnick; Frederick Smith; and Robert Schrank: each was helpful and to all, my gratitude is heartfelt.

Knox Burger, my agent deserves the best for his invaluable assistance; Barbara Campo, for rescuing me from grievous spelling errors and grammatical infelicities; and my wife, Harriet, for her loving patience.

Contents

Apprentice 3

Journeyman Fireman 20

Journeyman Machinist 39

Brookwood 65

Travels for Brookwood 87

Brookwood: Last Journey 108

Mediator 128

SWOC 158

Workers' Tribune 186

Causes of Industrial Peace 224

Mission to Greece 249

Mentor 315

WORKS CITED 353

INDEX 357

CLINT

Apprentice

THE REVEREND LAZARUS GOLDEN waited three months after the birth of his son before purchasing a ruled Keystone Notebook to write, "with God's help I would . . . improve a few spare moments . . . to call as far as possible . . . to remembrance many of the ways in which God has been leading me, and at the same time to leave behind me when I am gone something which may be a comfort and a source of encouragement unto my children and the friends who may live to mourn for me when I am gone." Golden had reason for not plunging into his memoirs on the birth of his son, for infants often died shortly after birth and his generation was one of survivors; he and a nephew were the only ones left of a large family "to perpetuate the Golden name." He had lost his first wife to the fevers of the time and considered himself, in his mid-fifties, fortunate to have married again, to a woman still in her thirties, handsome, of a good Yankee family and healthy. Indeed, he was so pleased that he named his son Clinton Strong Golden, the first name after his wife's hometown in upstate New York, where they had met, the middle after her family, as was the New England custom.

Lucy A. Strong was a descendant of Jonathan Edwards, the great New England divine and Calvinist theologian. Her grandfather, Nathan Strong, was among the early settlers of Clinton,

New York, "the first village founded by New Englanders on their way westward." He was born in Southbury, Connecticut, before the American Revolution, moved west to farm the fertile soil of the Mohawk Valley in 1805, and died, during the second year of the Civil War, at ninety-four. His fourth son, Selah, born of a second wife during the War of 1812, also farmed in Clinton. In 1839, Selah married Lucinda Wakely, the daughter of farmers in the neighboring town of New Hartford, and fathered, over the next eighteen years, nine children, two of whom died in their infancy. Lucy was the seventh child, born on August 12, 1853, at the old Strong homestead on College Hill. Her surviving brothers all became farmers, though one apparently tried to escape the family fate. Charles Augustus Strong enlisted as a private in the 115th Regiment, New York Volunteers, in 1863, fought in Florida, at Fort Fisher and before Richmond. He joined the regular army after the Civil War but soon left to return to Clinton to farm. Lucy's sisters married farmers from round about Clinton, but she waited.

Why, and what were her expectations? We do not know, though we do know that women married young then. But Lucy became a woman during the disturbed years following the Civil War, when many of the young men were either dead, wounded or off to the west. Her sister, Adelaide, a year older, married at sixteen, three years after the war, but another, Emmaline, who turned twenty mid-war, married at twenty-seven. Lucy did not marry until she was thirty-four. In any event, surely it was a strange meeting, the stuff of fiction, between a Yankee near-spinster and an elderly widowed preacher from South Carolina.

"I have been a sojourner in a strange land." The Reverend Lazarus Golden may have echoed Moses at Midian often, for he had preached across New York State for nearly thirty years by the time he came to Clinton to minister to the town's tiny

Baptist flock. What made him so singular a man, however, was not his restless preaching across the face of New York but the fact that he was something of a stranger in his own land, a Southern Baptist preacher who had chosen to begin his ministry among the colored freedmen of his native state. It was not the expected choice of a graduate of a college founded and headed by an ardent secessionist.

We do not know if the South Carolina Goldens owned slaves; perhaps so, perhaps not. A modern student of the social structure of revolutionary America estimates that three out of five South Carolinian whites were farmers; and four out of five farmers held property worth at least £200; of the typical poor low-country planters, half held slaves. Reverend Golden makes no mention of slaves nor of slavery.

He does, however, tell us something of the Golden ancestry, evoking Crèvecoeur's definition of an American, "that strange mixture of blood, which you will find in no other country." Lazarus's mother was of Scottish and Welsh parentage; his father's family was, for the times, exotic as he noted in his memoirs: "two bloods mingled in my father's family—one was a fierce or fiery blood, inherited from the Spanish or Portuguese. The other was a sober, thoughtful, pious blood inherited from the thoughtful and religious Germans." His paternal grandmother was a Sophia Pulaski. "I can't say she was related to General Pulaski who fell in defense of Savannah," Golden commented, "but I think she was." Her mother, however, was of Dutch or German extraction, "a pious woman and a very devoted member of the Lutheran church." Little is known of the Goldens ("my father only talked of relatives on his mother's side of the family"), but the original immigrant apparently came from Belfast sometime before the American revolution.

John Golden, Lazarus's father, was a native-born South Carolinian. He was "a blacksmith by trade; and with all he was quite a genius as a trades man. He had the physical strength and knew how to handle iron or steel; so as to make anything he wished out of this one or the other. He also owned quite a farm connected with the Homestead." The senior Golden, however, "was not a very provident man." According to his son, Lazarus, he earned "a great deal of money by his trade," but "he spent it even faster than he earned it. He was not careful either to collect the accounts which were due him from work."

Lazarus Golden was born on March 21, 1831 "in a very humble shanty (my father was building a new dwelling at the time)" in Prince William's Parish, Beaufort County, South Carolina. He was the sixth child, fourth son in a family of eight, five sons and three daughters. The Goldens lost their first-born son, who died in infancy, and their third son, fourth child, who sickened with "Bilious Fever," and died when he was only eight or nine years of age. Hannabel Golden, who "lived to maturity," volunteered as a soldier in the Mexican War and never returned; the family never learned what happened to him. Their youngest son, Oliver Perry, died of wounds received at Chickamauga in "the War of the Rebellion." Lazarus survived, as did his three sisters.

He clearly considered himself fortunate. He was born near his father's birthplace, "a country place; and generally unhealthy." Prince William's Parish is in South Carolina's low country, an alluvial region of tall pines and tangled swamps; a country of fevers. "There was much sickness in our family," Reverend Golden wrote a half-century later, "with frequent attacks of chills and fevers." His mother's health failed when he was about eight, and she died four years later of "dropsy," a possible inflammation of the kidneys or form of cancer. Lazarus looked back on no happy childhood; he was "sickly and feeble," consequently, "ugly, as they tell me, in my disposition." He recalled his mother telling him "that I had cried more and had given her more trouble than all of her other children. Perhaps she was herself at that time a little out of patience and also out of humour. I have no doubt however but that I was bad and very shy." But his health improved as he entered manhood; "I commenced to develop rapidly both in mind and in body, and in the course of a few years I became the strongest and most vigorous member in my father's family, except my father himself whose health was generally good, except when he had an attack of rheumatism."

A devout aunt, according to his son, insisted that Lazarus go into the ministry. Be that as it may, there was perhaps something more, for the Baptists, of all the Protestant denominations, insisted, as an 1859 Baptist *Directory* phrased it, on "*signs* and *evidences*" of a divine call on the part of their preachers. They also believed that "Nothing but *immersion* is baptism." Lazarus's youth was a time of rapid growth and conversion—by 1850 the Baptists were second among Protestants in membership, only the Methodists were more numerous. The Baptists were eager for recruits and a young preacher would find ready congregations eager to hear the word of God. But *the* call he had to have, one evidence of which, "and the greatest," is "the inward teaching of the Spirit, by which, after long, deliberate, and prayerful consideration, and perhaps painful conflict, the conviction becomes deep and permanent in the mind, that to teach the Gospel is the work which God has assigned to him."

This conviction is fed by contemplation of the Scriptures, a contemplation that must break out in speech. The Baptist *Directory* explains: "An increasing facility of expression, a freedom of utterance, when attempting to explain, enforce, or illustrate any particular passage of Scripture, in public meetings is a further indication of a call to the ministry. . . ." Young Lazarus met the test of faith by the time he was twenty-five, as a handwritten note in faded brown ink, found among his affects, attests: "This is to certify that the church of Christ called Sandy Run, having heard our beloved brother Lazarus Golden preach and approving of his gift, his good moral character, and real piety, have this day [January 9, 1856] authorized him to preach the Gospel wherever his lot may be cast, and do hereby recommend him to the affectionate regard of all Christians, particularly those pertaining to the Baptist denomination, praying that the Lord may be with him and abundantly help his labours of love." The license to preach was granted by "the unanimous order of the Church" and signed by Hardy Harrison and G. W. Williams, Pastor.

Later that year, the young preacher took an unusual step for the time and his age: he went to college. As a historian of his alma mater, Furman University, put it, "Vast numbers of Baptists were still suspicious of educational institutions and educated preachers. They loved the good old pulpit eloquence of the shirt-sleeve and plow-handle variety." Nonetheless, the Southern Baptists on their withdrawal, over slavery, from the antislavery national organization in 1845 proposed that the Furman Institute be the seminary of the South. By the time Lazarus Golden enrolled at Furman, the Institute was a seminary in the process of becoming a college. Theological students were required to take courses leading to a Bachelor of Arts degree. That Lazarus found the work sufficiently arduous may be gleaned from a letter written by a friend, G. Gaines. "Excuse my blotching," Gaines wrote in January, 1858, "my fingers are so numb that I cannot control them. I am glad to hear that you have turned ladysman to some extent, and have been 'doing up the agreeable' with the 'fair ones.' I think that after your year's hard study just posted you will find it 'good for your wholesome.' "

In 1859, the seminary broke away from Furman, taking a $26,000 endowment and a theological library to set up in another part of the town as the Southern Baptist Theological

Seminary. Lazarus, however, remained with Furman, graduating, in a class of fourteen, with a Bachelor of Arts degree in 1861. "The present war troubles preventing the use of the plate of the Diploma," President Furman wrote, "the presentation of the Diploma is for the time being deferred—and this certificate given instead."

On that note, the University closed its doors for the duration of the war. In October, Lazarus was ordained, "set apart to the work of the Christian ministry by prayer and the imposition of hands," and began his ministry in York, South Carolina. These were troubled times, as a Southern Baptist weekly noted in the summer of 1861, "Colleges have been suspended, some of them indefinitely. . . . Added to this gloomy picture, our Foreign Missions are paralyzed, our Home Missions almost suspended, and our State organizations unable to carry on their work. Ministers have been forced through stern necessity to leave their fields of usefulness in order to provide bread for their families." Reverend Golden, in June 1862, was exempted from "ordinary militia duty" and from "draft for Confederate service" but he was "liable to perform patrol duty, and . . . subject, as an alarm man, to be ordered to perform actual service in his Brigade."

Sherman marched through Georgia, swept north through the Carolinas, and the war drew to its close. In the spirit of President Abraham Lincoln's second inaugural, "with malice toward none," overtures were made by some Northern clergymen to their Southern brethren. As the editor of the New York Baptist *Examiner and Chronicle* put it, "Undoubtedly there are in our Southern churches multitudes of good Christian men and women, as good as are to be found; undoubtedly they have multitudes of good and faithful pastors, sharing with them a common lot of poverty. Let us establish, they with us and we with them, better relations . . . it is not as conquerors or oppressors that Northern Baptists would come to such cooperation, but as brethren seeking to restore wastes and turn them into joy and gladness . . ." But Sherman's troops had torched too many churches for the scars of war to be so easily healed even among those Baptists not necessarily hostile to Emancipation. Talk of the reunion of the two great wings of the Baptist Church in America "incensed" former Confederates, the American Baptist Home Mission Society reported in 1865. A Society meeting in St. Louis adopted a resolution, presented by a Virginia-born, Kentucky-bred pastor from Tennessee, the Reverend J. M. Pendleton, proposing that the Society undertake the responsibility for Baptist missions in Kentucky and Tennessee. Pendleton suggested that the Society name as missionaries such "suitable men" as could be found, and he spelled out his idea of suitable men as those of "unquestionable loyalty to the Government of the United States, men who approve the policy of the Government on slavery." The American Baptist Home Mission Society also appropriated forty thousand dollars for work among the freedmen. And among the twenty-five white brethren, ten colored brethren, and sixty-two assistant missionaries devoting themselves to "the evangelization of the freedmen," was the Reverend Lazarus Golden. He labored seventeen weeks in and around Catawba, preached thirty-nine sermons, baptized one person, and recruited 275 scholars for Baptist Sunday Schools.

Through his work for the Home Mission Society, the Reverend Golden came north to New York where he preached, interrupted by a single pastorate of two years in Pottsville, Pennsylvania, almost continuously for three decades. He labored at Boonville, Redwood, and Sandy Creek, upstate villages and towns, for 126 weeks, preaching 340 sermons and baptizing five. He undertook pastorates at Redwood, Sandy Creek, Fulton, Clinton, Newark and Ontario for varying terms, but never longer than four years. Fulton, whose folk shipped milk and fruit and manufactured woolen goods, paper containers and food products, was his largest pastorate, with a church membership of 142 when he arrived in 1879. Reverend Golden increased the membership to 164, raised the value of church property from seven to eight thousand dollars and the number of sunday school scholars from 100 to 215. "Paid for support of worship," $880.00 in 1879 and $850.00 in 1880. Golden was the Oswego Baptist Association delegate, representing fourteen churches, to the New York State Convention in 1881; he was also chairman of the Missionary Committee of the Oswego Association.

The Clinton Baptist Church, a white clapboarded building with a modest steeple, sits just off the northeast corner of the town common, facing the street running east where, next door, is found the parish house. In 1885, Golden came to preach to a congregation of ninety-seven that managed to pay $800 annually "for the support of worship." He had lost his wife, and had a young daughter with him. At fifty-six, he married Lucy A. Strong, a woman of thirty-four and of a good Clinton family. Within a year, Reverend Golden accepted a call to Pottsville, Pennsylvania, where a group of forty-four Baptists had just withdrawn from the First Baptist Church to form the Olivet Baptist Church. The Goldens moved into a small frame house on West Minersville, where Clinton Strong Golden was born on November 16, 1888.

The family did not remain long in Pottsville, leaving when Clinton was a year old for upstate New York, where the elder Golden accepted a call, first at Newark, a town on the old Erie Canal between Syracuse and Rochester, and later at Ontario, a town closer to the great lake. The Ontario Baptist Church had a fair-sized congregation of 106, with Sunday school scholars numbering 140-odd. In an autobiographical sketch found among his papers, Clint recalled his childhood as particularly penurious, his father's salary as "meagre," and though supplemented by free living quarters and an annual 'donation' of smoked meat, potatoes, turnips, cabbages and such at Thanksgiving," it "hardly sufficed to support the family and pay doctor's bills let alone provide savings for a rainy day." But he may have confused conditions after his father's retirement with those of the Ontario years. The Reverend Golden's salary—$672.28 in 1892—was beneath the ministerial average of approximately $800 a year, but it was well above that of teachers, about $270, miners, roughly $388, or railroad workers, $563.00 a year.

Even with another child, Clint's sister, Mabel, two years younger, to support, the Golden family circumstances were reasonably comfortable for the times. Ministers rarely starved, though they were not entirely insulated from the economic vissicitudes of the day. Reverend Golden's stipend did decline, dropping to $636 in 1893, perhaps reflecting the impact of the depression of that year on his parishioners. There was, too, a decline of discipline within the church. As Norman H. Maring, the Baptist historian, noted of the church by 1890 in *Baptists of New Jersey*, "With the larger memberships, it was almost impossible to have the kind of intimate fellowship presupposed as a requisite of a wholesome discipline." But of more immediate import was Golden's failing health. He was obliged to retire, and in 1895 the Goldens moved to Clinton where, when his health permitted, he "supplied the local Baptist pulpit," the Clinton church being without a pastor in those years, and where, according to his obituary in the *Clinton Courier*, he "represented various publications connected with some department of Christian life and work." He was asthmatic, and died in the early evening of Thursday, April 14, 1898, after a forty-five-day illness.

Clint Golden was then nearly ten years old. His recollections of his father are necessarily hazy, of an elderly and sickly figure, of the need for quiet about the house, and of physical distance—for how could a child clamber onto such a father, both forbidding and frail? In speaking of the pastors of Reverend Golden's generation, the Reverend William Rollinson once said, "The fathers were lovers of 'strong meat.' The sovereignty of God; His electing grace and eternal purposes; His changeless decrees; the impotence of man; the perseverance of the saints, and similar themes, were like manna to their souls and nourished a sturdy piety." Baptists, be it remembered, had no bishops or archbishops, no hierarchy. The congregations were independent and chose their own pastors. When one was baptized, one was "immersed" in the waters of faith, fully aware, having "experienced a saving faith in Christ." Infants could not be baptized "since they can neither exercise, nor profess that faith in Christ."

Clint was not baptizd in his father's faith; the labor movement was to become his "church." Late in life, he would claim to be "nominally a Baptist," a contradiction in terms, or so it surely would have seemed to his father. Yet, he would retain something of his father's beliefs as reinforced by his mother. A Baptist upbringing makes for independence in thought, a great individuality combined with an equally great sense of solidarity with one's fellows. Clint's choice of trade was particularly revealing. Machinists and railroad enginemen were imbued with the Protestant work ethic. An early organizational circular called upon machinists of "honorable, industrious and sober habits" to show "we are more worthy men and better mechanics than formerly, thereby proving to our employers and the world at large that we are justly entitled to standing and distinction." It was an attitude held in common with the operating railroad men and, in both instances, coupled with fraternity and self-reliance in a common cause. Clint, was reared in what William James called our American religion: "the faith that a man requires no master to take care of him, and that common people can work out their salvation well enough together if left free to try."

His father's death clearly troubled young Clint. His mother was hard-pressed to keep body and soul together, baking bread for sale, caring for an invalid and taking in a boarder or two. Clint was sent to live with his mother's sister, Emmeline, and her husband, William E. Crossman, a farmer in nearby Augusta. The rolling farmlands south of the Mohawk River have not changed that much over the years, though bungalows now edge the fields between the older farmhouses and barns and the farm tractor and gas pump stand where teams of horses once chomped on their bits. Crops were perhaps more diversified and farms somewhat more self-sufficient then than now. Wheat and buckwheat were raised to provide flour for bread and for buckwheat griddle cakes. Flint corn provided meal for "mush" as well as for feed for the horses, chickens and hogs. Cow peas were sowed with oats, cut as hay and cured for winter fodder as a supplement to timothy hay and clover. A grove of sugar maples provided sweetening for the home and another cash crop to go with the butter, eggs, cider vinegar, apples and cordwood sold or traded for such staples as cotton cloth, boots, shoes, coffee and sugar.

The seasonal round of upstate farm life—from plowing to harvest, the cutting and stacking of cordwood, the tug of a team of horses, the smell of manured fields, the wisp of smoke rising from the snow-surrounded sugarhouse—evokes powerful feelings of nostalgia. Clint would recall all his days the boil of sap, the sugaring off, with syrup congealing in a pan of snow, the farm shepherd dog's jaws caught in carmel-like maple sugar until it dissolved and the dog barked with the joy of release. But there were also the never-to-be-forgotten chores.

Clint's Aunt Emma and Uncle William were, as he described them in his autobiographical sketch, "hard-working, God-fearing people." They had no children, nor hired help. Clint, sprouting fast, and husky for his age, was expected to make himself useful and "earn his keep." As he recalled, "I tramped for hours behind a team dragging either a spring or a peg-tooth harrow after spring plowing." Then came hand-hoeing corn and potatoes, helping with the haying and harvesting. During the long winter, he helped fell hemlock, skid it onto sleds for hauling to a nearby sawmill, or cut beech for firewood. His uncle also had a shop with a small forge and anvil where he shoed neighbors' horses as well as his own, repaired wagon wheels and wagons, built his own bobsleds. Working alongside his uncle, Clint learned how to use hand tools and developed his lifelong love of craftsmanship.

Such pleasurable work was done between chores, the daily morning and evening tasks that the young Clint came to hate with a remarkable passion. To save pumping water from the well dug in the cellar of the house each time water was wanted, his uncle built a tank in the attic, and installed a hand-operated force pump; it was one of Clint's most tiresome of daily jobs to pump water to fill the attic tank. Another, he wrote, consumed the evenings: "What seemed to a restless boy as endless hours were spent in the evening rolling 'lighters' from strips of paper torn from old weekly newspapers or religious journals. These had to be rolled tightly to uniform lengths with one end loose. They were neatly packed in glass jars or boxes and were used to save 'stove' matches in lighting candles and oil lamps, the fire in the kitchen range or in the sheet-iron 'chunk' stoves that heated the house." As isolated farm folk will, Clint's uncle and aunt developed certain idiosyncracies, among them, an aversion to salt. Thus homemade breads, oatmeal, corn-meal mush, boiled potatoes, cooked vegetables—what might have been tantalizing farm-kitchen foods—tasted flat. Clint began skipping school and running away whenever he had the chance.

Clint never went very far, staying at most overnight or for a few days with compassionate friends or kindly relatives. But if the farm seemed harsh, school was becoming something of a nightmare, especially on Fridays, recitation days for the young scholars of Clinton. Pupils were expected to memorize poems or rhetorical set pieces and to recite them before the class. Gawky, with his knees bumping against his desk as he rose in his turn, Clint was miserable. Somewhere into the recitation, his mind would go blank and he would be unable to finish. Rather than go on through this, he skipped school Fridays and soon other days, too. His mother was unhappy, but unable to control her son. He was, at twelve, "overgrown; most people thought I was fifteen or sixteen." Today, troubled youngsters get counseling and are encouraged to remain in school but then it was felt by most of the Golden friends and relations, as Clint later put it, "that if I did not 'like' school or 'want an education' I should go to work."

Clint managed to get through the sixth grade, the year of his school troubles, thus he quit school two years under the median school-leaving age for his generation. "I am a bit sensitive about this," he wrote author Stuart Chase some forty-five years later, "but I try to gain confidence by recalling what Mark Twain said about having never let his lack of schooling interfere with his education. So all I know is what I've learned by experience and observation." He went to work as a mule driver in a recently reopened ore mine just east of the village of Clinton. The Franklin Iron Furnace was built in 1852, but it had been closed for seven years when M. A. Hanna & Co. of Cleveland leased and repaired the works in 1899. The mine was a slope mine, dug into a hillside, and the red hematite was smelted at the furnace, two miles away by rail. The mine soon shut down again, reopening two years later under local management to produce some six thousand tons of ore a month. Clint was taken on, then, as a drill tender, working six ten-hour days a week for six dollars. He lived with his mother, much relieved now that her son had a job that served to keep him out of mischief, and contributed to the family's support.

What she did not realize, nor did her son at the time, was that his education was about to begin. Clint "tended drill" for "Big John" Powderly, "a huge hulk of a man." As Clint recalled in his autobiographical sketch, he had "the largest and flattest feet I have ever seen on a human being." Big John was not, understandably, a walker; tending drill for him consisted of fetching supplies for the drill and tobacco for its operator: a constant running back and forth to the blacksmith shop, where drills were sharpened, and to the machine shop for repairs, and elsewhere about the "workings" for whatever Big John happened to need. Big John was a talker, too, railing against the Catholic Church and the Catholic bishop who had excommunicated his brother, Terrance, labor mayor of Scranton and former Grand Master of the Knights of Labor. He had tales to tell to the entranced lad of the Molly Maguires who had "done away" an arrogant, slave-driving mine boss, been betrayed by a fellow Irishman "gone over to the Pinkertons," and, best of all, "hanged in the very town where I was born."

Big John preached the gospel of the Noble and Holy Order of the Knights of Labor, "a union of all trades and callings," as his brother Terrance once put it, "furnishing the great heart through which the life-giving current may flow strong and healthy to every part of labor's mighty frame." Although the heyday of the Knights—their peak membership of over seven hundred thousand in 1886 was down to one hundred thousand four years later—was long past, Big John remained true to its vision of one, all-embracing organization for all workers. He imparted his enthusiasm to his young acolyte. "Their ritualism," Golden wrote many years later, "the secrecy with which their meetings were conducted, the signs and symbols that gave notice to their members as to when and where meetings were to be held, fired my interest and imagination and in my own mind I resolved that henceforth my lot was cast with that of the wage earners. I began to see class lines and distinctions. I discovered that there were people in America besides those who lived their lives upon farms that were largely self-sufficient. People who worked long hours for low wages in hazardous employment, lived in miserable tenements and hovels, whose very life depended on having a job, earning money but rarely more than enough to provide for the bare necessities of life."

Young Clint's conversion, the tales of class war that he carried home, angered his mother. She warned him against the "shanty Irish Fenians"—most of the miners were Irish immigrants with a few Welsh, Hungarians and Poles among them—and inveighed against "the trouble-makers invading our peaceful community." His poor departed father, Clint was assured, would turn in his grave.

Still, the mother could not hold out against her son when it came to doing something he wanted to do. Since he was still a lad, Barney Burns, a red-whiskered elderly miner, sought Mrs. Golden's permission for her "educated boy" with his "strong voice" to attend a Sunday meeting of the miners. There were letters to be read, and "could the boy come and give them a hand with the reading?" She assented, but reluctantly.

We can imagine how the young Clint Golden felt, standing before some hundred-odd workingmen and reading to them from letters written by other miners about efforts to organize in the face of great employer opposition. "After the first feeling of self-consciousness and fear . . . a feeling of confidence and strength . . ." Then the talk, the offering of a motion, the brogue of the Irish, the lilt of the Welsh, the argument excited the youth. "I was beginning to learn. . . ."

Life was full, but there was the itch to get on. The "workings" fascinated Clint as a work-place will a young man who is curious, has a bit of money in his pocket for the first time, and enjoys his first glass of beer with the fellows after work at Billy Ashcroft's saloon. Clint was assigned a new job, at the tipple, where loads of ore were dumped from mule-drawn cars into a railroad gondola. Clint "trimmed" the ore, breaking off slate from the lumps of iron ore with a small sledge hammer. At the tipple, he became friendly with the railroad men, Michael Murphy, the engineer, and "Butch" Sieselinier, the red-faced conductor. They teased Clint about working in the mines when he could become a railroad man. Learning of his liking for tools and the blacksmith shop, they suggested he try out for the machinist trade in the Utica railroad shops. But they also talked of "firing" the great steam boilers and of promotion to the top of the line, becoming a railroad engineer. Clint helped the brakeman let the empties down the grade as the loaded cars were taken out to the furnace, where the ore was to be smelted. Soon he was riding the old locomotive, dreaming . . .

And one day in 1904, when he was sixteen, Clint Golden went home and told his mother that he was going to work on the railroad.

Journeyman Fireman

WALKING HOME from the mine, after a day's work, young Clint could hear the trains chuffling, buffers clanking, at Clinton Station, a short way from the Golden home on Elm Street. Having watched the arrival and departure of the trains often as a schoolboy, he could easily conjure up the bustle at the station now: dapper drummers dropping off the daily "Flyer" to make their sales pitch to the town's merchants, "Sunday-best" townsfolk returning after a day in the big city, the hurried loading of mail and freight. On the long sidings, coal from Pennsylvania's anthracite region slithered in a black cascade into the hoppers of the Clinton Coal Company, milk cans clanged as freight-handlers loaded produce destined for far-off metropolitan markets.

"A railway aids travelling by getting rid of all avoidable obstructions of the road and leaving nothing to be conquered but pure space," wrote the sage of Concord, Ralph Waldo Emerson, in 1844. Within three decades railroads spanned the continent, and by 1904, nearly three hundred thousand miles of gleaming steel rails criss-crossed the nation. Railroad promoters had talked of opening up the West but the call of the wild, the westward movement, subsided as the young began to leave the farms for the big city. A gigantic steel harp, the rails sang of wealth and power, of movement and conquered space, of the seductive city. In Clint's youth, the railroads had all the excitement and promise that the automobile and the airplane offered subsequent generations of the adventurous young. Railroad work paid well, and railroad engineers were folk heroes, while conductors, with their gold watches and chains slung across blue-vested paunches, were important men, men whose opinions were weighed alongside those of village bankers or station-masters. Famous engineers designed their own whistles, building four-, five- or six-barrel "quills." When steam ripped through such whistles, the hills echoed with a wild laughter as the train raced through the valley below. One engineer, it was claimed, could play *How I Love Jesus* on his whistle, and Casey Jones could make *his* "say prayers or scream like a Banshee." The ballad of the brave engineer became a popular vaudeville tune the year Clint decided to seek work on the railroad.

For Clint, as for countless young men of his generation, the sound of the locomotive whistle on a summer's night was a call to adventure. Casey Jones was not the only engineer to push his "high right-wheeler" to its limit. Crews were constantly ordered, as in the classic railroad ballad, "The Wreck of the Old 97," to "put her into Spencer on time," to "get back on card," or to rigorous schedules. Others sought to establish a record, for the line or for the world. The Pennsy's crack train, the Broadway Limited, on July 12, 1905, hit a speed of 127.1 miles an hour between Ay Tower and Elida, Ohio. Running late, firemen built up great heads of steam. "No sane bystander stood close to a piece of level, straight Ontario and Western trackage when a scheduled train was due," a historian of the line wrote. "The suction was often enough to carry him half-mile free." To the end of his days, Clint enjoyed telling stories of his railroad days. "These were always stories about brakes going bad, getting stuck in snow drifts," according to his daughter Olive. One tale he often told is reminiscent of

Casey Jones' great crack-up, and the ballad's great line, "Number Four stared him right in the face . . ." As Olive remembers the story, her father had stoked up the fire "something fierce." "We were making good time out of Cadosia as night fell," he would say, "when suddenly a great light loomed up ahead. The engineer, an old-timer, gave me a solemn look, and gravely shook my hand. 'Jump,' he said, he went out one side and I, the other. And, you know," here Golden would pause, "that train of ours just peeled off to the right and the other sailed past without one touching the other."

Mrs. Golden was pleased when her son told her that he was leaving the mine and the roughneck miners. But she was worried about his working on the railroad, and for good reason. Train wrecks were featured in the weekly newspapers published in the towns strung along the New York, Ontario and Western Railway, from Oswego on Lake Ontario through Oneida, along the branch lines from Rome and Utica that passed the lower Catskills to Middletown and Cornwall and down the Hudson to Weehawken and Jersey City. Not two years earlier a northbound train had run head on into a southbound train, killing an engineer, a fireman and two others. The introduction of the Westinghouse air brake over the previous decade had reduced the accident rate among railroad employees by 60 percent. Still, the newspapers reported the death or maiming of firemen and engine men with a depressing regularity.* Between 1904 and 1912, 124 firemen were killed in accidents. Mrs. Golden was considerably reassured when her son told her he was going to work in the Utica roundhouse of

* Social note of the time: A member of the Norwich, New York, Historical Society told me in 1976 that, in those days, whenever road crews were injured or killed in an accident, the local papers would report, "Six Italians killed," never mentioning the victims by name. Engineers or firemen were always mentioned by name whenever accidents occurred.

the New York, Ontario and Western as a fire-cleaner and wiper.

The lanky sixteen-year-old actually began as apprentice to a machinist but, wanting to become a locomotive engineer, he willingly took on the grim task of wiping down oily locomotive parts. He earned more at the railway shops than at the mine, and the extra five dollars a week was welcomed at home, where Mrs. Golden continued "to make do" for herself, her daughter and her son by taking in boarders, baking, sewing and washing, the odd jobbery of widowhood. Already six-foot-one, young Clint had the reach some railroaders considered desirable in a fireman. As an old railroad story has it, "if a tall feller's got long arms he can do wonders." In another, an engineer claimed, "I had a fireman and I never saw him throw a shovelful of coal on the fire—his arms was so long he just reached and laid the coal on." And so Clint, just short of his seventeenth birthday, in September, 1905, became a fireman on the "Old and Weary." It was a proud day, a step up towards becoming an engineer. He also joined the Brotherhood of Locomotive Firemen and Enginemen, Lyon Brook Lodge, Number 216, based in Norwich, New York. On a faded clipping from the *New York Times*, dated October 21, 1950, announcing the closing of the New York, Ontario & Western, Clint jotted, "This is the railroad I went to work for in 1904 and where my practical labor organizational experience began."

Clint was taller than most of his fellow crew members, and loose-limbed, with a thin, longish face and a bristling mustache beneath a peaked cap; a photograph of him in his mid-twenties shows that he did not fill out crisply laundered blue-striped railroad overalls. After his sister's marriage to Harvey Head of Paris Station, his mother went to live with her stepdaughter at Unadilla, New York, a small town on the upper Susquehanna

River. Clint married Anna C., last name unknown, and sometime in 1907 moved to Norwich, New York. In 1910 he moved again, this time to Sidney, New York, a railroad town just downriver from his mother's new home. Clint became increasingly active in the Lyon Brook Lodge of his union, which met the first and third Mondays of every month in Andrews Hall, at Norwich.

Though railroad firemen and enginemen, or engineers, were the aristocrats of labor during the early years of this century, their well-established unions had a lively, radical intellectual tradition. Eugene Victor Debs, the grand old man of the socialist movement, had been a railroad fireman, served as the grand secretary-treasurer of the union and editor of the *Locomotive Firemen and Enginemen's Magazine*, from 1881 to 1894, and still enjoyed a considerable following among railroad men during Clint Golden's years on the New York, Ontario and Western Railway. The *Magazine*, too, remained infused by a kind of Debsian socialism, and carried alongside the monthly "study course," with its technical material on the Westinghouse brake, electric railways and the like, sturdy condemnations of "the master class," reports on developments in the labor movement, accounts of economics and "industrial democracy" by such radical and socialist intellectuals as Harry W. Laidler, Scott Nearing, and L. D. Hosman. Other issues urged a "nationwide cooperative system" and "a people's press." Clint devoured each issue as it came out, for he was hungry for ideas, for facts, and eager to apply them to his job and to the world around him.

John Stuart Mill, in *The Subjection of Women*, described the plight of the self-educated. "A clever self-educated man," Mill wrote, "often sees what men trained in routine do not see, but falls into errors for want of knowing things which have long been known. He has acquired much of the preexisting knowledge, or he could not have got on at all; but what he knows of it he has picked up in fragments and at random." For a worker with an inquiring mind but without habits of study, random reading often makes for a spotty education indeed. Rudyard Kipling once remarked on the quality of self-learning in America, a high tribute to the reading and writing fundamentals as taught in the traditional little red schoolhouse. It seems that Kipling and a friend were out driving in the hills behind Brattleboro, Vermont, one afternoon and had drawn up in a farmyard for a drink of water. They had been engaged in friendly argument and while refreshing themselves, the friend fired off a quotation at Kipling to clinch a point. The farmer, who had been listening, interjected, " 'Twarn't Montaigne, 'twere Mon-tes-que."

Clint was close to this tradition of self-education, forever scored in our memories by the portrayal of young Abraham Lincoln reading by the light of a log cabin fireplace. However brilliant the individual, solitary reading without intelligent exchange with others often gives rise to mere eccentricity, the dottiness of the village atheist or the queerness of the radical workman. Ideas need to be tested against other ideas as well as experience. As a young fireman active in his union, Clint gained an invaluable grounding for his continual refining of his ideas of industrial democracy, first gleaned from the pages of the *Locomotive Firemen and Enginemen's Magazine*. It was the socialist movement, however, that was to be Clint's Yale College, his Harvard.

There was an active socialist group in Utica, and Clint may have been recruited there, possibly by a Debsian fellow fireman or shopman machinist, but he entered Socialist Party history in Delaware County soon after moving to Sidney. "Between the elections of 1908 and 1912," according to historian David Shannon, "the Socialists enjoyed their greatest growth." The Party membership nearly tripled, rising from 41,751 to 117,984 and in the presidential election of 1912, Eugene Victor

Debs polled 897,000 votes, about 6 percent of the popular vote. Socialists Victor Berger and Meyer London were in Congress, and in 1911 there were thirty-three socialist city and town administrations, including that of colorful George R. Lunn, mayor of Schenectady. The Socialists of pre-World War I America were strong believers in industrial unionism, evoking in Clint's mind the passionate teachings of his first mentor, John Powderly. In *The Socialist Party of America* Shannon sums up the nature of the Socialist Party of those times:

> Most of the differences between Debs who believed firmly in industrial unionism in the economic field and militant Socialist agitation in the political field, and more conservative Socialists such as Hillquit, Maurer, and Victor Berger, leader of the Milwaukee organization, were differences of emphasis. They all believed in industrial unionism, but the conservatives, who made great efforts to win elections, were willing to speak only softly on this issue for fear of antagonizing some elements in the AFL; all of them believed in the immediate demands of the Socialist platforms, but the conservatives, in the hopes of attracting non-Socialist reformist votes, often made these demands paramount and minimized the distinctively anticapitalist aspects of the Socialist program, much to the disgust of Debs.

If these differences made for tension, it was, for a time, fruitful tension, overcome, in good part, by the charismatic Debs, who, as the poet James Whitcomb Riley put it, was,

> . . . a man 'at stands
> And jest holds out in his two hands
> As warm a heart as ever beat
> Betwixt here and the Jedgment Seat.

Once settled in Sidney, Clint stepped up his activity on behalf of the Socialist Party. In December, 1911, he was named by the Delaware County organization to the New York State Executive Committee, then chaired by Algernon Lee. It sounds a bit more grand than it actually was, for though the committee met quarterly, the upstate members rarely attended. The committee would meet upstate once a year, usually in the summer and usually with a full turnout of the forty-odd members. Soon after Clint became a member, however, in April 1912, new Delaware County locals were chartered at Fish's Eddy and Rock Rift. Both towns were located on the New York, Ontario and Western line, socialism riding on the rails as it were, prompting the state committee to note, on April 16, 1912, "Delaware County has at present eight locals while there was not a single local less than one year ago." Clint campaigned for Debs, presumably in Sidney as well as elsewhere in Delaware County. On November 6, the *Sidney Enterprise* reported the local tally: 14 socialist votes, 59 for the Prohibitionists and 119 for the Theodore Roosevelt Progressives, to 404 Democratic and 501 Republican votes. (Woodrow Wilson was elected President.) Undaunted, Clint continued organizing. "Several locals in Delaware County," the State Executive Committee noted, "report on the need of a local paper for the county and the steps taken to publish such a paper as soon as the required funds can be raised." That educational touch was pure Golden.

Clint continued to read widely, especially socialist and trade-union literature. T. V. Powderly's autobiography, *Thirty Years of Life and Labor*, and Edward Bellamy's *Looking Backward* were two books that impressed him greatly at the time. A folder of clippings from the 1914 *New York Call*—"Socialists have no interests separate and apart from the Working Class as a whole," its logo proclaimed—gives some idea of the range of his interests at that time. He, of course, followed Socialist party developments within New York State, clipped tips about organizing and propagandizing. "Literature is superior to soap-box speaking," one such bit of advice reads. "The energy of every Comrade should be enlisted and centered upon a systematic and persistent distribution of Socialist leaflets and periodicals," to be followed up by visiting enrolled Socialist voters. Socialists, another such clipping reads, can reach "rural man through the rural mail." A dollar buys one hundred one-cent wrappers so that "each month one hundred farmers can receive a well-selected Socialist leaflet" or a copy of the *New York Call.* Clint also clipped and treasured articles and editorials on economics, foreign affairs, industrial conditions, strike accounts, quotes from Robert G. Ingersoll, John Spargo, Clarence Darrow, Charles Proteus Steinmetz, James H. Maurer and Debs. Walter Rauschenbusch's "Prayer for the Cooperative Commonwealth," a note of social gospel that may have contained reverberations of dimly remembered sermons: "Thou hast called our people to freedom, but we are withholding from men their share in the common heritage without which freedom becomes a hollow name . . . We pray to thee to revive in us the hardy spirit of our forefathers that we may establish and complete their work, building on the basis of their democracy the firm edifice of a Cooperative Commonwealth, in which both government and industry shall be of the people, by the people, and for the people."

Lillian Wald's statement to the U.S. Commission on Industrial Relations that workers' organizations were more effective than the law in reforming working conditions caught Clint's eye, as did an editorial on industrial accidents. The editorial indicted "the system"—"You have made it more profitable for employers of the working class to make life unsafe than to make it safe"—inadvertently touching on a solution while boasting that Socialists were "pioneers," as indeed they were, in fighting for workmen's compensation and factory inspection.

Clint was interested in accounts of how the city of Zurich housed its workers, how socialist municipalities provided parks and recreational facilities for working people, how cooperatives succeeded in reducing the cost of living for their members. Socialist condemnation of war, support of the suffragette movement, and a proposal that the United States post office be an employment bureau as well were grist for Clint's intellectual mill. Much of this, one surmises, provided data and argument for Socialist local branch discussions and Firemen's Lodge meetings, where similar issues were often raised.

Militarism, for example, was very much on Socialist minds at the time. War had broken out in Europe, and the United States had invaded Mexico in pursuit of Pancho Villa's revolutionary forces. The militia had been called out in Colorado to maintain "peace and order" in the Colorado Fuel and Iron Company strike. Striking miners having fled the company-provided housing to live in tent cities, the largest, outside Ludlow, had been fired upon and burned, killing men, women and children. Patriotism and unionism, therefore, was discussed within the labor movement. As W. S. Carter, president of the Brotherhood of Locomotive Firemen and Enginemen, put it in an editorial in the *Magazine*, on the eve of American entry into World War I, "In the United States a military system has been cultivated with the understanding that its principal activities will be limited to the suppression of strikes. The Master Class has secured laws and appropriations for the erection of bastille-like 'armories' in the larger cities, not for the defense of the nation but the suppression of riots that their own avarice and greed might provoke." This suspicion lay behind unionist opposition to the Compulsory Service Bill of 1916. Even the Boy Scout movement came under suspicion, with A. A. Graham echoing Socialist criticism in the *Firemen and Enginemen's Magazine:* "I am not the first by any means to notice that the 'Boy Scout Movement' is for the purpose of organizing the boys of the 'better classes' into a citizen soldiery for the purpose later, when called upon, to kill the 'working classes,' should they become 'troublesome.' "

The railroad unions, the largest sector of organized workers, with over a million members by 1917, were interested in nationalization. After World War I, they endorsed the so-called Plumb Plan named after its author, Glenn E. Plumb, general counsel for the associated railroad labor organizations, which called for a permanent government takeover of the wartime-seized railroads. Owners were to be fully compensated and the railroads to be operated by a corporation without capital stock and controlled by a board of directors, one-third of whom were to represent classified employees, "to be selected by those employees." It is not difficult, given the interest among railroad workers in government ownership, to imagine an eager young fireman rising at a lodge meeting to quote Charles Proteus Steinmetz, the popular scientist at General Electric in nearby Schenectady, on industrial evolution. "The railroads must consolidate. Supervision over them must lead to government management. Then you have ownership. And so with all our industries . . . And that is socialism."

Clint, too, enjoyed those calculations of society's potential, rudimentary conceptions of productivity, that so enamoured Debsian socialists and other radicals of the time. August Bebel once figured that about one million workers could supply the entire needs of the population of Austria, some twenty-two million, in sixty days, and from this deduced that, taking the entire able-bodied male population into consideration, "we find that they would have to perform only about 2½ hours of work daily." "Nor will anyone deny that tremendous, incalculable progress may still be made in perfecting the process of production . . . many requirements will be satisfied that only a small minority can satisfy today, and with the higher development of civilization, new requirements will arise that will also have to be satisfied." Socialists really believed that "a new world's in birth," one that, in Bebel's words, "will not elect to lead a proletarian existence. It will demand existence of a highly civilized people for all its members from the first to the last. But it shall not only satisfy all the material requirements; it shall also grant to all ample opportunity and time for the study of science and art, and for recreation." Starry-eyed, but nonetheless rooted in a notion of productivity as the necessary coin for all wealth.

Socialism also embodied a concept of democracy that would remain with Clint all his life. A treasured clipping from the *New York Call*, a brief statement by John Spargo, contains that credo:

> Socialism does not propose to surround itself with a network of laws in the vain hope that it will make men perfect and remodel human nature by legal enactment, but it does propose to destroy, as far as that is possible by collective effort, all those anti-social conditions which compel men to live vain, hopeless, sordid, brutal and unworthy lives.
>
> It does not expect, nor will it attempt, to override the great laws of human nature and make men equal, but it does make the proposal that all those things which deny equal opportunities and create unnatural inequalities should be destroyed.
>
> It claims for every child born into the world its heirship to the vast resources of wisdom and knowledge so painfully fathered by the race through the long ages; it claims for every child equal opportunity for the fullest and freest development of all its power, leaving only natural inequalities to manifest themselves.
>
> That is the "equality" of Socialism.
>
> To be more specific: the form of government essential to its very existence is a complete political democracy,

resting on the broad base of adult suffrage. It thus elevates woman to the plane of political and social equality with man.

Industrially, the State—no longer representative of a class, but of the whole nation—will be as democratic as it is politically.

That is the kernel of Golden's concept of industrial democracy.

The "collective effort" that John Spargo saw as essential in order to destroy "those anti-social conditions" that compel men to live hopeless lives was, for Clint, the trade union movement. As he would write many years later, "Workers organize into labor unions not alone for economic motives but also for equally compelling psychological and social ones, so that they can participate in making the decisions that vitally affect them in their work and community life." And young Clint was eager to participate, whether it was a debate over socialism, a town fight over the water supply, or a grievance of a fellow worker. He rarely missed a Lyon Brook Lodge meeting, rising to speak on issues of local and national interest to the railroad firemen. Though the railroad unionists were given to lofty discussions—it was the era of Chautauquas, of educational lectures as entertainment, after all, not of television or even radio—they were also pragmatists, bread-and-butter unionists of great negotiating skill. While a man of words received a ready welcome, one of work won their support. As the son of a railroader, the noted labor journalist Merlyn S. Pitzele, once put it in an article about Clint, "Within their organizations there were no meteoric rises; a man came to leadership only after long seasoning." In August 1914, Clint's fellow firemen elected him, at age twenty-five, chairman of Lodge 216, Lyon Brook, Norwich, New York. It was a signal honor.

It was not, however, a full-time job. Clint continued to shovel coal, taking runs out of Sidney south to Scranton and north to Utica. These were make-or-break runs for young firemen, shoveling ten to sixteen hours a day in 120 degree heat, heat so terrific that thermometers broke when trains ran through tunnels. Arbitration proceedings in April 1913, reported in the *Locomotive Firemen and Enginemen's Magazine*, give an idea of what conditions were like. Guy Turck of Cornell, New York, a fireman on the Erie Railroad, testified that he shovelled "on an average of 24 tons, or almost two tons an hour. I often throw into the furnace 146 shovels of coal an hour, and still a man is expected to keep a lookout for signals just the same as an engineer." Turck worked eight to ten trips a month, ten to twelve hours a day, often without a chance to eat, was away from home twenty-two days a month, and averaged sixty dollars a month in pay.

"Speaking of shoveling coal," Joseph Flegal told the arbitration board, "I handled exactly 2,192 shovelfuls on one trip. . . ."

"How do you know?" Judge William L. Chambers, chairman of the Board, asked.

"Well, you see, I've been shoveling coal for so many years I just decided that some day I would count 'em, and I did."

James A. Bell, a New Castle, Pennsylvania, fireman, testified that when away from home firemen often put up at "rest houses" owned by the railroads. "They rent beds as low as 15 cents a night. The beds have high partitions on both sides and there is barely room enough for a man to get in to go to bed. Other beds, more comfortable, are rented at 50 cents a night. These 15-cent beds are the limit for a man after a long, hard run. You're lucky if you get any sleep."

What about meals for the aristocrats of labor?

"The minimum is 25 cents, and then you get a piece of steak about the size of a fifty-cent coin. Believe me," added Bell, "a man would starve on those meals. We work hard and we must eat, Judge."

Bell averaged a hundred dollars a month, and Judge Chambers wanted to know what, if anything, he contributed to his church.

"Oh, about 25 cents."

"How much for theatres?"

"Oh, about 15 or 20 cents."

"Then you must go to the movies?"

"Sure, that's the best I get."

Expenses away from home, Bell, who had a wife and a child to support, testified, were about thirty dollars a month. He and other firemen complained about the grade of coal: "I wouldn't call it coal; it's dirt." Firemen had to put wicks in lanterns and tack signal flags to sticks before leaving on their runs. Laborers in New York City, they complained, were getting 40 cents an hour to the fireman's 27 to 30 cents an hour. Living costs, too, were rising. A Youngstown engineer, David B. Robertson figured that on an engine of a certain class in 1907, a fireman's daily wage was sufficient to buy 12.9 pounds of sirloin steak but in 1912 the same wage bought 10.9 pounds. (In 1970, for comparison, an average railroad worker could buy 23.89 pounds of sirloin steak with his eight-hour-day's pay.) What the firemen gained out of the arbitration proceedings, incidentally, was a reduction in hours to ten a day and a raise in daily rates, depending on class of service, to a minimum of $2.45 and a maximum of $4.00 a day. But the 1913 award was a disappointment to the firemen, who wanted an eight-hour day.

Clint took on more responsibility and, in 1915, while serving as local chairman, he was elected a state legislative representative of Lyon Brook Lodge and, later, elected general chairman for the New York, Ontario and Western system. Lodges, then, were not co-terminous with the railroad; grievance committees, however, were organized on a system-wide basis. Clint, as general chairman, negotiated wages and working conditions with the management of the NYO & W. It was an important post for a young man of twenty-six, and he was soon caught up in the rail unions' struggle for the eight-hour day.

The disappointing arbitration award prompted a call for unified action by all railroads, and their engineers, firemen, conductors and trainmen. Leaders of the four operating brotherhoods came together and, in August 1915, submitted a referendum on the question, and 95 percent of the membership voted to submit the eight-hour, 100-mile-run minimum demand to the railway managers of the country. The railway managements organized a General Conference Committee of Railroad Managers of the United States to combat the workers' move for a shorter work week. The railways claimed that it was physically impossible to reduce the average run to eight hours. The demand for shorter hours was a hoax, they charged, a ploy for more overtime.

On March 30, 1916, the demands of more than three hundred thousand railroad men were formally submitted to the managers of 458 roads, and the managements were given thirty days to reply. The railroads rejected the eight-hour day proposal; the union leaders declared that they would never accept arbitration. On June 1, Clint traveled to New York City to join some six hundred and forty division chairmen from the four brotherhoods in what labor historian Selig Perlman termed "the most momentous wage conference in the history of the United States." It was Clint's first experience with major bargaining. The chairmen insisted that the eight-hour day proposal was neither subject to compromise nor to arbitration. The railroad managements insisted on the latter. Negotiations went on for fifteen days without result; finally, both sides broke off all talks.

Clint returned to Norwich to prepare a strike vote. Nonunion as well as union workers employed by the New York,

Ontario and Western Railway, as was the case on all the other railroads, were allowed to vote. Management drafted open letters, issued warnings, pleaded for loyalty and threatened to abrogate pension rights. Clint, and men like him, remained firm, patiently explaining to the men why arbitration was no go. As W. G. Lee of the Trainmen put it, "It is impossible to secure men sufficiently familiar with railway operation fairly to decide all questions submitted to them . . . There is no question but that the neutral arbitrators assume a task that carries so much responsibility that they really should not be called upon to assume, that it is unfair to ask them to sit in judgment on something we know they do not understand." The counting of ballots in early August showed a vote in favor of the strike ranging by district and occupation from 84 to 98.7 percent of the total votes cast. Clint took special pride in the Firemen turnout, 69,570 for strike and only 1,204 against.

Alarmed at the possibility of a national tie-up of transportation, President Woodrow Wilson intervened personally. He held separate conferences with both sides, and in an address to the general chairman on August 17 in the East Room of the White House, he asked that they accept the immediate installation of the eight-hour day with all other issues, notably the question of time-and-a-half overtime, being submitted to arbitration. The chairmen accepted; the carrier representative balked. On August 28, Clint and the other chairmen headed for home, each carrying a sealed envelope containing a strike call, set for September 4 at seven in the morning, and detailed instructions on conducting the strike. Three faithless chairmen revealed the contents of the secret instructions to the railways. Management released the story to the press.

President Wilson appealed to the rail unionists to cancel the strike orders, but was politely told that the matter was out of their hands and in those of the men. The President then called a joint session of the Congress, and on August 28, 1916, summarizing the course of the dispute, said, "the whole spirit of time and the preponderant evidence of recent economic experience spoke for the eight-hour day." After discussion, Congress responded by adopting the Adamson Act, which established the eight-hour day for train-service employees as of January 1, 1917. The strike was called off, and the law upheld by the Supreme Court in a five-to-four decision on March 16, 1917.

It was a notable victory, but 1917 proved to be a disturbing year for most Americans. Germany resumed unrestricted submarine warfare in February, sinking neutral as well as belligerent ships bound for Britain and other Allied ports. The United States broke off relations with Germany, and war followed on April 6. Clint registered for the draft under the new Selective Service Act and was placed in Class 2, the son of a widow, dependent on his labor for support, and Class 4, the father of a motherless child, under ten, dependent on his labor for support. He left Sidney to live in Utica that spring, moving again in the fall, to Ilion, New York, where he may have gone to work as a machinist in the Remington arms factory.

Why he decided to leave railroading is uncertain. He was, after all, a leader and clearly on the rise within the ranks. Yet, the New York, Ontario and Western Railway was not a major road, and so, perhaps, he felt he could go no higher. He had passed his "Book of Rules" examination in April 1915, but firemen had to wait eight to sixteen years before promotion to engineer, and Clint still had two more examinations—machinery and air brakes—ahead of him, and already he had put in twelve years on the railroad as a fireman. Perhaps, as Merlyn S. Pitzele suggested in his *Saturday Evening Post* article on Clint, "he succumbed for the only time in his life to the lure of high wages and went back to the machinist's trade," where the money was indeed good and the work a good deal safer. Or, it may have been some personal tragedy; we know nothing of his first wife, presumed dead on the evidence of his draft classification, or of his first child. In any event, one day in the fall of 1917, Clint Golden left upper New York State for Philadelphia, where he went to work as a machinist.

Journeyman Machinist

PHILADELPHIA, where Benjamin Franklin published *Poor Richard's Almanac* and where lusty patriots cracked the Liberty Bell, had become in the years before World War I, in the words of iconoclast H. L. Mencken, "the most peck-sniffian of American cities." The Philadelphia story was fashioned on the main line of the suburban railway where bankers and lawyers spent their lives, in poet Archibald MacLeish's telling phrase, "practicing prudence on a long-term lease." The Stotesburys, a noted banking family, equipped their bathroom with gold fixtures ("You don't have to polish them, you know"); and a Kitty Foyle could not marry a Winn Strafford, even in the Golden Twenties. Philadelphia, in short, was synonymous in the American argot for staid, stolid and stuffy. But in 1919, for working men and women, it was a boom town.

There had been a complete turn-around in the labor market. Unemployment had run as high as 30 percent among machinists and toolmakers along the eastern seaboard scarcely two years before Clint Golden's arrival in the City of Brotherly Love, where he was initiated into Lodge 159 of the International Association of Machinists on September 26, 1917. Machinists were in great demand, especially in shipbuilding, the railroad shops, for toolmaking and in munitions work. As machinist business agent William A. Kelton reported in the *Machinists' Monthly Journal* for October 1917, "Big things are doing in Philadelphia, not alone in business but in the I. A. of M. as well. . . . Conditions, generally speaking, in and around Philadelphia have improved since my last report; wages have advanced, and we are taking in a great many new members." Encouraged by these developments, Kelton added, "Now is our golden opportunity, and organization is in the air. I am hoping that we may see our life time chance and get Philadelphia organized." He ended his report, however, with a caution: "I would suggest to our brothers who receive offers from firms in and around Philadelphia not to start for less than sixty cents per hour and then have it in writing, as so many brothers have not received the rate promised them when they arrived."

Clint Golden had no trouble finding a job; he was, after all, a skilled craftsman in a seller's market. Given his skills, he might well have emigrated to any industrial center, but he chose Philadelphia, one surmises, because of the opportunities within the machinists' union as well as those of the job market. In the six years from 1914 to 1920, unions expanded like balloons. The overall gain of about 2.3 million nearly doubled the size of the trade-union movement, bringing it to a peak of 5,047,800.* Most of the increase went to established unions in railway transportation, shipbuilding, metalworking, and apparel. The railway clerks bounded from a bare 7,000 members in 1917 to over 71,000 two years later; the electrical

* The figure includes some 166,600 Canadian members of international unions with locals in Canada. The labor movement at this time comprised the American Federation of Labor with 111 national and international union affiliates; the four operating railway brotherhoods—Engineers, Firemen, Railroad Trainmen and Conductors (not affiliated with the AFL); and several other independents, notably the Amalgamated Clothing Workers of America, which affiliated with the AFL in 1933. The examples of growth cited are all of AFL affiliates.

workers grew from 42,000 to 131,000 over the same period. The meat cutters and butcher workmen sprouted from a tiny organization of 10,000 into a substantial 85,000-member trade union. But few unions grew so rapidly or so large as the International Association of Machinists; roughly 74,000 in 1914, the union was 127,484 strong when Clint moved to Philadelphia in 1917 and would reach a peak of 331,449 two years later.

But the Machinists were something more than just a fast-growing craft union. Many among the rank-and-file of the AFL's third largest affiliate were socialist-minded, and a Socialist, William H. Johnson, was elected president of the union at the 1911 convention in Davenport, Iowa. The union was considered "radical" by other AFL unionists. The initiative, referendum and recall, the instruments of a populist democracy, were repeatedly used to frame policy, to force officers into elections, and to otherwise enliven the internal affairs of the union. The union favored the amalgamation of all metal-trade unions into an industrial union in the belief that that would extend the advantages of collective bargaining to those who were not craftsmen. While there was a substantial minority, if not a majority at times, within the union who were convinced of the soundness as well as of the inevitability of socialism, one must keep in mind that it was a simple sort of socialism. As Mark Perlman noted in his history, *The Machinists*, "to them Socialism meant no more than anti-Gomperism, industrial unionism, Populism, and increased political action." Mild stuff nowadays but a radical—and heady—brew back then.

Clint Golden drank deeply of that particular draught. It infused his normally pragmatic mind with a rare romanticism. "We are living in an age of steel and metal," he wrote, several years later, in an article for *The Amalgamated* [Clothing Workers] *Illustrated Almanac—1924*. "Our civilization is a machine civilization. Whatever way we turn, we see the products of the skill of the machinists." He continued with a rather remarkable tribute, in which we can sense how he must have felt about his craft.

> It is he [the machinist] who has developed both the gigantic steam and electric locomotives, the internal combustion engines or motors that propel our automobiles and cause the airplanes to annihilate space, the marvelous turbines that drive ships over the seas of the globe. It is he who devised and builded [*sic*] the type-setting machine, the printing presses, the electrical equipment that brings the peoples of the earth into quick and easy communications, the machines that weave the cloth and furnish us with raiment, and likewise the sewing machines and even down to the smallest needles that are used to fashion the garments we wear. His skill has produced the marvelous instruments of modern surgery. Turn wherever you may and on all sides will be seen evidences of the contribution the machinist has made to modern progress and civilization.

The model is Debsian; this panegyric is followed by political exegesis:

> But the things which he has created have become, in the present industrial order, a modern Frankenstein [*sic*] which has all but destroyed him. His interests, his creative instincts, and his life are bound up with those of his fellow workers. His social vision is greater perhaps than that of his fellow worker in a less important trade or occupation. As a rule he is an idealist, a dreamer. Too often and in too great numbers are machinists theorists. Because of their skill, of their contribution to civilized society, it may be that he and his kind have been impractical. But their hearts are right. It is safe to predict that when the final

> struggle comes, for a new and better order, where all shall receive in proportion to what they contribute, the machinist will be among those who will bear the brunt of the struggle and who will make the greatest sacrifice, if need be, to establish that order.

Over the years, Golden would drop many of these socialist notions and most of the socialist rhetoric, but he never would lose his sense of the marvelous in the machine age, nor of the contribution of the worker. He draws a distinction between the skilled and unskilled. The machinist's "social vision is greater *perhaps* than that of his fellow workers in less important trade or occupation." In the quick sketch of the machinist, Clint clearly projected something of himself—or, his perception of his self—"idealist," "dreamer," a theorist somehow lacking in practicality. Others often saw in Clint an idealist while he considered himself a pragmatist, though not without ideals. What we have above is Golden's identification with those machinists whose "hearts are right" but at one remove. The machinist's role is presented as central to industrial society, "turn wherever you may" and the machinist's contribution is evident. (Railroad firemen and enginemen held similar views as to the importance of their crafts.) Then, there is an odd, perhaps revealing juxtaposition: The things which the machinist has created have become "a modern Frankenstein, which has all but destroyed him." The nearly destroyed man is intrinsically linked to his fellow workers in lesser trades and occupations. This, of course, is his redemption, making safe the prediction that in the final struggle for a new and better order, the machinist will be among those who will "bear the brunt" and "make the greatest sacrifice." Golden was always a craft-proud man with a touch of the Baptist about him.

He plunged into the agitation, organization and internal life of his union with an evangelical fervor. While working at the J. G. Brill machine shops, Golden lead his first strike. One evening in July 1919, after a stint on the picket line, he crossed the street to look up a fellow recently returned from France and said to be a militant machinist. Emil John (Jack) Lever was born in Russia in 1894, emigrated to this country with his family at age twelve, and served during the war in Battery D, Third Field Artillery. He was a diemaker, an ex-Wobbly (the Wobblies were members of the Industrial Workers of the World) who had helped to organize the Philadelphia longshoremen before going off to war, and Golden sought him out to enlist him in the struggle to reform the local Machinist district organization. Lever became a lifelong friend, something of a protegé. Golden won the Brill strike but lost his job, a seeming paradox, but not unusual in those pre-National Labor Relations Act days when management was not compelled by law to hire back workers fired because of union activity. A strike could win higher wages or improved working conditions without securing the reinstatement of fired "troublemakers." That kind of layoff was tantamount to blacklisting, but Golden avoided that fate largely because of an acute labor shortage.

He found another job at Westinghouse, where he kept up his drive for reform of District 1 of the IAM. Gorged with a suddenly enlarged membership, many of whom were more interested in a quick dollar than in the craft, the IAM was a fractious union at the time. Though IAM president Johnson enjoyed considerable popularity, his personal hold as titular leader of the "Progressive," or Socialist faction was never very strong, and he was unable to win over the more conservative "pure-and-simple" oppositionists to some form of support for his administration though in office fourteen years. As Mark Perlman concluded in *The Machinists* "the history of Johnson's regime is one full of friction and quarrels." But for all the turmoil and tummeling, relatively few members were involved. When the pro-Johnson general executive board (three to two) proposed, in a 1918 national referendum, a per-capita increase raising the monthly assessment to $2.00 for journeymen, $1.50 for helpers, and $1.00 for apprentices, it was defeated 22,818 to 21,769; there were 300,000 eligible voters. In another referendum a few months later 13,944 voted to endorse Samuel Gompers' candidacy for reelection as president of the AFL with 12,111 opposed. In an earlier referendum in March 1917 on whether or not to admit women, 13,394 voted yes; 2,387, no. While a great victory for the progressives, it was no great turnout.

Philadelphia District 1, with 15,000 members in 1919–1920, was in the hands of so-called "pure-and-simple" unionists, mostly supporters of the previous national administration headed by James O'Connell. They were traditional craftsmen, friendly towards the AFL and suspicious of the radicalism of the progressives. There may have been some petty racketeering going on, too. Headed by Golden, the reformers won the election held in December 1919. In "setting our house in order," the new administration "investigated and exposed the activities and destructive tactics" of some former officials of the District. It "rid the organization of at least one man it could well spare." This account, given by Golden in the *Machinists' Monthly Journal* of July 1920, was necessarily discreet. Under Golden's leadership, the reformed Machinists joined other union reformers in the Painters, the Metal Polishers, the garment unions and the Textile Workers to clean up the corrupt Philadelphia Central Labor Union.

When Golden was elected business agent for the District, he immediately instituted "many sweeping changes in methods and policies," including a joint organizing committee, a widespread distribution of Machinists' literature, an education program and the establishment of a weekly paper, the *Metal Worker*. The District itself was reorganized, pulling the seven marine locals together into a new Marine Erectors District No. 95, and leaving Golden in charge of fourteen locals composed of men employed in the machine shops in various branches of the industry. Jack Lever was named District Organizer; he began going after the repair shops, and plans were laid for an assault on the Baldwin Locomotive Works, described by Golden in the *Monthly Journal* as "Philadelphia's most notorious long hour and low wage institution." A class in public speaking was organized, transforming ten "hitherto 'speechless' machinists into as fine talkers, orators and debators as have appeared on the platform in various lodges in a long time." The union also acquired "a fine six story building located in the heart of the city." The Machinist Temple, located at Thirteenth and Spring Garden streets, became a center of labor activity, providing meeting halls and offices for a number of other unions as well as the two Machinists districts.

"Realizing that one of the greatest problems with which we had to contend was that of keeping the new member within the organization after he had been induced to join," Golden reported in the *Monthly Journal*, "the present officers . . . have felt it necessary that the organization should function in a manner that would not only inspire confidence in it by the rank and file, but would also hold its respect." Their success, he added, "is best shown by the large increase in membership, the organization of several shops heretofore unorganized and the subsequent wage increases secured by the shop committees working in conjunction with the District Office." The report, the first of many (Golden filed nine reports in 1921, six to eight more than any other business agent did; his were also the longest), spelled out the District's progress under its new leadership.

Many members who have dropped out of the organization in the past have reinstated and a movement to establish the 44 hour week with a $1 per hour minimum has been launched. The entire local gas meter making industry has been organized, the workers of which are members of Meter Makers Lodge No. 368. These brothers have been on strike since April 26 [Golden is writing in late June] for a 15 percent increase in wages and a 48 hour week, and while comparatively new in the organization they have conducted the strike like veterans and their ranks are still unbroken. A local of instrument and dental equipment makers has been formed and efforts are being made to completely organize this branch of the industry which has several hundred workers employed in this city. A rate of $1.10 per hour has been established for machinists and 75 cents for helpers on building construction work. At this writing negotiations for a 44 hour week and an hourly rate of $1.25 for brewery machinists are in progress with excellent chances for a settlement. The brass workers, while comparatively recently organized, have been successful in securing increases ranging from 5 to 15 percent. The growth of Auto Mechanics Lodge No. 1002 has been most remarkable during the past few months and this lodge bids fair to become one of the largest in the city.

It was an auspicious beginning for the newly elected business agent. But the meter makers would be out for twelve weeks, a strike, though victorious, that foreshadowed a time of bitter struggles. In the 1920s, as labor historian Irving Bernstein pointed out in his fine account of the period, *The Lean Years,* American society "was a society in imbalance and workers enjoyed few of its benefits." It was a time of dislocation, with awkward shifts in the economy from production industries to service industries, from blue-collar to white-collar employment. There was persistent unemployment—10 percent or more from 1924 to the year of the crash, 1929; industry was becoming mechanized at an increasing rate, and the word "robot," imported from Czechoslovakia, became a part of our language. During World War I, the federal government secured organized labor's cooperation in the formation of national economic policy. President Wilson appointed William B. Wilson, a former secretary-treasurer of the United Mine Workers, Secretary of Labor. A Federal Mediation and Conciliation Service was established to encourage peaceful collective bargaining. The government operation of the railroads resulted in an extension of trade unionism, since the government as employer granted full official recognition to collective bargaining, a recognition that was carried over, not without difficulty, when the railroads were returned to private hands. But what was achieved on the railroads was not accomplished elsewhere.

Initially, as Golden's first reports to his fellow machinists indicate, labor was optimistic. Encouraged by the Wilsonian recognition of labor's rights, the American Federation of Labor prepared to organize the steel industry. On August 1, 1918, a National Committee for Organizing Iron and Steel Workers was formed, composed of the representatives of twenty-four participating unions, including the Machinists. With John Fitzpatrick, the popular president of the Chicago Federation of Labor, at its head, and with William Z. Foster, a prototype American radical workman and later a leading Communist light, as secretary-treasurer and chief tactician, the drive gained momentum, and by early 1919 over one hundred thousand steelworkers had joined up. But a request for discussions with management was promptly turned down. Speaking for the industry, Judge Elbert H. Gary, chairman of U.S. Steel, declared, "Our corporation and subsidiaries although they do not combat labor unions as such, decline to discuss business with them." Some 98 percent of the organized steelworkers voted for a strike, and when attempts to meet with company officials were further rebuffed, a strike began on September 22, 1919. Before the month was out, some three hundred to three hundred fifty thousand workers were out on strike. Foster estimated that the strike was then 90-percent effective.

What happened next was to provide the script for the so-called American Plan. Company police, local militia and state troopers were mustered against striking workers. Public and/or union meetings were quashed in company towns to prevent the unions from reaching the strikers with the truth about the state of the strike. Since so many of the nation's four hundred thousand steelworkers were recent immigrants, speaking many tongues and anxious about their citizenship, industry propagandists assiduously spread the idea that the strike was un-American. Industrial spies whispered stories of Italian defections into Serbian ears and of Serbian back-to-work movements into Italian ears. Giant posters appeared on steel-town walls proclaiming the failure of the strike and with a giant Uncle Sam, finger pointed at the onlooker from over the smoke stacks of a steel mill, shouting, "Go Back to Work," "*Idite Natrag Na Pasado,*" "*Chodte Nazad do Boboty,*" etc., in seven languages. Slowly but surely, the companies broke the backbone of the strike. Terrified workers began to drift back into the mills. On January 8, 1920, the strike was called off. The workers had sustained twenty deaths, and wage losses of between $86 and $112 million in a three-and-one-half month battle in nine states that had involved more than three hundred thousand workers.

The steel industry's success gave the post-World War I anti-union drive a running start. While organized employers drew upon tactics that ranged from cowing individual workmen with court injunctions to gunrunning strikebreakers past indignant picket lines, the basic strategem of the American

Plan was brilliantly simple and remarkably direct. The idea propagated was that the closed shop was bad *and* un-American while the open shop was good and patriotic. The whole arsenal of union-busting techniques was wrapped in red-white-and-blue bunting. What could be more American than the notion of the open shop, a place "with equal opportunity for all and special privileges for none," where nonunion and union workers were treated alike. The ugly truth, of course, was that the open shop was one closed to trade unionists. As President Buffington of the Illinois Steel Company put it, "We don't discharge a man for belonging to a union, but of course we discharge men for agitating the mills." On December 10, 1917, the U.S. Supreme Court, in the *Hitchman Coal Company* v. *Mitchell* case, held that an individual contract not to join a union was valid, that inducement to join a union was a breach of that contract, and that the right to strike was not a right to instigate a strike. Armed with injunctions barring violations of what workers came to call "the yellow-dog contract," employers could call upon the forces of the law to break almost any strike.

The American Plan arrived in Philadelphia during the summer of 1920. As Golden informed the readers of the August issue of the *Machinists' Monthly Journal*, "the Manufacturers Association and Chamber of Commerce have fired their first shot in a campaign to establish the 'open shop' . . . throughout the city and adjacent territory. They have publically announced that they intend to bring pressure to bear upon all bankers to refuse credit to employers doing business with organized labor or conducting a union shop."

The Machinists had been selected as a key target of the anti-union drive. The National Metal Trades Association was among its most vociferous and active adversaries. Metal trades employers eagerly sought the blacklisting, spy, and strikebreaking services offered by the Association, which boosted its dues and initiation-fees income from $127,696 in 1918 to $541,236 in 1921. NMTA's effectiveness may be measured in terms of the precipitous decline in the membership of the IAM from 330,000 in 1920 to 77,900 in 1924.

Philadelphia became a crucial battleground of the war between capital and labor that continued throughout the 1920s. Employer sorties, at first, stiffened worker resistance. IAM locals, formerly unaffiliated with Philadelphia's central labor body, now joined, crystallizing, as Golden phrased it in the *Monthly Journal*, "progressive sentiment in the Central Labor Union" and preparing "for a closer degree of cooperation on the part of all organized labor than ever before." Philadelphia's workers, according to Golden, "are taking greater interest than in the past in political matters," indicating that "in the fight the employers and business interests are waging against us, the forces of organized labor in this city will be welded closely together with the result that the master class will get a full taste of the workers' solidarity."

When employer spies infiltrated their ranks, the Philadelphia Machinists enjoyed some success in driving them out. "We have been able to locate some of these chaps," Golden informed fellow Machinists, "and in one instance we were able to secure his picture and publish same in our weekly paper—*The Metal Worker*—together with a description of his activities, his number as an operator and the name of his employers. Within twenty-four hours after his picture appeared in the paper, he was virtually run out of the shop in which he was employed by his irate shop mates."

To recruit men for "confidential investigation," the agencies that provided men for anti-union activity ran blind advertisements in the local newspapers. Golden ran a similar help-wanted advertisement, requesting "previous connections, experience, and qualifications," for several weeks. The lead—"wanted machinists"—was changed intermittently to read "carpenters," "printers," "boiler makers," and other skilled unionized trades. "The response to this was somewhat startling," Golden wrote in a memorandum for the National Labor Relations Board fifteen years later. Somewhere between three and four hundred letters were received. Many, of course, came from desperate men wanting work, but "the astonishing thing was that a large number of active union officers and committeemen, particularly in the Machinists organization, answered the ad, indicating that they had worked for such agencies as Railway Audit and Inspection, Pinkerton, Burns, and others. . . ." Among the respondents was a recording secretary of a local Machinist union and a member of Golden's lodge who boasted of his subversive role in the 1919 steel strike. The president of the Philadelphia Central Labor Union and a former business agent of Machinist District 1 were also exposed as agents on the payroll of strikebreaking agencies.

But the union was not so successful in resisting the broader onslaughts of the well-organized employers. The Philadelphians got their first taste of what lay ahead in the shop of the Ace Motor Cycle Corp., manufacturer of the Ace "Fleet as a Flier" four-cylinder motorcycle. The company adopted the American Plan, and dismissed the entire shop committee after it lodged a protest against "the excessive hours" worked and the low rates of pay. When another committee was elected to request the reinstatement of the fired workmen, its members too, were let go. The Ace shop was well organized, and the workers immediately hit the bricks on behalf of their fired spokesmen. "One of the most magnificent fights ever waged by the machinists in this city has been put up," Golden declared, "and our members with the support of the other locals will, no doubt, win."

Golden, however, was much too sanguine. In February 1921, he gloomily reported, "conditions are worse than they have been since 1914. Very few shops are working with a full force on full time and thousands of local men together with large numbers of traveling brothers are out of work." Wage reductions and longer hours were the orders of the day, "with long lines of unemployed bidding against one another for a chance to live." It was not an opportune time for workers forced out on strike. "Our members who were locked out by the firm of Hess & Barker last July are still keeping up the fight and this is also true of the lockout at the shop of Merchant & Evans. Since July 23rd we have maintained a most effective picket line at this shop with the result that the firm has been unable to secure any skilled mechanics." Thousands were being laid off at the Baldwin Locomotive Works, while some were rehired at ten to twenty cents an hour less. The American Can Co. plant was practically shut down by a combination of layoffs and strike action. "We had but four members employed there when the strike was called and we succeeded in getting them out," Golden wrote, "but the wave of unemployment had just struck us and the remaining non-union men there evidently felt that by sticking to their jobs they would have steady employment throughout the business depression. Our latest information is to the effect that practically the entire force of machinists have [*sic*] been laid off and the plant practically closed."

The major test of the American Plan in Philadelphia took place at Wm. Cramp & Sons' Ship and Engine Building Company. The firm employed some eight thousand workers and was under contract to complete five light-battle cruisers for delivery to the navy by October 1, 1921. The federal government had encouraged labor and management to work with one another in shipbuilding, a policy that called for union recognition on the part of the industry's employers. The Cramp firm had been a signatory to an agreement between the Atlantic Coast Shipbuilders Association and the Metal Trades Department of the American Federation of Labor.

Cramp president Harry Mull, however, was also an active member of the Chamber of Commerce Committee on Industrial Relations, a group dedicated to the American Plan. On January 1, 1921, the company posted a notice that it had "discontinued" its agreement with the metal trades. The notice was the prologue to the American Plan drama.

> We decided to discontinue the agreement with the metal trades department of the American Federation of Labor, and to deal directly with our own employees on and after January 1, 1921.
>
> We are convinced that closer and more satisfactory relations can be maintained between you and ourselves by direct intercourse, rather than through individuals disinterested in the welfare of this plant and ignorant of practical shipbuilding, but more concerned over self-advancement and self-gain. The welfare of this plant means much, not only to you and us, but also to our families and the community in which we live. You employees also know that practical shipbuilding cannot be conducted efficiently and economically when throttled by craft regulations.
>
> We are indifferent as to whether our employees are members of labor organizations or not. Nondiscrimination will be practiced by us and we insist that our employees shall act in a similar manner.
>
> We expect our employees to ignore all laws enacted by labor organizations for the restriction of output. It is our intent to deal fairly and justly with the rates of pay, and we shall expect our employees in return to give us an honest output for each hour of employment.
>
> We will reinstitute our rules governing late checking and we request our employees to be prompt. Due consideration will be given to our employees whose late

checking is caused by conditions beyond their control.

We shall receive our individual employees for conference when they desire.

We assure our employees that they will share with us the prosperity of the firm. Our prosperity depends upon the efficiency and economy which increases production and lowers the cost thereof.

We trust that the new year will bring continued prosperity to our employees.

Although the fourteen craft unions organized among the Cramp employees were brought together, in part as a consequence of World War I government policy, under one agreement, and a simple one at that, for all it provided was that all discussions between employer and employee should be through representatives of the union, the unionists were far from united. Some five hundred metal workers walked off the job in mid-December, anticipating the "discontinuation" of the agreement with the company. In January, Cramp dismissed committeemen representing the Boilermakers, who then struck. The Machinists "came out" and were followed by all the other crafts, except the Patternmakers, until well over 7,000 workers were out on strike. A month elapsed before a central strike committee could be formed, comprised of one striker from each of the trades involved. As business agent of the Philadelphia Machinists, Golden was deeply involved in the Cramp strike and left an invaluable account of the affair in a series of monthly reports to the *Machinists' Monthly Journal*, starting in May and running through November 1921.

The company recruited scabs, advertising daily for all classes of workers in the local newspapers. In mid-February, 800 lined up at the shipyard, seeking employment, and the city detailed 250 policemen to protect the job-seekers. The streets adjacent to the Cramp property were sealed off to prevent union picketing. "Police to the number of over 1,000 including many mounted men are on duty and have formed a 'dead line' throughout the restricted area," Golden reported in the April 1921 issue of the *Machinists' Monthly Journal.* Cramp increased the number of its plant guards and armed, as Golden reported, "imported thugs and gunman . . . in the guise of workmen."* Shots were fired from time to time and when strikers disarmed several "workmen" the police searched strikers at union meetings. "No weapons of any description were found." Unionists countered, in effect, by picketing the Kensington district of Philadelphia where the Cramp yards were located. Scabs were hounded to and from work, blows were frequently exchanged, and, in at least one instance, windows were broken in the home of a "Cramp man." The strike committee hired an airplane to fly over the plant to take photographs to expose Cramp claims that the yard was working. The airplane also dropped leaflets, a reprint of Finley Peter Dunne's Mr. Dooley and Mr. Hennessey's exchange on the open shop, rumoured to be Communist propaganda. A motor patrol on the river reported to the strikers that they had

* As a consequence there was a good deal of what is best described as random violence. An irate captain of the Cramp security force walked into the Boilermakers' office and threatened to kill the union secretary, Stanley Ratajeski. (The strike committee had refused to sanction the employment of a striker, who was a relative of the guard, as a Cramp company police officer.) Ratajeski grappled with the irate man, the gun went off and hit the union official in the knee cap.

Golden's description of the next day's events gives some idea of the atmosphere surrounding the strike. "The day following this shooting affair one of the scabs armed with a revolver also attacked some of the pickets by firing his revolver from his coat pocket. He was seized by other strikers in an effort to prevent his wild shooting and in the melee the scab shot himself twice through the groin. The promiscuous arming of these notorious strike breakers has been the cause of many riots that have terrorized the Kensington district. A servile press has laid the entire trouble at the doors of the strikers and a supine police force has permitted these thugs to traverse the streets of the city armed after the fashion of brigands of bygone days."

heard "distinctly" the sounds of exactly three air hammers at work.

The strike was well organized, and provided Clint with a lifelong store of experience on which to draw. Finance, relief, legal aid and publicity committees were formed; wives, mothers, sisters, sweethearts of the strikers were organized into auxiliaries. Once a week they jammed into Harmer Hall, over a thousand in attendance, to hear Pauline Newman of the Women's Trade Union League, Dr. Edith Hooker of Baltimore and Grace B. Klueg, of the IAM's Ladies Auxiliary and others speak "on many phases of the social question" as well as on the issues behind the strike. A ten-piece orchestra was formed to play concerts and the Philadelphia Local of the Theatrical Stage Employees Union staged a three-days' entertainment, raising three thousand dollars for the strikers. The strikers established a commissary that managed to accommodate the "many nationalities" with their "differences in their accustomed mode of living," as they parcelled out food to the families of the strikers. Through the Direct Trading Committee of the American Cooperative Commission, the strikers were able to secure hundreds of bushels of potatoes direct from nearby farmers at a saving of approximately two dollars a bushel over prices charged at chain stores. Over three hundred arrests on charges of inciting to riot were made, and nearly two hundred thousand dollars in bail had to be raised to secure the release of the arrested strikers pending their trials.

When the American Legion and "other organized bodies of 125 percenters" planned a parade on All-American Day, April 14, the strikers, as Golden put it, "felt that a little parade of their own would not be out of place." When the workers and their supporters left crowded strike meetings and filed down the street, two by two, "in perfect order," they were met by a mass array of mounted police. Golden tells what happened next:

The first few that left Friendship Hall, where the Machinists hold their meetings, were charged by the mounted bulls, rounded up and driven into waiting patrols. They were taken to police headquarters and charged with inciting to riot. That evening some thousands of strikers and their families again paraded, with the police dashing from one end of the line to the other in motorcycle side-cars and on horses. Some excellent snapshots, showing these "guardians of the law and order" beating up innocent bystanders and charging the strikers were secured. The following day a prostitute press carried shock headlines stating that the police had been obliged to charge a crowd of strikers who were marching on Cramps' shipyard, intimating that they were bent on seizing the plant.

At midsummer, Clint summed up the strike situation, not without a touch of bravado.

Twenty-four weeks of this fight for justice has transformed 6,000 men, for years accustomed to the usual routine of going to work, working all day or night as the case might be, returning home and then repeating the formula every twenty-four hours, into a solid compact body, fully cognizant of the extremes to which the master class will go in their mad efforts to crush the workers; well disciplined, learning more each day of the war of the classes, and after each day of battle resolving that some day, some time, they will put an end to a system that permits a parasitic minority to control the lives and destinies of the many by the ownership of their jobs, as well as the press and State. And could these masters of industry but realize to what extent their arbitrary and unsocial actions have aroused the working women, and wives, mothers; yes, and the children of these thousands of shipbuilders, they would feel their control fast slipping away from them. Instead of flying into hysterics and beating the air with their protests against every expression of a desire of the workers for a better and bigger life, they would take stock of their actions and try to find a way to at least ease the suffering of their victims.

The strike, as the discerning between-the-lines reader will notice, was not going well. In Golden's words, "conditions remained 'unchanged' in so far as the spirit and solidarity of the strikers are concerned." But the unions had run out of strike benefits; Cramp's had a shipyard full of scabs. The strikers had hoped that the government would intervene to enforce its wartime policy of encouraging labor-and-management bargaining relationships. The United States Department of Labor made one attempt, but the company offer did not include the return to work of *all* strikers and was turned down. In the end, the navy refused to intervene, and granted the company an unlimited extension of time in which to complete work on the battle cruisers; on September 22, 1921, the Machinists voted to call off the strike. The strike had cost the union $173,864.56, most of it in cash relief and strike benefit payments. It also ended on a discordant note. As Golden commented, "It is to be regretted that the members of the Boilermakers' organization could not see their way clear to call off the Cramp strike at the same time the Machinists took action. However, a sharp difference of opinion existed in this respect, the Boilermakers thinking that they can successfully and effectively continue the strike without the assistance of the machinists and other crafts, and without the payment of strike benefits." The Cramp strike ended in a victory for the open shop. It reinforced Golden's belief in industrial unionism and of the necessity for a union shop.

"The chief lesson to be had from these many and varied struggles with an organized master class," Golden declared in a comment about the Cramp and similar strikes in the clothing, construction and printing trades, "is the fact that there is not the degree of unity and cohesion essential for success in the present form of craft organization. In all the cases cited we find the most damnable crimes committed against the workers; in some instances by their own leaders and all in the holy name of trade autonomy."

Perhaps the most difficult thing a trade unionist can do is negotiate a wage reduction and at the same time preserve the fundamental rights of union members. Widespread unemployment made wage cuts inevitable during the early 1920s, and gave the employers the cutting edge in their attack on unionism. That Golden managed to salvage something out of this was something of a miracle. His negotiations with the employers in the printing machinery repair shops demonstrate his ability to wrest the most out of a given situation. Within that industry, a verbal agreement as to hours, rates of pay and working conditions had existed for a number of years, when the employers served notice, in the spring of 1921, of a wage reduction. Golden immediately called a series of conferences between the employers and the shop committees, a series of talks that finally worked out a 10-percent wage reduction for a six-month period but also retained the schedule of hours, overtime rules, working conditions and the union shop in a written agreement. The starting rate for new men, seventy-five cents an hour, was unchanged and an effective shop minimum of eighty cents an hour established. In a settlement negotiated with John Wood Mfg., a producer of range boilers and air tanks, Golden secured an understanding that should trade conditions warrant, negotiations would be opened to revise wages upwards. Of greater significance, however, was a provision that called for foremen, when new openings developed, to advise the shop stewards and committeemen, who, in turn, would hire the new workers. As Golden remarked, "A greater degree of shop democracy and control by the workers exists in this shop than in any other shop in this section of the country." It would be a model for years to come.

Golden's notions of the degree of unity and cohesion essential to trade-union success were broad indeed. He was active in the founding of the Philadelphia Labor College. Brookwood, the nation's first workers resident college, won his support. He publicized Brookwood in the pages of the *Machinists' Monthly Journal* and arranged a scholarship for Jack Lever, who became a member of Brookwood's first class in 1922. Golden organized a local branch of the American Labor Alliance for Trade Relations with Russia. The bad news about the outcome of the Russian revolution had not as yet filtered back to the United States. "Our members feel," Golden wrote, "that the resumption of trade relations with Russia will not only in a large measure contribute toward relieving the present unemployment situation, but it will also give the Russian workers an opportunity to further develop their new social and industrial state." He worked with other unionists to organize the Producers & Consumers Bank, one of a wave of workers banks established in the 1920s. (The only survivors, incidently, are the Amalagmated Clothing Workers Banks of New York and Chicago.) He helped form the Quaker City Cooperative Association, a consumer group that hoped to enter the building business, to acquire land for building, and to manufacture, buy and sell "all kinds of commodities." Workers, he said, "are now thinking and acting along constructive lines," and Golden expressed the hope in the Machinists' *Journal*, "that a new scheme of things is being developed within the shell of the old order."

To further that objective, Golden became active in politics. He served as secretary to the local branch of labor's Citizens Non-Partisan Political Association, an operation largely run out of his office. He also participated in the 1921 launching of a

Labor Party in Philadelphia, which had the backing of the Central Labor Union. The party fielded a full ticket—"all of whom were union men and women"—in the municipal elections, garnering some thirty-two thousand votes but nary a mention in the local daily press. Labor Party partisanship, however, did not prevent's Golden's endorsement of William J. Burke, an officer of the Baltimore & Ohio R.R. Conductors, in the Republican primary of 1922. Burke ran against George Wharton Pepper, "handyman of Big Business and the Pennsylvania Railroad." Golden's varied activities, however, always came to rest on his trade union concerns. Unemployment was a pressing problem; in January 1923, he reported in the *Machinists' Monthly Journal*, that "fully 75 percent of our membership in District No. 1 were unemployed [for a period of nearly eighteen months]."* The District organized an Unemployed Relief Committee, comprised of delegates from all the Lodges, to raise funds through collections at membership meetings, assessments where possible and other fund-raising activities. Meal tickets were issued for meals at a restaurant in the basement of the Machinists' Temple, operated by the Temple Association. Again, an effort was made to purchase potatoes and other foodstuffs directly from nearby farmers. Eviction cases were referred to the Tenants' Protective Association, formed to "combat the greedy landlords and profiteers in housing." The point of all this activity being, as Golden declared, to "demonstrate to numbers of the public generally that we are not only interested in shop conditions, hours and rates of pay, but also in the personal welfare of every individual member."

How much convincing union members needed is uncertain.

* The machinists were in a bad way the country over. On August 24, 1921, the staff officers of the union—the international president, ten vice presidents, the secretary-treasurer, and seven auditors—decided to refund their salaries for August to be used in relief of unemployed members. It was a gift of $10,000, a large sum for the time.

The union hall was for many trade unionists, especially craftsmen, a natural center of their lives. Whatever protection they possessed against economic vicissitudes was to be found in their union. There was, then, no social security, no unemployment compensation, few if any employer-financed health and welfare benefits, little, in fact, beyond that which they might secure through their trade union. In an age when movies were still in their infancy, radio as yet a thing of magic crystals and television undreamed of—and long before the automobile would spin workers off into an ever-growing surburban ring—unionists found their entertainment, much of their social life in union gatherings. Golden gives us a glimpse of that long-forgotten world in his May 1922, report in the *Machinists' Monthly Journal*, one of the last he would file.

> More than 800 members of the various lodges, their wives and families, came to the spacious auditorium to enjoy an evening of entertainment and education. Glenn E. Plumb was the principal speaker of the evening and his splendid address was listened to with deepest interest.* Following Mr. Plumb's address, a solo was rendered by Herman Thoma of Lodge 1018. Little Elizabeth Zappo, 6-year-old niece of Secretary P. J. Zappo of District 1, gave a wonderful exhibition of toe dancing for a youngster. Mrs. Viola Coffman and Miss Steen of the newly organized Ladies' Auxiliary rendered a duet which called for several encores. Patrick Tinney, versatile Scotchman and a union patternmaker, out-Laudered Harry Lauder. Music was furnished by an orchestra of striking printers, members of Typographical Union No. 2 and the Musicians' Union as well. A feature of the evening was a presentation of the charter for the Local Ladies' Auxiliary to the officers . . . At the conclusion of the entertainment

* Glenn E. Plumb, general counsel in the railway unions, was the major advocate of a proposal to nationalize the American railroads.

union made ice cream and home made cake was served in plentiful quantities to all present. Adjournment was then taken to the splendid ball room on the first floor of the Temple, where young and old alike tripped the light fantastic to their heart's content.

The dance drew to a close, however. The machinists had entered upon hard times. Golden was nominated in 1922 as a candidate for the editorship of the *Machinists' Monthly Journal*, but he lost to Fred Hewitt, the incumbent, 19,555 votes to 36,384. District 1 was in bad shape financially. Jack Lever later recalled, "Three of us, machinists and tool makers, young fellows, pledged to ourselves to give one-third of our pay to keep Clint on the job." Golden, according to Lever, received one hundred dollars a month from the Grand Lodge, the international union, and "we provided $30 a week, between the three of us, which was a little more in my case than one-third of my pay, because a toolmaker's wage at that time was all of $27 a week. We held the thing together for several years." But they could not hold out against the American Plan *and* unemployment. Golden was asked by the Amalgamated Clothing Workers to undertake a survey of conditions in the clothing industry of Pennsylvania, preparatory to a state-wide organizing drive. Jack Lever took over the job of District 1 business agent during the summer of 1923, but a service-connected illness put him into the hospital and he had to resign. The office was closed and the Machinists' Temple was put up for sale.

Brookwood

WHILE IN Philadelphia, Clint Golden became active in a number of labor and liberal causes. During the railroad shopmen's strike of 1922, in which the machinists were involved, he served as the secretary of a relief and defense committee and, drawing upon his experience at raising funds for the Cramp shipyard strikers, he raised some twelve thousand dollars from sources outside the labor movement for relief purposes. He also secured the loan of thirty thousand dollars in Liberty Bonds for use as bail for strikers arrested during the walkout. When the Amalgamated Clothing Workers general strike of the Philadelphia market for union recognition ran into trouble, Golden along with Jack Lever organized a committee of public-spirited citizens to investigate civil liberty violations by the courts and the police. The committee also worked "to bring about peace" within the industry. It was, however, something of a lost cause. There just was not sufficient weight to liberal public opinion to counter an injunction issued by Judge Joseph P. Rogers, who held, "This organization is no corporation, should have no legal recognition, and should be driven out of all existence as a menace to the nation." The major clothing manufacturers succeeded in defeating their workers with the aid of the courts, the police and gangsters in yet another variation of the American Plan.

Golden's efforts, however, were much appreciated by the Amalgamated Clothing Workers.

The country, in truth, was in the grips of a self-induced hysteria, a product of the recent war and the collapse of its high-minded aims. Though employers, in fact, were winning strikes and therefore, presumably, in control of industrial matters, broad segments of the public persisted in seeing red revolution behind every picket sign. Attorney General A. Mitchell Palmer envisioned a national emergency. "Like a prairie-fire," he wrote, "the blaze of revolution was sweeping over every American institution of law and order a year ago [1919]. It was eating its way into the homes of the American workman, its sharp tongues of revolutionary heat were licking the altars of the churches, leaping into the belfry of the school bell, crawling into the sacred corners of American homes, seeking to replace marriage vows with libertine laws, burning up the foundation of society."

The Immigration Act of 1918 provided for the expulsion and exclusion of aliens advocating the overthrow by force or violence the government of the United States. Between November 1, 1919 and April 26, 1920, 3000 aliens allegedly in this country in violation of the law were arrested. After hearings, 762 were deported—455 Communists and 307 members of the Union of Russian Workers.

Steelworker Jacob Dolla, of Lebanon, Pennsylvania, was a victim of Palmerite passions. A Hungarian immigrant, he was a natural leader of men and became very active in the 1919 steel strike. When an alleged Pinkerton detective, passing himself off as a steelworker, placed two bombs up against a boardinghouse where several scabs roomed, one bomb went off and no one was hurt. But Dolla was arrested, prevented from calling witnesses who could prove that he was out of town on the fateful day, and convicted on five counts, including a felonious attempt to kill. He lost his home and what little money he had saved in making his defense. His wife, a frail woman, had to find work in a factory to support their two children. While in prison, Dolla wrote to James Maurer, a leading Socialist and president of the Pennsylvania Federation of Labor, who asked Golden to look into the matter. Many years later Jack Lever recalled, "We organized a civil-liberties committee in Pennsylvania to get Jake Dolla out of jail." Golden raised some money from the council of steel-industry unions and from friends of Esther Harlan to aid the Dolla family and to carry on a campaign for his release. Golden prevailed upon Governor Gifford Pinchot—"I personally know that he has very little love for the state cossacks," he wrote to William Hannon, secretary of the steel-unions council—to appoint an investigator to look into charges raised by Lebanon Steel Company attorneys in attempts to forestall a pardon. After two years of effort, Dolla was pardoned with a full restoration of civil rights.

Typically, Golden did not let matters rest there. He arranged a vacation for Dolla. As he wrote to John Rothschild, who with Charles Garland and several others operated a cooperative farm at Coopersburg, Pennsylvania, "I think you can understand about how a fellow might feel who has spent nearly five years in prison for no reason at all. . . ." Golden, who was always a realist in these matters, however, cautioned the middle-class idealists at Hazletts Orchard, "Dolla is a typical proletarian. He is a somewhat impulsive character and one who apparently never tires of talking about the injustice that has been done to him. This, of course, is not a difficult matter to understand when one is acquainted with the facts of the case. It may mean, however, that should he come to stay with your group, that he will nearly talk all of you to death during his first week or two and this may become somewhat tiresome. I feel that you have a right to know of this inasmuch as you have been good enough to express your willingness to take him in and to help him get on his feet." While Dolla recuperated at

Hazletts Orchard, Golden raised funds through Roger Baldwin and R. W. Dunn of the Civil Liberties Union and from the generous Miss Harlan to carry the family through relocation to Pittsburgh and until Dolla secured a job, which he did with assistance from Golden's old friend and associate Andrew T. McNamara of the Machinists. Golden and McNamara also managed to prevent Dolla's deportation as an "undesirable alien" later in the same year, 1924.

The Dolla case was not the only such case Golden worked on during the Palmer days. "We remember, too," Jack Lever wrote in 1961, "the civil liberties case of that Italian 'anarchist' tailor who got too vocal about wanting a union and whom, with one more court order in your hand, you snatched off the boat at Gloucester immigration dock the very moment it was pulling out." A letter to Golden from August Bellanca, a member of the Amalgamated Clothing Workers' General Executive Board, puts these cases into an international context, a chilling foretaste of things to come, though in this instance one with a happier outcome. "Your success in staying the deportation of these comrades Joseph Baldasarre and Oswaldo Eusekki has not only given fathers to their children, but you have also saved two sure victims of the barbarous and criminal Fascisti movement which is in control of Italy today." Mussolini, incidentally, was being praised at about this time by such as muckraker Lincoln Steffens as "a romantic figure," a "willful man of action," boss of "historically discovered and experimentally proved going concerns." As tourists of history, they saw Mussolini running trains on time. It was not a mistake that the labor movement, or Golden, ever made.

Golden was indefatigible on behalf of the victims of the 1920s flash of hysteria, pressing Governor Pinchot, pleading with senators and federal officials. Where he could not win a legal case, he did not hesitate to beg for clemency. He wheedled senators George Wharton Pepper and Magnus Johnson into intervening on behalf of Catoni Ticci, an Italian shoemaker caught in a raid while collecting a debt from an acquaintance who, apparently, was a Communist. Though Ticci belonged to no "subversive" organization, he was slated for deportation until Golden saved him. Again, Golden took a personal interest in the family of those in trouble. Often, he would just "drop in" to see how they were doing, to see if they needed anything in the way of food, clothing, or rent money. On one such visit, he came in the kitchen door and nearly fell over a kneeling woman wiping up an oven spill. A child was ill, and a group of women were helping out, and Dora Oleve had volunteered to bake a pie. But she had dropped it taking it out of the oven and there was Clint Golden, looming large over her embarrassment.

Dora Oleve was a shirtmaker, the third youngest in a family of eight, born of immigrant parents, Jews who had fled the pogroms of czarist Russia. Her father operated a small candy store, ran a picture framing business, farmed a bit outside Philadelphia and taught Hebrew. He was a Zionist, and Dora thought of her family as being "conservative." Her sister married a Wobbly, Grover Perry, and the Oleve girls got to know Jack Lever. Through him, Dora became active in a volunteer group that pitched in to help out families of workers in trouble. That is how she and Clint Golden met; they were married on April 24, 1923.

That summer, as a general organizer for the Amalgamated Clothing Workers, Golden mapped a drive to unionize the industry in the state. New offices were opened on Arch Street; "among the best appointed of those occupied by the trade unions of Philadelphia," according to a report carried in the *New York Call.* Room 7, the report continued, "is fitted up for use as a reception, reading and conference room. Charts showing in a graphic manner how the various units in the structure of the Amalgamated are related to each other and to the general organization; others showing the difference between the wage scales in the organized and unorganized markets, the growth of the Amalgamated, the extent of season employment, etc., decorate the walls of this room. All publications issued by the various departments of the general office are also available for reading and study by those interested." The charts reported the findings of a survey conducted by Golden: twenty thousand workers, 60 percent women, eligible for membership in the union, producing in Pennsylvania $65 million worth of men's clothing annually and $40 million in men's shirts. Pennsylvania shirt factories produced 4,965,700 dozen shirts in 1922, Schuylkill County was the largest producer, with a total output of 1,133,700 dozen; Philadelphia ran second, with 782,000.

Throughout eastern Pennsylvania, coat, pants and vest contractors worked for New York and Philadelphia houses, and while a few "country town contractors" had modern, sanitary shops, others utilized private houses, barns and other outbuildings. Amalgamated organizers cited one old wooden barn housing a large cutting room as typical. "The place is overrun with rats. Running water and sanitary toilets or wash rooms are unknown." Similar shops, the Amalgamated General Executive Board report for 1924 added, "exist in communities so small that there is an insufficient supply of labor. Auto trucks fitted up to accommodate from ten to twenty people are sent out through the adjacent territory to pick up wives and daughters of farmers and bring them to the shop in the morning and deliver them to their homes at night. In other cases, country town contractors distribute the unworked garments by auto trucks over a large area to the homes of Pennsylvania Dutch farmers where the women and children toil long hours with foot power sewing machines and by hand." Wages, Golden found in his survey, were low. In Philadelphia, where the union had had some impact, workers averaged $20.64 a week, but throughout the state, they averaged only $14.40 a week.

Open-shop employers, however, continued to dominate the Philadelphia clothing market. As the Amalgamated General Executive Board report of 1928 acknowledged, "Union control in factories was lax. Manufacturers made demands for reductions and adjustments in wages. [This followed a partially successful strike in the summer of 1923 that gained one to three dollars more a week for Amalgamated members.] Workers of six . . . shops were locked out for weeks and other employers were causing troubles." A general strike was called on August 6, 1924, and twenty-five hundred workers responded. But the union's weaknesses were apparent in Golden's prestrike statement of intent. "Those manufacturers who will settle with us," he said, "will receive every possible co-operation and will experience practically no cessation of production. Their workers may remain out for a day or so merely as a demonstration but following this they will get full co-operation from the union. Those who will not meet with us must take the consequences. . . . We propose nothing but civilization of the industry and make no demands which will mean an increased wage scale or an increased cost of production. The issue is clean cut. It is merely for the placing of the industry on a higher plane. The conditions, particularly of sanitation and home work, are different in each shop. It is an individualistic matter, one that must be talked over in conference with individuals and as individuals. It is no proposition where we make a series of arbitrary demands that must be either accepted or rejected. The strike is a humane strike for the bettering of conditions."

The strike, the union later claimed, was a success "as far as it went," but "there were no settlements with the larger manufacturing firms." By August 14, 95 percent of the strikers had returned to work under union conditions. Settlements were made with forty manufacturers and fifty contracting shops, who agreed to the registration of contractors, as a guarantee against wage cutting and assurance of a strict forty-four-hour week; elimination of home work; and all cutters belonging to the Amalgamated. But these firms were all small units; the greater portion of the industry was left in the hands of open-shop employers. It would not be organized until the 1930s.

Unions were having a difficult time and the lesson to be drawn from this, Golden concluded, was "that labor must be self-sufficient." He had the craftman's self-assurance and a belief in the fundamental soundness of his fellow workers and a confidence in their ability to manage. He remained a socialist, though apparently no longer a member of the Socialist Party. In *American Labor's Who's Who*, published in 1926, Golden stated "no political affiliation at present." "The way to save ourselves and American civilization," he wrote in April 1922, for *Labor Age*, "is to kill the profit system, and introduce the idea of service in industry." He took heart from the AFL endorsement of the Plumb Plan for the nationalization of the railroads and the Mine Workers' support for public ownership of coal. But he foresaw dangers in nationalization "if workers control does not go with it. There must not only be a distinct voice in management, but always the recognition of the right to strike and to bargain collectively. If these rights were denied, it would be better to go on with our present messed-up situation. For otherwise, we would have Bureaucracy." Cooperation attracted Golden as an alternative, "though still largely a matter of hope." The Machinists were trying it, as they did during the Cramp strike, forming cooperatives to act as commissary departments in strikes, and so were miners in at least one West Virginia town. "Why should not the workers, through their unions, run factories—clothing, metal works, building, etc.? They could probably do it much better themselves." Golden deplored what he saw as a tendency in some quarters to settle on one technique—nationalization, cooperation, etc.—"as the be-all and end-all of the social scheme. The American labor movement cannot stand for that sort of dogmatics. It will only lead to little bickering groups, fighting each other harder than they fight the common enemy." Each way has its merit, "in beating down the defenses of Profit-Making. Let us give a hand to all of them—consumers cooperation in the food and kindred businesses, producers cooperation in the factory industries, and Nationalization in the big basic industries. That means a general advance on all wings for the establishment of *service as the business of work and life*."

Writing in the *Machinists' Monthly Journal*, published in the same month, Golden confessed that recent developments, "together with the acquisition of additional knowledge as a result of intimate contact with the large section of the 'public' known as wage workers," had "served to dampen the ardor of the once enthusiastic advocate" of "Public Ownership and Democratic Management." His doubts were occasioned by the large influx of workers into the machinists trade, "more interested in the dollar than the craft," who deserted the union once times were bad. Golden expressed a growing belief in education, a belief reinforced by his experience with the Philadelphia Labor College. "If we are hopeful and believe that at some time we are not only going to *manage* but *own* the industries of this country," he wrote, "is it not time that we began to make preparations for the future responsibilities that we will be obliged to assume?" In *Labor Age*, Golden declared, "workers have too long depended on their brute strength and bare hands to bring them results and have failed to use their heads except as cushions for the riot sticks of the State constabulary." Too many unionists, he added, know nothing of parliamentary procedure, cannot keep minutes of meetings nor follow through on important correspondence, and keep woefully inadequate financial records. Workers, too, need "to make use of expert knowledge as a weapon in their struggle for justice," as well as "to pry into what have heretofore been unknown facts relative to production, management, ownership, capitalization, overhead and other mysterious factors in modern industrial society."

Workers' education then was in its infancy. The socialist movement, which had provided an education of sorts for self-educated working men and women, was in disarray. Few universities or colleges—Wisconsin was a notable exception—offered courses in labor history, economics or labor-management relations, nor were many, then, interested in education tailored for adult working men and women. Unionists, many of them immigrants or the children of immigrants with an uncertain grasp of the language, desperately needed training in the fundamentals, just as their unions increasingly would need investigators, research workers and economists. Bryn Mawr and the YWCA began workers' summer schools and weekend institutes. Upwards of a dozen labor colleges were founded in the 1920s. Courses in the basics—how to run a meeting, organize or write a leaflet—were given at hours convenient to working people. The more ambitious schools offered courses in labor economics, history, even literature and the arts. The idea was to educate workers, but there was a growing emphasis on activists and those likely to become union officers or staff. "No more constructive work on the part of district councils, central labor unions, system federations and local unions," Golden argued, "could be undertaken than that of establishing free scholarships in resident workers colleges and of selecting the intelligent, capable and ambitious workers from the rank and file for the training. . . . By developing and controlling our own institutions of learning for the men and women of our movement, we will educate the workers into the service of their fellow workers rather than away from the labor movement, as is so often the case when the ambitious unionist enters the average university."

Golden linked labor education to "the aspirations of the workers for liberty, justice and democracy," and himself with those who viewed labor education as a means of reforming the leadership and policies of organized labor. Many of those active in the growing labor education movement of the 1920s shared Golden's views and were of one socialist persuasion or another. The leadership of the American Federation of Labor did not take kindly to what it considered unjustified criticisms of craft unionism or of alleged racketeering, nor did they care for proselytizing on behalf of industrial unionism, the nationalization of industry or a labor party. Such stuff, said AFL president William Green, was "highly objectionable from a Trade Union point of view." The Federation took control of the Workers' Education Bureau, formed in 1921, to eliminate, as John P. Frey, secretary-treasurer of the Metal Trades Department, put it in a letter to Green, "those conditions which we thought were unsound, and to build up the W.E.B. so that it could carry on the work the A. F. of L. desired." The Bureau was not to concern itself with trade-union policies but to function strictly as an educational and research organization. As a consequence, as historian James O. Morris demonstrated in his *Conflict within the AFL,* most of the labor progressives of the 1920s centered their activities at Brookwood Labor College, in the Labor Publication Society, publisher of *Labor Age*, and, later, in the Conference for Progressive Labor Action.

Golden was not happy working for the Amalgamated. As he wrote to A. J. Muste, head of Brookwood, "I feel somewhat unsettled." In part, this was the natural let-down that followed the collapse of his Machinists' hopes and that flows from certain kinds of career change. Golden had been an elected officer of the Machinists, and a leader with a growing base within his own union and within the larger labor movement. With the Amalgamated, though appreciated and valued, he was nonetheless on staff and could never hope to establish the kind of base he had enjoyed within the Machinists. At the same time, he lost his mother on Decoration Day. "She had lost her mind completely and pretty much of her eyesight in the few weeks preceding her death," he wrote to Andrew T. McNamara, an old friend and Machinists representative in Pittsburgh, adding that "Jack Lever is in pretty bad shape as a result of another operation." By fall of 1924, even though "some matters in connection with the policy of the General office of the Amalgamated in relation to the Philadelphia situation have been ironed out," Golden was looking for "some other field in which I can render a useful service to the movement."

He had been named to the board of directors of the American Fund for Public Service, becoming a vice-president in 1925. It is one of the ironies of radicalism that its activities are often sustained by the monies of the very rich, and the Fund, widely known as the Garland Fund after its benefactor Charles Garland, was a case in point. It would not be too great an exaggeration to say that it kept a good many radicals and their cause alive during the flush, capitalistic golden twenties. Young Garland inherited in 1922 over a million dollars from his father, a Wall Street broker. The family had amassed a fortune from the manufacture of stoves and ranges. At first, he wished to renounce the inheritance, but friends, notably Roger Baldwin, the noted civil libertarian, prevailed upon the young idealist to accept the money and to endow a "socially-conscious" foundation with nine hundred thousand dollars. The fund's capital was invested in common stock of the First National Bank of New York and the great bull market of the 1920s boosted its value to nearly two million dollars. As David A. Shannon put it in his history of the Socialist Party, "The furious activities on Wall Street were creating money for the Garland Fund faster than the radicals could spend it."

Garland Fund bequests were made by a self-perpetuating board of directors, self-described in an annual report as having been "picked out as persons of diverse connections with radical, labor and liberal movements, who, despite philosophical differences, are practical minded enough to deal harmoniously with immediate issues." James Weldon Johnson, executive secretary of the National Association for the Advancement of Colored People, served as its president for many years. (The Fund expired in 1941.) Roger Baldwin served as secretary, Morris L. Ernst, famed civil libertarian lawyer, was treasurer, and Walter Nelles, counsel. Others on the board were Elizabeth Gurley Flynn, Benjamin Gitlow, Freda Kirchwey, Scott Nearing and Norman Thomas. They gave money to Brookwood, the Communist publication *New Masses,* the Socialist League for Industrial Democracy, the Rand School Research Department, *Labor Age,* the anti-fascist *Il Nuovo Mundo,* the Vanguard Press (Golden was on the Press's board of directors), the Brotherhood of Sleeping Car Porters, the NAACP, the Sacco-Vanzetti Defense Committee and many other such causes.

As Roger Baldwin recalled many years later, "We backed the new experiments in labor education with fancy sums—Brookwood Labor College, then the leading institution, which later went bankrupt, getting far too much for its own good. We employed one trustee, Clinton S. Golden, a staunch labor man—recently knighted by Harvard with an honorary degree—just to go around the country and find wise ways of spending our money to educate unionists. He found them." By 1924, the Fund was matching Brookwood's student and union income with an equal amount not to exceed ten thousand dollars annually. Later, the Fund waived the requirement for matched funds, and by 1926 it gave Brookwood over one hundred fifty thousand dollars. (Golden secured another one hundred thousand dollars in appropriations for workers' education over the same period.) Brookwood was, as a consequence, well enough heeled to loan the International Ladies' Garment Workers' Union one hundred thousand dollars (which it had received from the Garland Fund) to help defray expenses of the New York Cloakmakers' strike of 1926. But the initial grant to Brookwood was not made without "misgivings," as Baldwin reported at the college's fifteenth anniversary. "Some of us thought we could not see ahead for ten years in any enterprise clearly enough to commit ourselves so far in advance. Indeed there was so much doubt in the board that the appropriation carried by only one vote. Some were skeptical as to whether Brookwood could maintain a nonpartisan basis of labor education. Others doubted the wisdom of fixing definite annual amounts in a diminishing ratio so far in advance. They were dubious as to whether the trade union movement could be induced to support Brookwood in an ever increasing ratio as the Fund's aid declined."

Golden, no doubt, helped to allay their fears. He was their working-class connection. But he was also a factor in their "misgivings." A. J. Muste, Brookwood's director, had explored with the Fund the possibility of hiring a field director, who would "investigate" workers' education throughout the United States with an eye to drafting proposals for assistance, and who would also assist Brookwood "by spreading its gospel and propaganda" as well as by recruiting scholars. Golden was suggested for the post. James H. Maurer, the doyen of labor progressives of the day, a leading socialist and president of the Pennsylvania Federation of Labor and a member of Brookwood's Labor Co-operating Committee, was enthusiastic. As he wrote Muste on September 17, 1924, "If Clint Golden can be secured, then I, unhesitatingly, say, engage him. I have known Golden for some years and cheerfully recommend him. He understands both the labor movement and workers' education. Besides he is an able speaker, a good mixer, makes a good appearance, has the courage of his convictions, is progressive, and just the man for the job." Both Baldwin and Nearing were enthusiastic but, as Nearing wrote to Muste, "He is on our Board and we can't very well hire ourselves," and as Muste reported to Golden, "Roger is absolutely positive that you would have to resign from the American Fund if you took it." Norman Thomas wrote Muste that he "personally would not be in favor of his resigning" and Golden was hesitant about leaving. As he told Muste, "They do not seem to have very much direct contact with the Labor Movement as it really is and I therefore feel that if the movement is to get anything from the Fund there should be a practical unionist on it." But, he added, "I am rather keen about the field secretaryship."

Muste and Golden conducted an informal canvass of the Garland Fund board, talking up the idea with Thomas, Ernst, Gurley Flynn, and several others. At the November 1924 board meeting, Muste's letter proposing Golden's appointment as field secretary for Brookwood was read, and Morris Ernst took the position that Golden must remain with the Garland Fund as well. "Quite a discussion followed," Golden later wrote to Muste. "Roger was practically the only one to object and he did this purely on 'ethical' grounds. A motion was finally made to approve of my appointment and for me to remain on the Board and it was passed without a dissenting note. Even Scott seemed to favor it." Golden resigned from the Amalgamated, effective December 13, 1924, and by December 28 the Goldens had leased their Philadelphia house and were ready to move to the Mount Vernon-like estate isolated on a wooded hilltop in Katonah, New York, that housed Brookwood, labor's first residential college.

Brookwood was the product of a Utopian strain in American history that threads its way in and out of working class efforts at organization and self-help. Helen and William Fincke were pacifists, active in the Fellowship of Reconciliation, and they had participated through the liberal Committee of Forty-Eight in the founding of the Farmer-Labor Party. Their radicalism was closer to the cooperative Associationism of Fourier and the founders of Brook Farm, evoked in their choice of name for the new Katonah venture, than to the Marxian-oriented thought of the liberals of the 1920s and 1930s. Still, like the middle-class idealists and visionaries of the 1840s, the Finckes were drawn to labor, and pretty much for the same reasons. The workers were an inchoate mass, seemingly caught up in revolutionary turmoil, with their unions envisaged, at least by reformers, as the only possible vehicles for progressive or even radical change in a country dominated by a heartless corporate capitalism. At first, the Finckes set up what young people call a "free school," a preparatory education free of coercion and full of love and mutual respect. The school, however, did not succeed, and in 1921 the Finckes, influenced in part by Toscan Bennett, an acquaintance from Hartford, Connecticut, who had been a corporation lawyer and was then interested in labor, decided to call a conference to consider a college for working-class adults.*

The founders issued a statement of purpose. "We, laboring men and women and labor educators . . . decided to unite with the American labor union movement a force of education that will serve American labor with trained, responsible lib-

* Present were the Finckes, Toscan Bennett, James Maurer, John Brophy, president, District 2 of the United Mine Workers, John Fitzpatrick, president of the Illinois Federation of Labor; Rose Schneiderman, president of the Women's Trade Union League; Joseph Schlossberg, secretary-treasurer of the Amalgamated Clothing Workers; Jay G. Brown, president of the International Timber Workers' Union; Abraham J. Muste, executive secretary of the Amalgamated Textile Workers of America (independent of the AFL); Abraham Lefkowitz, vice-president of the American Federation of Teachers; and Charles Kutz, a Machinists business agent and editor of a Pennsylvania labor paper.

erally educated men and women from the ranks of the workers." They hastened to assure union officialdom that the new college "is not intended to act as a propagandist institution. Thoroughly in sympathy with the aims and aspirations of labor as a whole, the college will closely cooperate with the national and international labor groups, also with the various local colleges and schools that send to it working men and women who show promise and need further education in order to best serve the labor movement and through it society."

The Finckes and the Bennetts hoped to operate the college together with the labor people but they soon left, for reasons that remain obscure but were apparently personality conflicts rather than ideological ones. Before leaving, however, William Fincke left a lasting mark—he gave the school its property, fifty-three acres of land and a fine old farmhouse, and he picked A. J. Muste to head the new college. The two had much in common. They were fellow war resistors, graduates of Union Theological Seminary and had served in the pulpit. (Fincke was a Presbyterian; Muste, a Dutch-Reformist *cum* Congregationalist.) Two of the college's strongest advocates were Norman Thomas and John Nevin Sayre, sharers in a roughly similar Protestant social idealism, who were also colleagues and friends.

A. J. Muste was a natural choice as chairman of the Brookwood Faculty. Of all the radical ministry, Muste had become the most involved with the labor struggles of the day. On leaving his fashionable Newton, Massachusetts, pastorate in a dispute over his opposition to war, Muste had become involved in the 1919 Lawrence textile strike. As a consequence, the lanky minister helped found the independent Amalgamated Textile Workers of America. Strike victories, notably in Paterson, Passaic and Hudson counties in New Jersey, established the forty-eight-hour week and a 17 percent wage increase within the industry and boosted the membership of the union to nearly fifty thousand. But when the depression hit the industry in 1920 to 1922, the union crumbled and Muste, then the union's secretary-treasurer, despaired of what he called an "unremitting desperate effort to establish a beachhead . . . of unionism in a chaotic industry." So, the call to Brookwood came at the right time and was accepted with alacrity and with relief.

The college was an immediate success. Muste recruited an able faculty—David J. Saposs, a contributor to John R. Commons' monumental histories of labor and the author of several works of his own, taught trade unionism and labor problems; Arthur W. Calhoun, a noted sociologist, gave classes in sociology and economics; Mark Starr, who came from the National Council of Labor Colleges of England on an exchange program, remained as a special tutor and lecturer; Josephine Colby, a teacher's union organizer, taught English; Helen Norton (who married Mark Starr at Brookwood), daughter of a railroad worker and a graduate of Kansas State College, taught journalism and oversaw the editing of the school paper; Tom Tippet came from the Mine Workers to run Brookwood's extension service. Muste taught a course in the history of civilization, using as texts James Breasted's *Ancient Times* and H. G. Wells's *Outline of History*, and requiring a five-thousand-word paper on the theme, "From Ancient Egypt to the English Imperial Control of Egypt."

A stream of visitors and guest lecturers enlivened the school year. James Maurer, who was long remembered for his fine aim with chewing tobacco and headed the school's board of labor advisors, shared his fund of knowledge about the labor movement. Norman Thomas came to talk of socialism and industrial democracy. Roger Baldwin, Stuart Chase, Oscar Ameringer, Sumner Slichter and Sinclair Lewis were among the many who dropped in for a day, an evening or a weekend.

During the summer and on holiday weekends, Brookwood specialized in offering institutes—to labor educators, building tradesmen, railroaders and other special groups within organized labor. Minority groups were given attention, which was unusual for the time. Charles S. Johnson of the Urban League, B. W. Bagrall, representing the National Association for the Advancement of Colored People, and sociologist E. Franklin Frazier participated in a discussion, "Negroes Can Organize," and in the same year, 1927, the college held "the first institute for women's trade union auxiliaries ever held in the United States."

For the students, most of whom were trade unionists ranging in age anywhere from the late teens to the early forties, Brookwood was a heady place to be. As Len DeCaux, a graduate and later the left-leaning CIO publicist, wrote in retrospect, "To the miner, Brookwood was green, clean, all above ground—no coaldust, no cricks in the back. To the machinist, Brookwood was greaseless days far from the grinding roar of metal against metal. To makers of suits, dresses, hats, Brookwood was fairy-tale country . . . ," a sharp contrast to "trash-strewn cement valleys of Manhattan or Chicago. To those who had known poverty, Brookwood offered ease, security, the fresh-air pleasures of the well-to-do." Brookwood deliberately sought out students of different labor backgrounds, taking in one year, for example, fourteen "nationalities"—Negroes, Scots, Norwegians, and Hungarians were listed—from eighteen industries. Initially, students were required to have been union members for at least a year, but this policy was discarded in the late twenties in order to enroll workers from the unorganized mass-production industries. For the most part, the vast majority of Brookwood students in the 1920s were trade unionists who came, in large part, from the needle trades' and coal miners' unions.

Poet Sarah Cleghorn, who taught English for a brief time at Brookwood, discovered that her students "were what I called

Labor Puritans. They wanted literary feeling, personal expression, not for life in general, but for the Labor Movement alone. To this they were consecrated like Cromwell's Ironsides." Most, indeed, were to become fiercely loyal to Muste, at least for a time; they were dedicated to the labor movement, and many would make significant contributions to the birth and growth of the Congress of Industrial Organizations in the late 1930s. Some went into labor education, helping to found or influence some six labor colleges—Baltimore, Philadelphia, Salem (Massachusetts), Wilkes-Barre, Pittsburgh, and Shenandoah—soon after graduation. Others became union organizers, elected trade-union officials. A 1931 survey of 186 Brookwood graduates found that 80 percent were still active in the labor movement in some capacity. It was no mean accomplishment for the times. As Cara Cook, school librarian and sometime secretary to Muste, later recalled, "In the next half-decade, [Brookwood] built itself up through the labor and love of progressive trade unionists, educators and contributors, a devoted staff, and a succession of eager student groups, until in 1926 when I went there it was no longer spoken of as an 'experiment,' but as an established institution. It even had traditions, and could reminisce about the 'good old days.' 'The faculty had to wash dishes and scrub floors then,' was one frequent reminder."

Muste set the tone and developed the college's character. As he stated in *Worker's Education*, a WEB publication, "Brookwood believes in what has been called the 'factual approach.' We would have the organized workers confront every situation not with prejudices, superstitions, mere notions or feelings, personal animus, but with the willingness to seek out the facts and to base judgment and action on the facts. If we negotiate with employers, let us not go with opinions or 'hot air' but armed with facts. When a town is to be organized, let us proceed not by guesswork but with careful knowledge about the place, its workers, their conditions." While Brookwoodians considered workers' education a practical trade-union tool, they also conceived of it as a means of emancipating the working class. James Maurer put labor education into perspective for the labor progressives at a WEB conference. "The underlying purpose of workers' education," he said, "is the desire for a better social order, the desire of workers for a richer and fuller life, individually and collectively. These things gave the movement its birth and must remain its treasured inheritance. Labor education aims at the ultimate liberation of the working masses. It seeks to help the workingman to function most effectively both as a citizen and a worker in the solution of our many complex social problems. Unless it is education looking toward a new social order, with more wisdom and justice than exists in our present order, its right to existence is questionable."

Maurer and Muste, these were Golden's kind of folks, visionaries with a practical bent. Brookwood would prove to be both a home for the Goldens and a refuge from the general collapse of organized labor in the terrible twenties. Golden helped fashion it into America's foremost labor school as well as into a center for labor progressives out of which would emerge talented organizers committed to an aggressive industrial unionism. Edmund Wilson once observed, "There is a Musteite type quite distinct from those of other radical groups. The Musteites differ from the Communists in maintaining the conventional dress, literate language and polite approach of intelligent middle-class people. They might be students or instructors from any college, and the influence of Muste himself has perhaps had the effect of making them a little like the students of a divinity school. On the other hand, they also differ from the truly academic radicals possessing the conviction and courage which carry them into industrial battles and make them do thankless work and venture into situations which few middle-class people care to face." It is not a description that fits Clinton S. Golden exactly, but it is close and helps to explain the working relationship he established over the next six years of his life with the lean Netherlander.

Travels for Brookwood

The last half of the Golden Twenties was a lean time for the American trade-union movement, but, paradoxically, a stimulating one for labor education. Over the five years of 1925 to 1930, Clint Golden visited nearly all the major centers of labor activity from Salem, Massachusetts, to Portland, Oregon. He cajoled local unions into creating scholarships for deserving union activists, interviewed and recruited potential students, raised funds, and propagandized for Brookwood. "At no point," he reported to the Brookwood faculty, "have I found an antagonism on the part of trade union officials toward educational activity, providing it was of a character that had some definite relation to the labor movement. There seems to be a general recognition on the part of all elements in the movement on the need of having trained leaders and active rank-and-file members. Experiences growing out of the disastrous results of the shopmen's strike, failure of cooperative enterprises and other business ventures of labor organizations seem to furnish the incentive for interest in education activity. In none of the classes or colleges visited is there any manifestation of a demand for the teaching of 'revolutionary' theories. A consciousness of the desirability and need for new and better social order seems to exist in *every* group visited and observed . . . there seems to be a recognition of the fact that the Labor organizations as such are not as efficient in advancing and protecting the interests of the workers as they could and should be . . . In other words, the whole movement is passing through a state of experimentation. . . ."

Golden traveled along what might be called an "old boy" network of socialists, independent radicals, railroad men, machinists, and their various friends. From Portland, Oregon, Golden wrote Muste on March 15, 1925, "I have met Ben J. Wilson, a prominent old time socialist and a brother of ex-mayor J. Stitt Wilson of Berkeley, California. Also George D. and Grace Wilson, two former prominent members of the staff of the old Appeal to Reason. They tell me that there is no use whatever in visiting Bakersfield, California, and that time would be utilized to a much better advantage in Frisco and Los Angeles."

Brookwood's first graduates were already established in the labor movement and active in labor education. Jack Lever and Charles L. (Buck) Reed, for example, headed labor colleges in Philadelphia and Salem, Massachusetts, respectively. (Reed, a Salem machinist, later became president of the Massachusetts State Federation of Labor.) A. J. Muste's antiwar colleagues helped. Cedric Long, the pacifist Congregationalist minister, provided Golden with a list of people to visit in Boston, including the wealthy Boston matron Mrs. Elizabeth Glendower Evans, who provided both moral support and financial salvation at crucial moments, particularly for the Mustes.* Jim Maurer's

* In a January 15, 1925 letter to A. J. Muste, Golden reported: "I met Mrs. Evans yesterday and had a long talk with her. I think I made something of a hit with her. She is greatly interested in knowing what we can do about financing married men with families who may want to enroll as students. I told her that I was trying to get a line on such people and when we knew just about what the problem was, we would be in a position to talk more accurately about it. She is a little peculiar but I think she could get quite excited about helping in this direction."

blessings were invaluable in Pennsylvania and elsewhere in the labor movement, although by 1925, Clint found him "getting pretty old and cranky and . . . talking about resigning." Maurer, Golden added, "can't decide on anyone to take his place [as head of the Pennsylvania State Federation of Labor]. . . . Jim has been running pretty much a one man show and I shudder to think of what may become of the Federation if it is turned over to some of those who are supposed to be active in it."

After short sorties into Pennsylvania and Massachusetts in January and February of 1925, Clint traveled across the country seeking support for Brookwood. Dora went along on a second honeymoon. Combining, however, business with pleasure, she learned to type and spent long days in lonely hotel rooms transcribing her husband's letters and reports to A. J. Muste while he met with union activists and addressed local union meetings. "She is developing into an honest to God stenographer," Golden wrote Muste from Chicago, "and is handling all my correspondence for me together with lots of other helpful work." By the end of May, Golden had visited nineteen states, fifteen city central labor bodies, thirty-six local unions, twelve worker education enterprises, including some eight labor colleges, and two state conventions. His welcome was enhanced by the knowledge that he could recommend and secure much needed financial aid for labor's educational efforts from the Garland Fund. Six institutions were so aided–labor colleges in Boston and Salem, Massachusetts; Philadelphia; Denver, Colorado; Portland, Oregon; and in Seattle, Washington. Salem, for example, was given five hundred dollars to be matched by a like amount from the local unions, enabling Buck Reed to devote "his entire time to the development of educational activities in a circuit of towns fairly close to Salem."

While the educational news was good, at least in these instances, the labor movement was "pretty well shot to pieces," as Golden reported from Wilkes-Barre, after arriving "about 2 A.M. Saturday in the midst of a blizzard that nearly tied-up the train enroute," on January 4, 1925. Ten days later, he wrote to A. J. Muste from Fitchburg, Massachusetts, where "the Finns [active cooperators and publishers of a socialist newspaper, *Raivaaja*] seem to be the only alive, active and constructive group." "The organized labor movement seems to be in a state of coma," Golden continued. "The Machinists have virtually disbanded and the Local is not functioning. There was a local of textile workers which won a strike and then gave up. The Carpenters are said to be practically the only ones who have a Local. . . . The secretary of the Central Labor Union . . . could not be found." In Worcester, he found the railroad trades "demoralized." The Boston & Albany Railroad had settled with the shopmen, but "scabs were permitted to remain at work," which caused "a lack of faith and confidence in the organizations and there is no enthusiasm for Union activity whatever, among them." The Central Labor Union, when headed by Daniel R. Donovan, had "taken a fairly progressive position," joining the La Follette campaign with vigor, but incurring "a heavy deficit which is a drag on the organization at the present time." Donovan, at the time of Golden's visit, was "making a precarious living in the insurance business," having "lost everything he ever had in worldly possessions since he was taken off the staff of organizers of the I. A. of M." At forty-eight, with a wife and three small youngsters, he had been blacklisted, though he managed to work three months under an assumed name. "He is a splendid chap," Golden informed Muste, "makes a good appearance and a fine talk . . . and is the type that in the next ten years could probably make a big contribution to the movement. [But] it can hardly be expected that he would have much enthusiasm under the circumstances." The new CLU president was "not a progressive by any means and is a personal friend of Judge Webster Thayer who handled the Sacco-Vanzetti trial."

Before leaving Massachusetts, Golden attended a memorial meeting for AFL president Samuel Gompers. It was a pretty drab, uninspiring affair, according to Golden. "There were less than two hundred in attendance. The speech was written and Green [Gompers' successor as president of the AFL] read it and it was broadcasted. They blamed the radio for the lack of attendance. The whole affair lasted one hour. The comments from even the old moss back C.L.U. crowd was anything but enthusiastic. I think Green is more interested in educating the public than the rank and file of the movement."

The state of the labor movement was not much better elsewhere. Stopping off in Baltimore to see Brookwood graduate William Ross, later Philadelphia Joint Board manager for the ILGWU, Golden reported back to Brookwood, "there is an awful amount of unemployment . . . I am told that less than one-half of the Carpenters are paying their dues . . ." From Pittsburgh, he wrote "I have been on a starvation diet most of the week [his stomach had upset] and this would have been reflected in my expense account had it not been for some of those with good appetites but no money, whom I ran into around Pittsburgh. Not all of them were rank and filers either, by the way." In Chicago, where Brookwood had counted on financial aid from Amalgamated Clothing Workers, Golden "learned from other sources that the unemployment insurance payments [unique in the labor movement at this time] have exceeded the income from payments by employers and workers by more than $150,000 to date [February 16, 1925] and this is climbing up every week."

On the west coast, Golden found Spokane "hard hit by the depression. Unemployment has been very general in the city and has continued for nearly two years. The shop crafts strike dealt the movement a solar [*sic*] blow as the shop craft workers were among the most active and progressive. Their locals have just about ceased to exist there. The Machinists who formerly had a membership in pre-war times of about 400 of the 600-odd employed in the city, now have less than 100 but they alone seemed to be the only group really making an effort to come back." Seattle unionists had invested hundreds of thousands of dollars in various cooperative and other enterprises and, so Golden discovered, "all [had] blown up without a single exception other than the laundry and this is being operated on a strict corporation basis." He cited to Muste the example of the Boilermakers, who had put thirty thousand dollars into the *Union Record*, a labor paper, and some twelve thousand dollars into another enterprise. The paper ran into trouble and a private group was trying to rescue it. "There is a slight chance that some of the Unions may recover a part of that which they have dumped into it. That is—at some future time." One corporation, organized along the lines of the Brotherhood of Locomotive Engineers' holding or investment concern, collapsed to the tune of over a million dollars. "These experiences," Golden wrote, "have made the people in the movement very sore and very reluctant about supporting other enterprises of any nature. And they have lost about all they ever had in the shape of finances and money."*

* In the 1920s, unions invested in cooperatives, even some businesses, and founded some half-dozen banks. The Amalgamated Clothing Workers banks, in Chicago and New York, were the only ones to survive. While the Goldens were on their cross-country trip, the Producers & Consumers Bank in Philadelphia failed. "Our interest and mortgage money was all deposited there," Golden wrote Muste, "and Dora was greatly upset." As well she might be, as bank deposits in those days were not insured. "The closing of the bank," Golden's account to

Los Angeles unions were having "a hard struggle to maintain themselves"; there were over sixty thousand unemployed in that city.

Yet, Golden was also able to report back to Brookwood, "I have never seen any more interest manifested in one of my talks than that of the Central body delegates. There were about 100 present and I guess nearly everyone tried to shake hands with me or ask questions . . . They are anxious to get a local Labor College worthy of the name established and then put up the Brookwood scholarship as an inducement for students in the Local classes." Wherever he went, Golden not only preached the gospel of workers' education but he also organized to get education underway. In Pittsburgh, for example, where he spent five days in early February, "getting in touch with Local Union and Central Body officials in the day time and in the evening attending various meetings," he got the movement's "live wires" to present a motion to name an education committee at the Central Labor Union following his talk before that body. The motion was carried, and a seven-man committee was named by the CLU chairman. Golden was asked to prepare a memorandum with suggestions as to how best proceed. "It appears to be a pretty live committee," he wrote Muste, "and I believe they will get something going."

At the outset of his first trip, Fannia Cohen, the educational director of the International Ladies' Garment Workers' Union and a leading member of Brookwood's Labor Co-operating Committee, warned Golden against "the crowd interested in the Bryn Mawr experiment" in labor education and expressed her fears that the "Y.W.C.A. crowd" might take over Brook-

Muste continued, "has created a most difficult situation for not only some thousands of individuals but for a great many unions in Philadelphia. The Labor College balance is tied up there (some $700.00), teachers are unpaid and virtually all the unions including principally the ones most interested in the college, have all their funds tied up."

wood. "I also received plenty of instruction about the communists and warnings about 'isms'," Golden continued in his report to Muste, "and I will purchase an extra pair of glasses to make sure that I discern any attempts on the part of 'isms' to capture me."

Golden, however, needed more than glasses to avoid the pitfalls of faction and the antagonisms of the deeply divided partisans in the labor quarrels of the time. Brookwood sought the broadest possible base of support from the labor movement without, however, loosing its own distinctive character as a labor education institution. The Communists were already something of a problem for democratic radicals. They had split the Socialist Party earlier and in the mid-twenties pursued a divisive policy within the unions through "boring from within." (In 1928, the Party began to sponsor dual unions in opposition to the Federation.) In Minneapolis, for example, Golden found that the Central body had become a "sort of forum for the discussion of everything except those subjects that related to the everyday work of the movement." One entire session, he reported to A. J. Muste, "was devoted to a discussion, precipitated by the Communists, of Dr. Abrams Theory of Electronic Reactions, after which the body solemnly approved the 'Theory' and then appointed a committee to call on the County Medical Association and urge its adoption by their members. I understand that this is somewhat typical of what had been going on for several months."

Brookwood came under attack; the *Daily Worker*, the official Communist organ, editorialized against Brookwood's "class-collaborationist . . . teachings." Where the Communists managed to control or influence labor education, Marxian economics and the problems of the Russian revolution predominated. Arthur Calhoun, Brookwood's brilliant sociologist, contended, though he denied being a Party member, that Brookwood should adopt a policy of communism and that those who took a contrary stand were "betrayers of labor." (The board and faculty asked him to leave in the summer of 1929 because of his insistence on Marxian purity.) Golden, who held little brief for the Communist Party, nonetheless drew some distinctions, possible in those days before the Russian Party's control became absolute, between the hard-and-fast, the crazy, and those he considered "Communist . . . but quite sane." Among them, apparently, were some Brookwood students. Asking for a place on the May 29, 1925 commencement program for "a sort of heart to heart talk with the graduates in particular," he added, "I think I can give them some sound advice without losing my temper with the Communists."

Golden concluded, after observing Communist worker-education efforts, that they were destructive, tended to drive away students—as at the Communist-controlled Boston School of Social Science where he found "only a negligible number of organized workers" enrolled—and, finally, "the moral seems to be that propaganda institutions will not flourish as labor colleges. That has been the record to date all over the country."

On his travels, however, Golden often had to exercise considerable tact. In Cincinnati, Israel Mufson, a Brookwood graduate who would succeed Jack Lever as head of the Philadelphia Labor College, and Phil E. Ziegler, editor of the *Railway Clerk* and a member of Brookwood's Board, introduced Golden to Max Senior, a wealthy liberal businessman, in the hopes of raising scholarship funds. At sixty, as Golden described him, Senior was "extreme in his views and somewhat erratic. He supports a Labor Forum . . . which does not attract many other than a handful of communists and he meets the deficits incurred for any showing of Russian films, etc." Golden thought him "sentimental," and believed that if a project caught his imagination, it would get his full support. Senior assured his visitors that he would underwrite a scholarship, adding that he hoped that when the student returned to Cincinnati, he would "lick hell out of Kummer," the president of the AFL Central Labor Union, an associate of John P. Frey, the chief of the Moulders' union and a powerful figure within the American Federation of Labor.

Frey had been named to the executive committee of the Workers Education Bureau by AFL president Green, and Brookwood, eager for AFL support, did not want to alienate him. While in Cincinnati, Golden paid Frey a long visit, talking about labor and education and Brookwood. His report of that talk to Muste is interesting in the light of Frey's subsequent opposition to Brookwood. "He is a peculiar type," Golden wrote, "and I fear he has a rather stultifying influence on local educational activity." He had advised the Ohio labor education chairman, he told Golden, against creating "any enthusiasm whatever," preferring educational activity among the unions to be pursued through University extension courses. Frey expressed opposition to the AFL's support of the WEB, much to Golden's astonishment. On the other hand, Frey expressed "a real interest in Brookwood and a desire to come up and look the place over and see how they were doing things." He praised the development of a young moulder, Leonard Craig, a Brookwood graduate soon to become educational director for the Pennsylvania State Federation, while "continually calling his own International officers 'chair warmers.' " Frey may have been dissembling, though that is not in character; Golden, who was perceptive about such things, believed him sincere. Golden concluded, "I will be blessed if I can figure him out."

Though often fractured and weak, the labor movement of the 1920s was often lively, fascinating. While in Milwaukee, the Goldens attended an annual Socialist Masked Carnival where nearly ten thousand turned out; "it seemed as if everyone connected with the labor movement, state federation of labor and county and municipal governments were present," Golden wrote Muste. The unionization of Butte, Montana, intrigued Golden, who reported, "I doubt if there is another such city in the country." The Retail Clerks, he continued, with about one thousand members, "take in everyone employed in any kind of store who will not be taken in by another organization. They have the delivery wagon drivers, a group which the teamsters locally do not want. As a condition of joining the Clerks International Union they have been told that they must get rid of these drivers. This and other reasons are given for their refusal to join the International. Phonograph repairmen, watchmakers, demonstrators of household appliances, etc., are all members of their organization." Four hundred women, who worked as dishwashers in cafés, chambermaids, domestics, and so on, "including about every working woman in the city who is not eligible for membership in any union," were organized into a Working Woman's Protective Union and affiliated directly to the AFL as a Federal local. The Sheep Shearers, "a migratory crowd," were organized, roughly a thousand, in the Sheep Shearers Union of North America.

While Butte's workers were nearly 100 percent organized, the copper miners were not. The seven thousand miners, Golden reported to Muste, "have always been a difficult group to handle and more than one rebellion has taken place within their ranks. This has created a situation where their fellow workers in the mines, the employers and the workers generally have no confidence in them and look upon them, when organized, as a singularly destructive factor in the local labor movement. All the other trades in and about the mines including some of the most important, such as the hoisting engineers, electricians, etc., are 100% organized and have a collective relationship with copper companies. These workers claim that if there was any way of determining that the miners would subject themselves to ordinary union discipline and behavior, they could organize them and companies would be compelled to do business with them." If relationships with Butte employers seem rudimentary, they were, nonetheless, effective, as a Golden anecdote shows. "The Berkin Motor Co.," he wrote, "employing *one* machinist and some helpers, refused to pay the Machinists scale and sign an agreement and in June 1923 chased the business agent off the property with a 'gat.' Whereupon the Machinists placed the Co., on the unfair list and 'packed a banner agin thim' which means that they hired a man to parade with a banner announcing the unfairness of the firm, in front of the firms place of business six hours a day for nearly 18 months. It was not until the Automobile show was to start that they were successful in effecting a settlement. They had succeeded in having this firm barred from the show unless they settled. They then came to terms, sent for O'Brien the Machinists Business Agent while I was there and wanted to make a settlement. O'Brien armed himself with his 'gat,' went to see the firm and compelled them to pay $800.00 in wages for the service of the man who 'packed the banner agin thim' for the past 18 months. This sum represented just one half of the amount actually paid the banner man. And they *paid* and settled. If this sort of action is 'radical' then the Butte labor movement is radical for this is a typical case I am told."

The 1920s were an experimental time for the labor movement, as Golden discovered in Haverhill, Massachusetts, "a union town" where the labor movement had "supported socialist candidates for office in years gone by and last year had a Socialist mayor" and "where the communists are very scarce."

The Shoe Workers Protective Union, an independent union headed by an old-time Socialist, James J. Rooney, was the largest organized trade in the city. They owned "a splendid four-story building, modernly equipped in every respect." Conditions within the organization, however, were "chaotic," in part because of a new approach to industrial relations that fascinated Golden. "They have undertaken," he wrote to Muste, "to establish impartial arbitration machinery." Edwin Newdick, formerly of the Labor Bureau, Inc., served as impartial chairman. "Mixing with the rank and file of the workers at the noon hour and at other times about the Union headquarters and listening to the conversations lead me to believe that the workers do not understand what is involved in this form of industrial relationship. Unfortunately, the machinery was set up apparently at a time when the wages were at peak rates. Some were entirely out of proportion, apparently, to the amounts others received. One of the first duties of the impartial chairman was to recommend some readjustments that had the effect of reducing the wages of some of the higher paid workers. This, then, gave the machinery a bad name in the minds of the uneducated and unimaginative members. There is no enthusiasm among the members for the machinery. The leaders themselves do not seem to sufficiently understand the possibilities of using it to establish their organization, to in any way inspire the rank and file. There seems to be no tendency to look to the future. Yet there are some fine types of workers in the Union and especially among the so-called [by immigrant workers] Americans."

Golden suggested to Rooney that he get a group together interested in studying the experiences of other organizations with impartial arbitration. David Saposs, at Brookwood, was asked to draw up a reading list, and Golden wrote to Jack Lever asking him to send some copies of the monographs and pamphlets published by Hart, Schaffner and Marx on their agreements with the Amalgamated Clothing Workers. The story of Brookwood, said Golden, "seemed . . . a breadth of life and encouragement" to the shoe worker activists of Haverhill.

Impartial arbitration, an idea first developed in the garment industries, was but one aspect of industrial democracy, an idea widely propagated for the first time in the 1920s. The 1923 Portland, Oregon convention of the AFL called industrial democracy a goal of the labor movement, suggesting that labor in some way must come into wider control in industry and must take up some of the responsibility of management. Golden, Muste and their associates at Brookwood and around *Labor Age* were intrigued by the possibilities opened up by worker cooperation in production plans, particularly when the idea was advanced by strong unions. Muste, as general secretary of the Amalgamated Textile Workers, had had first-hand experience with such a plan. The New York silk-ribbon workers, a branch of the ATW, negotiated an agreement with their employers that established a joint workers-employers council chaired by an impartial figure who was the final arbiter in conflicts over wages and working conditions. Success, the parties agreed, would depend on "the suppression of the militant spirit by both parties and the development of reason instead of force as the rule of action." Golden had a similar experience while working for the Amalgamated Clothing Workers, which made impartial machinery of some sort the cornerstone of its bargaining.

Elton Mayo, the noted sociologist and a pioneer proponent of worker participation, was teaching at the Wharton School of Finance, at this time having just arrived in the country from Australia where he had taught Workers Education Association classes. He heard of the Philadelphia Labor College and looked up Golden, who helped him launch a study of industrial fatigue and human behavior in a textile mill. The two became close friends, and Golden was influenced greatly by Mayo's work.

When the Baltimore & Ohio Railroad, as a consequence of the 1922 shopmen's strike, entered a production agreement with the shopcraft unions—boilermakers, electricians, railway carmen, machinists and sheet metal workers—Brookwood took a more than ordinary interest. One of the college's first institutes, in the summer of 1925, brought together elected officials and rank-and-file railroadmen for extended discussion of union problems as well as explorations of the B & O plan.

The Communists attacked all such plans as "class collaboration" and as "sell-out." Golden was said to be "sympathetic to Taylorism," a scientific management system felt by many workers to be a disguised speed-up. The March 1924 issue of *Labor Age* defended the B & O plan, carrying a long article by O. S. Beyer, Jr., a consulting engineer for the shopcraft unions who broached the plan to the railroad, and another by Jack Lever, whose thinking on the question was close to Golden's and Muste's. What leftwing critics overlooked in Beyer's proposal, wrote Lever, was its greatest merit: "teaching workers the technique and management of their own industry . . . The more workers know about the management and operation of their own industry the stronger the unions, the more self-reliance on the part of their memberships–the more progress at a faster pace." *Labor Age,* speaking for Golden, Muste, et al., moreover stressed that "The B & O idea adds to the workers' demands for decent wages and hours, a further demand that puts them on the first rung of the ladder toward the securing of power. It gives them, as organized workers operating through their regular union, a voice in the destruction of industrial wastes . . . By taking up the job of wiping out these wastes, the union workers not only benefit themselves, but prove the validity of their attack on the present Capitalist System." Pointing out that the group of unions involved in the B & O experiment in shop control also demanded the public ownership of the railroads through their support of the Plumb Plan, *Labor Age* concluded that the idea was "a fine step forward for Labor" since the unions did have "*the bigger program before them.*"

The B & O plan embodied current notions of what today is called "the humanization of work" as well as "worker participation" in management decision-making. As Beyer put it in *Labor Age*, "*The shop men, through their unions and accredited representatives, assume a brand new place in the structure of the shop. They participate in its management.*" Bi-weekly local cooperative meetings were held between the shop committee comprised of elected representatives from each of the crafts and the ranking local management officer and his staff. Every two or three months, the system federated committee, composed of the general chairmen of the crafts, conferred with the B & O general Superintendent of Motive Power and his staff. Shop, yard and roundhouse operations were reviewed. Material supply, care and saving, methods for doing work, coordination and scheduling of work, tools and tool equipment, job analysis, quality of work being done, group records of work turned out, general shop performance, conditions of shops, grounds, machines, stabilization of production and employment, education and training, and recruiting were matters discussed and acted upon.

The plan ended the notorious "contracting out" of work to nonunion labor as a means of ensuring "steady work" for the shopmen. The "fair-sharing of the gains of cooperation" was realized through improvements in working conditions and wage income. As Beyer explained the plan, "These improvements will be established from day to day as the cooperative program helps in bettering shop conditions and methods, and from time to time through negotiations with management, based among other things upon actual showings made through cooperation. The cooperative program does not contemplate any form of increasing wage income, other than through steady work and increases in wage rates. In other words, no piece work or similar system of payment is feasible or permissible in the development of cooperation."

Golden followed the B & O experiment closely with eyes sharpened by his own experience as a railroader and machinist.

Whenever in Baltimore, according to Bill Ross, he would look in on the B & O shops to see how the plan was going. He was a guest speaker at the B & O Federation [of unions] convention, which took place in Cincinnati over May 4 to 6, 1925, and the reception "almost took my breath away." His report to Brookwood reflected his enthusiasm and interest in the B & O idea:

> There are about 200 delegates present representing the six shop crafts organizations. A splendid, clean cut lot—some as young as 25 perhaps, others between 50 and 60 years of age with a probable average age of about 33.
>
> Reports indicate that at the time a settlement was made following the big strike, they returned to work with less than 50% of the workers as members of their respective organizations. Today they have between 85% and 90% of the organization and steadily climbing. The unorganized element is largest at the Mount Claire shops, a point where it has always been difficult to keep the men lined up on account of peculiar local conditions existing for many years.
>
> There are no "wings" manifest in the convention. Doubtful whether even a communist sympathizer could be found with a powerful microscope, among the delegates. There has been no appearance of communist literature at any of the sessions—even the "manifestoes" which are becoming so familiar at every labor gathering are conspicuous by their absence.
>
> No one is doing the thinking for this bunch of delegates. This is evident by the frequent spirited debate—delegates often vigorously opposing positions taken on the floor by their officers.
>
> No one seems to be worrying about the advantages accruing to the company as a result of the "Cooperative

Plan." Much more attention is being given to proposed changes in the agreement which will bring increased advantages to the membership in the shape of improved rules, changes in overtime rates, increased wages (altho their rate is now higher than on most roads). "Stabilization of employment" is a phrase frequently heard and a "Committee on Stabilization" consisting of 7 delegates is meeting frequently and will bring in a report.

Not a single company official or representative of any character has put in an appearance at the convention. Contrast this with what occurs at meetings of the Pennsy workers—when the company gives them permission to hold one under the "employee representation plan."

All the delegates present represent the members of their *own organization*—they are selected at their own local meetings in which no one who is *not* a member has a vote. The local committees similarly selected are those who represent the workers on the "Cooperative Committees." Not a single non union worker has any voice or vote or representation and all talk about the election of committees and representatives being held in the shops is all *pure bunk.*

President Jewell made a masterly presentation of the evolution of modern industry and of the evolution of the trade union movement from the guilds down to the present time. He clearly states that there "is a fundamental conflict of interest between the modern employer and wage worker that eliminates any such thing as 100% cooperation and this condition will continue as long as the present system endures." "There are other interests" said he, that "are not so fundamental, where there can be a degree of cooperation between worker and employer that may result in *some measure* of benefits to both, but there can be no reconciliation of the fundamentally conflicting interests under the present profit system."

Several delegates announced that local officials of the company had distributed cards and other literature among them with the request that this be passed out in an effort to "assist the company in getting more business." This literature did not bear the Union label and they had refused to distribute it. Discussion developed the fact that the B. & O. maintained its own printing plant where train schedules, advertising and other similar work was done, that the Printing Trades Unions were apparently making no effort to organize the workers in this shop but if they would, the shopmen would give them every possible assistance and support.

A report by the Committee on Organization indicated that most of the arguments advanced by non members of the Unions (who for the most part are the scabs who were permitted to remain at work under the terms of the settlement) as reasons for not joining the shop craft unions are that the officers are "fakers," "grafters," that the policy is that of "class collaboration," that the Unions are not "militant" etc., etc. The committee (rank and filers) characterized the excuses advanced for not joining with their fellow workers in the unions as "ranging from the sublime to the ridiculous."

As an observer at the convention I could not help but feel that:

These shopmen are articulate—they know what they want and they intend to get it.

They are interested in "cooperation" with the bosses just to the extent that it will enable them to have more pork chops—which means more wages, steadier employment, less laborious work, added protection, etc.

They have not lost their "militancy."

That they desire to use every opportunity granted under the "Cooperative Plan" to strengthen their organizations, to demand through them more and more of the better things of life.

It was good to see a bunch of workers assembled in convention, carrying on their work efficiently and earnestly, free from the rancor and hatreds that are so manifest these days in so many organizations of workers.

Golden's travels on behalf of Brookwood greatly strengthened the college's ties with the labor movement. By mid-1926, when Golden had been appointed business manager as well as field representative, he had secured, or helped to secure, the official endorsement and the financial support of thirteen national and international unions—the United Textile Workers, Hosiery Workers, American Federation of Teachers, the Machinists, the Brewery Workers, Coopers, Maintenance-of-Way Employees, Railroad Clerks, Railway Carmen, Painters, Hat and Cap Makers, the International Ladies' Garment Workers, and the Amalgamated Clothing Workers. Most of the financial aid was in the form of scholarships, enabling one or more union members from the contributing union to attend Brookwood. Four other unions, although they did not endorse Brookwood, spoke highly of its achievements—the Telegraphers, Electrical Workers, Boilermakers and Upholsterers. In a February 9, 1926 memorandum covering the work of the field representative A. J. Muste praised the publicity gained for Brookwood by Golden's activities in labor papers throughout the country and "the stimulus given . . . to the cause of Workers Education in almost every important labor education center in this country." This stimulus, Muste added, "seems to us to have been one of the most important influences in the field of workers' education in the last year."

In March 1926, the editor of the *Journal of Electrical Workers and Operators* summed up the prevailing view among unionists informed about Brookwood by Golden. "If you are discouraged about labor's future, if you have about lost hope, pay a visit to Brookwood Labor College . . . You will be surprised. You will be thrilled . . . It's a big place, a live place. It's not 'red.' It's not reactionary. It teaches facts–not theories; conditions–not propaganda . . . Yes, it's quite refreshing. Brookwood means real progress. It provides real encouragement. It is the most promising, the most hopeful spot in the American Labor World today."

Brookwood: Last Journey

THE GOLDENS settled in at Brookwood with evident pleasure. After catching trains, arranging meetings and conducting countless interviews, and sleeping in a succession of hotel rooms, the seclusion of Brookwood was a welcome relief and the faculty cottage, a delight. Golden was now business manager as well as field representative, so he traveled less and was home more. His salary was assured—$250 a month and keep—and the prospects for the college were promising. Dora tidied the faculty cottage assigned for their use, and prepared for the birth of their child, Olive.

Life at Brookwood was intense, for Muste fostered an atmosphere of deep solidarity and, as a consequence, a sense of spiritual comradeship flourished. Campus upkeep and expansion were a community concern, with both students and faculty participating in a daily manual-work schedule. College policies were arrived at through consultation among all residents. Individual conduct was guided by self-respect and the desire to keep Brookwood above the reach of harmful social criticism. Meals were taken in common, though those faculty members who wished to cook for themselves were entitled to a cash allowance of $50 a month to cover that expense. Brookwood's Saturday nights were famous for their entertainment, whether serious or in a lighter vein. Baseball, tennis and volleyball allowed for zestful competition, while community walks on Sunday morning restored communion.

Golden had what Helen Norton Starr remembers as a "very rich voice, like the lower notes of a pipe organ, with remarkable carrying power," as well as notable presence. "When he spoke, you listened," another faculty member once commented. After a going-away party for one of the students, Ed Falkowski, an ex-anthracite miner and Brookwood student, noted in his diary: "Clint Golden came, huge, wholesome man with bellowing basso voice—a big-hearted person, filled with information and anecdotes." He was often pressed into speaking, giving a talk on vocational education and the labor movement over radio station WEAF on one occasion, at the dedication banquet for the Philadelphia Labor Institute on another, and, almost routinely, at local union meetings wherever he traveled. He was once cajoled into playing the part of "Mr. Moneybags" in a Saturday-night Brookwood production. He was the college's fund-raiser, after all, and rather looked the part—tall, businesslike, with steel-rimmed glasses accenting the smoothness of his light-colored, rather serene face. "He had only a couple of lines," Helen Norton Starr recalls, "but he sort of muttered those down his chin rather than coming right out with them. He was most uncomfortable, clearly he didn't like to do it."

The Goldens are rememebered as being somewhat removed from the rest of Brookwood. In part, naturally, this was because Golden still traveled a good deal and so was not always involved in the day-to-day affairs of the school. Still, he often returned with tales that fascinated the younger staff and student body. Once, for instance, he traveled thirty-five miles into the back hills of Ohio to speak at a miners' meeting at Piney Forks only to have it nearly upset by a shooting affray between some bootleggers and some miners. His descriptions of trade-union officialdom were intriguing. Patrick Gorman, the president of the Meat Cutters and Butcher Workmen, Clint reported in a letter to Muste, was "a young fellow, about 35, fine looking but a good bit of the fast living, sporty type of labor skate. He has been in office three years and has brought back their organization from 7,000 (during the war they had 188,000 members) to about 20,000." But at Brookwood, Golden's role was something of an anomaly, not quite faculty, though he sometimes lectured, and certainly not a student. Dora was in an analogous position. She became the school's bookkeeper in the fall of 1929 and taught a course in bookkeeping yet was not considered "faculty." In his capacity as business manager, Clint also served as a kind of strawboss, supervising the school's many building projects, and he was impatient with student theoretical nit-picking, especially when they were supposedly working. "Clint," Helen Norton Starr recalls, "was quite happy to be going around with a wrench in one hand and a screwdriver in the other and in bibb-overalls."

Brookwood expanded, adding a dormitory here, a faculty dwelling there, volleyball and tennis courts, garages, and in 1929, a 460,000 gallon "drought proof" swimming pool. Through its classroom training, institute and conference programs, and its dominating influence within the Labor Publication Society, the publishers of *Labor Age*, Brookwood became a center for labor progressives, a lodestone for liberals and radicals with an interest in the working class. From the first, Brookwood cultivated the AFL unions with care, soliciting their support at every turn, but, over the years, Brookwood became increasingly critical of the established Federation leadership. Union structure, organizing the unorganized, and labor political action were matters of passionate concern to Brookwood. Initially, Brookwood favored amalgamation as the means of transforming the craft unions into industrial unions. But the failure of the railroad shopmen's strike, which turned on pulling the shop unions together, and the failure of the Machinists to convince the metal trades that amalgamation, by converting the AFL Metal Trade Department into an umbrella union was the key to organizing the metal trades, especially the steel industry, soured Brookwood on amalgamation. The answer was to create new industrial unions. And this Brookwood began to preach during 1926 and 1928.

The new industrial unions were to be created by organizing the unorganized, chiefly in the basic industries where some 80 percent of all nonunion workers were then employed. Industrial unionism, so the progressive argument ran, would virtually eliminate intercraft jealousies, race prejudices, and jurisdictional disputes and would greatly enhance union power, enabling workers to confront the giants of capital dominating the mass-production industries. This, however, was not to favor the creation of dual unionism, a policy adopted by the Workers' Party (Communists) in 1928 when it abandoned the policy of "boring within" AFL unions. Not rival unions but new unions, Brookwood's banner might have proclaimed. Nonetheless, Brookwood exhibited little sympathy for, and even less understanding of, craft unionism. Muste, in the April 1927 issue of *Labor Age*, declared that the mass-production industries would never be organized by the kind of unionism that considered assembly-line workers unorganizable or by a labor movement concerned with trying to prove itself "respectable," by a labor movement "wedded to an arbitrary idea of craft unionism," or by a labor movement which feared, or considered itself superior to, the workers' education movement.

Golden's reports from the field reinforced Brookwood's view of America as a land of suicidally competing craft unions. From Buffalo, where the seven thousand workers at the Lackawanna plant of Bethlehem Steel were all members of a company union, and where a big rayon plant, Fisher, manufacturer of automobile bodies, Pierce Arrow, and Houdaille Shock Absorbers (with which all Model A Fords were equipped) employed several thousands, Clint wrote a report for the June

1929 issue of *Labor Age.* "One would expect that here would be a live, vigorous, aggressive labor movement. But exactly the opposite proved to be the case. The building trades, to be sure, were the backbone of the local movement. Some of their members are employed by contractors installing new equipment at the Lackawanna, but there is little evidence that they are very much interested in whether the Lackawanna has a company union at all. An unorganized revolt of workers employed by the Houdaille Company, growing out of excessive speeding-up which in turn had resulted in an increase in production of 500 percent in 12 months, with wages remaining stationary during the same period, had evoked no interest at all. Rather, a committee of strikers had been informed that their action was 'illegal' from a trade-union point of view. The fact that the Pierce Arrow workers were restless and dissatisfied with the speed-up method introduced by the Studebaker Company when it took over control of the Pierce Arrow provided no reason for initiating a serious attempt to organize these workers. And those self-appointed guardians of the proletariat—the Communists—could not be found with a microscope."

John Fitzpatrick, the venerable head of the Illinois State Federation, gave Golden yet another illustration of craft-union impotence. "Several hundred workers in the biggest radio plant in Chicago revolted and struck," he wrote to Muste. "The plant employs about 8,000 workers. [Fitzpatrick] went out to organize them and they said they thought they could get the rest of the bunch out as they were only making 30 to 70¢ per hour daily. He found out that most of the workers would come under the jurisdictional claims of the Painters, Millmen [Branch of the Carpenters] Electricians and Machinists. He sent for representatives of each of these to enlist their aid in organizing this bunch. The result was that the Painters refused to accept them or to help out because they used spray guns for painting and were getting less than their scale; the Millmen because it was their slack season and they did not want to 'bother' with the matter; the Electrical Workers and the Machinists would have nothing to do with them because of the 'trouble' that it would cause them. So Fitz said, 'and you are going to double the membership in 1929, eh.' He tried to help them . . . told them to organize in an independent or any other old kind of a Union and he would personally do all he could to aid them. They stayed on strike for some two months but it petered out. I don't suppose we ought to quote Fitz on this for his own protection. He feels that the situation is pretty hopeless and there is not much that he and the older men can do about it. It's the old story of 'vested interests' all right with a vengeance."

Actually, it was not all that simple, as Golden, at other moments, realized. Industrial America was undergoing a great change during the 1920s. In Buffalo, for example, as Golden noted, investment in new machinery for the Lackawanna steel plant had doubled production since 1920 while reducing employment from over twelve thousand to about seven thousand in 1929. At the same time, the auto industry was creating, both directly and indirectly, new employment for countless new workers. New techniques for recruitment had also evolved. In Toledo, Golden found an employers' association utilizing the radio, beaming broadcasts one week at Kentucky, Tennessee and Virginia, and the next, aiming at another area, announcing that X number of workers would be hired by Toledo firms. "Within 36 hours," he reported, "antiquated flivvers" crowded Toledo streets, bringing in "a healthy quota of husky workers untainted by modern industrialism and to whom a wage of $3 a day had previously been munificent." The psychological effect of suddenly earning twice as much money plus "the fascination that goes along with their first introduction in a modern industrial establishment," Golden acknowledged, posed a problem for union organizers.

Superficial observation suggested that the industrial union

appeal would in and of itself provide sufficient incentive for workers to organize. Golden, however, had seen unsuccessful efforts by the IWW and by the United Auto, Aircraft and Vehicle Workers, an industrial predecessor to the present auto union, to organize in Detroit. Their failures, he argued, indicated something more was needed. "When one witnesses the spectacle of tool and diemakers getting an hourly rate of well over $1 an hour and working a 5 day, 40 hour week, quitting their jobs in such number as to create probably the largest turnover in the city, to accept jobs where there is a chance of working overtime and getting from 70 to 80 hours per week at a lower rate, then one wonders just what sort of an approach is to be made to the problem of organizing nearly a half million totally unorganized auto workers."

Clint had put his finger on the weakness of the Brookwood case against craft unionism's *immobilisme.* As historian James O. Morris later put it in *Conflict Within the AFL*, "The progressives of the twenties did not seem to realize that at the time there was really no strong sentiment for unionism in the big industries. They were barking up the right tree, but alone and in the wrong season." Nonetheless, Brookwood believed that there was something out there that ought to respond to the right appeal. As Clint perceptively put it, in a June 1929 *Labor Age* article, "To say that there are unsurmountable obstacles to organization work in either Detroit or Toledo is to ignore constantly recurring symptoms of industrial uneasiness and unrest. . . . Hundreds of thousands of pieces of literature ranging from that distributed by the trade unions of the more skilled workers such as the Machinists, to the periodic 'shop papers' issued by the Communists and Auto Workers Union, are eagerly picked up or purchased and read by the workers; spontaneous departmental strikes are of almost daily occurrence, and an undercurrent of unrest and social irresponsibility is easily discernible." Moreover, the auto industry "attracts great numbers of young coal miners who have been literally squeezed out of that industry in the past few years; other thousands have come from the railroad shops, the war time shipyards and last, but no means least, the farms have supplied another large quota." As Golden added, thousands had been members of unions before coming to Detroit and other auto centers. "Some day," he prophesized, "all those who can be helpful in this gigantic task will mobilize their forces, make use of modern methods of organizational work and approach the problem in an intelligent and scientific manner."

But Golden—and Brookwood—had little hope that the AFL would do the job. As he wrote Muste on March 7, 1929, from Milwaukee, "When the A.F.L. was going to organize the auto industry, Paul Smith of the Miners and A.F.L. came in and tried to get conferences with Nash and other big men among the employers. He refused to even discuss with the Union representatives methods of getting to the workers first and then later on getting to the bosses. Failing to meet Nash and the employers, he left town, and nothing since has been done. This is almost exactly the course that was followed in Detroit, I have been told on good authority."

Brookwood's growing criticism of the AFL leadership placed the college in an awkward position. Teaching and politicking in internal union affairs, as Brookwood came increasingly to do, is always risky, but especially so if the institution wishes to raise money and support from those it criticizes. Brookwood was on shaky ground even intellectually. As Morris pointed out, there were no craft-union proponents on the staff, and few students came from the old-line craft unions. So the debate, such as it was, over craft versus industrial unionism was one-sided. This, given the ideological bent of labor educators at the time, was perhaps understandable, but for an institution that prided itself on its intellectual as well as organizational contribution to the labor movement, it was something of a disgrace. As for the craft unionists, and this was not the best of times for any trade unionist, it was increasingly difficult to discern the fine line between Brookwood's advocacy of the need for *new* industrial unions to organize the unorganized in the mass-production industries from the Communist organization of dual unions. Would not, after all, the proposed industrial unions destroy the tiny craft beachheads already so precariously established in industry?

"Brookwood," Professor Morris observed in his study of the conflict within the AFL over craft versus industrial unionism, "could not expect to get and keep the endorsement and financial support of conservative unions and, at the same time, cast doubt upon and advocate changes in the basic principles of these unions." Brookwood, however, had its share of human perversity, and that is exactly what they expected. Muste, as Jo Ann Ooiman Robinson observed in her perceptive study, *The Traveler from Zierkzee*, in cultivating close ties with the AFL and writing as its severest critic, "revealed his old predilection for trying to ride two horses at once—a conservative steed and a radical charger." When the former turned nippy, Muste and the rest of Brookwood were shocked, hurt and then angry.

The AFL attack, when it came, was unfair. AFL President William Green asked Matthew Woll, as chairman of the WEB, to investigate Brookwood. Woll's report to the AFL Executive Council, made in August 1928, charged that anti-AFL and antireligious doctrines were being taught at Brookwood and that "pro-Soviet demonstrations had occurred there." That the Communists had attacked Brookwood washed no hands for Woll; his report had but one aim, as John Dewey, writing in the January 9, 1929 *New Republic*, wordily phrased it, "to eliminate from the labor movement the schools and influences that endeavor to develop independent leaders of organized labor who are interested in a less passive . . . social policy than now carried on by the American Federation of Labor." Woll, no doubt, would have put the thing in less verbose terms than the philosopher. In any event, the end result was identical: The Federation advised all its affiliates to withdraw support from Brookwood.

Golden once again took to the road to rally union support for Brookwood. His own union, the Machinists, despite the recommendations of its committee on education, severed its connection with the college. The Carmen and the Painters were among other past supporters to follow suit. The Mine Workers, annoyed at the support Brookwood had given its dissidents, commented with asperity as it withdrew backing that many had wondered "why any labor union would embrace Brookwood." John Fitzpatrick, "deeply grieved on account of the way in which this matter was handled," nonetheless resigned from the Brookwood board. As he told Golden, he felt "blue," and in view of recent developments within the labor movement, "did not know what to do." He reminded Golden, "rather significantly," as he reported to Muste, that the AFL "never did 'officially' recognize Brookwood" and "indicated that we should go ahead with our work regardless of them."

Fitzpatrick, however, did carry on what turned out to be a losing battle within the Federation for a hearing for Brookwood, as did some two hundred prominent individuals and a number of unions. Golden's mission was successful in holding the loyalty of the American Federation of Teachers, the Textile Workers, Hosiery Workers, Railway Clerks, and Lithographers. The ILGWU and the Amalgamated Clothing Workers, too, sided with Brookwood. In February 1929, at a conference of labor educators at Brookwood, the labor progressives prepared a counter-offensive. Jack Lever argued for a "line of communications across the country for progressives" and David Saposs declared that their task was "to permeate the labor movement." From the field, Golden reported, "A little further digging into the labor movement would, I think, result in finding some worthwhile labor folks, but they will hardly be among the present leaders." In the May 1929 *Labor Age*, he declared, "The sentiment for action is there, the need for organization is greater than ever, and there are an encouraging number of people, well-informed and capable of contributing much to a large section of the nation's workers who, with inspiration and a certain amount of helpful direction, will go forward and make new history in the workers' movement."

It was decided to call a conference of labor progressives in the spring. Golden was asked to draft a plan for the organization of labor progressives around the country to present at the conference scheduled for May 25–26 in New York City. From Cleveland, he wrote to Muste, "I think by the time I reach Minneapolis I will have collected sufficient data and observations to draft a tentative plan. . . . In these places I have so far visited I have found a number of people in each who want to do something but who beg for a plan to guide them." One thing that could be done right away, he added, "is to have someone, preferably like Budenz, for instance, following me two or three weeks behind, meeting with these groups that could be called together by a local person prior to his arrival, talking further about the situation and getting subs for *Labor Age*." At the conference of some 151 trade unionists, representatives of the Socialist Party and "friends" of organized labor, Golden presented a ten point program for adoption.* In sum, it called for the organization of regional conferences, the establishment of local groups, research, publication and a speak-

* Leonard Bright reported in the June 1929, *Labor Age:* "Of the 129 persons who attended the first day's meeting, 82 were described as active trade unionists, 11 as representatives of the Socialist Party, and 36 as persons sympathetic to the labor movement. . . . They came from 31 cities in 18 states, were associated with twelve educational classes or institutions, and were members of, although they did not represent, 33 unions, most AF of L affiliates."

ers' bureau, that *Labor Age* become the official publication of the Conference for Progressive Labor Action, the encouragement of union activists in their advocacy of "militant progressive labor policies," the support of strikes and workers' struggles, and contact with the unorganized to interest them "in forming study and discussion groups to consider problems of organization both economic and political."

Back on his travels, Golden handed out copies of "Where Brookwood Stands Now," a leaflet defending the college against its detractors, solicited subscriptions to *Labor Age* and assisted in the formation of CPLA branch organizations.* Soon there were at least seventeen branches located in such strategical industrial cities as Philadelphia, Pittsburgh, Youngstown, Cleveland, Detroit, and Chicago. Brookwood, through the CPLA, became more deeply involved in the labor struggles of the day. Brookwood graduates, more often than not, provided the nucleus for CPLA organization and extended its influence within the labor movement. As CPLA leaders and members, Brookwood faculty and graduates encouraged and participated in the several attempts made between 1930 and 1933 to create a "clean, fighting, intelligent" coal miners' union. With remarkable prescience, Muste argued that such a course would greatly increase the chances of organization of steel, auto and other unorganized industrial workers. Elmer Cope, another Brookwood graduate and CPLA activist, organized the Brotherhood of the Mills in eastern Ohio, publishing and circulating the *Mahoning Valley Steel Worker* among workers in the steel industry of the region. Alfred Hoffman and Lawrence Rogan were in the Piedmont organizing southern textile workers, and

* His assistance was invaluable in other areas of activity as well. He requested, for example, a grant of $2,400, at $200 a month, from the Garland Fund for the support of *Labor Age*. At the July 14, 1929, meeting of the CPLA executive committee, he reported that $600 had been voted and that the question of further support had been referred to a committee to bring in a recommendation in September.

turned to the CPLA and Brookwood for assistance. Golden raised $3,000 from the Garland Fund for "educational work in the Southern field" and secured an initial payment of $200 to send Brookwood graduate William Ross south to investigate the situation and to draw up plans and a budget for further work. And so Brookwood was drawn into the textile strikes that flared up in North Carolina and that, as historian Irving Bernstein noted in *The Lean Years,* foreshadowed "the turbulent labor history of the whole nation in the decade that followed."

The CPLA was an agitational and ideological precursor of the industrial unionism that coalesced in the Congress of Industrial Organizations during the late 1930s. At the founding of the CPLA, Muste asserted: "We are more loyal to the A.F. of L. than many of those who attack us. We will show our loyalty to the A.F. of L. by fighting for the principles of progressive trade unionism." This, however, did not forestall, as Muste so fervently wished, a Federation condemnation of the CPLA as a "dissenting or dual" organization. CPLA leaders were characterized as a "group of professional tingling souls who dream of a Labor Party." As for the Communists, William Z. Foster attacked the CPLAers as "little brothers of the big labor fakirs" and as " 'left' Social-Democrats" who wanted to form a rival political organization to the Communist Party.

For Brookwood, however, with its resources strained by the crash of 1929 and the great depression that followed, the CPLA posed a problem of a different order. For Muste, Tom Tippett, Golden and some others, it was an opportunity to expand Brookwood's influence, though requiring that Brookwood adapt to changed circumstances. Tippett was brought in from the mine fields of Illinois to undertake the development of an extension program that Golden and Muste envisioned as extending Brookwood's influence throughout the country.

While there was broad support among the faculty for the extension idea, others worried over the drain on Muste's time—away from Brookwood—to CPLA activities. Fannia Cohen, for example, resigned—along with others in 1929—from the *Labor Age* board of directors, cautioning the progressives against reading themselves out of the labor movement. H. H. Broach, a vice-president of the International Brotherhood of Electrical Workers, whom Golden had recommended as a replacement for a member of the Brookwood board of labor advisors, wrote Golden on July 23, 1939, "Frankly, I feel—certainly hope you will take no offense—that the job of yourself and Muste is to look after Brookwood and put it on a sound foundation. Such men as you are, of course, needed in the South and needed for raising funds for strikers. But I feel you are needed much more in doing your job for Brookwood. People simply cannot separate you from Brookwood, and when you go out and act and participate in other situations, this only weakens Brookwood and prevents you from doing the job which you want so much to do."

In his reply, Golden suggested that he, Broach and Muste get together for a talk, and added, "Perhaps it is sufficient to say at this time that in spite of everything that we have done in the past eight years to try to cooperate and work with the bona-fide trade union movement, there are not, in addition to yourself, more than half a dozen prominent leaders in the movement who have actually tried to cooperate in the real sense of the word."

Out in the field, Golden remained optimistic, despite difficulties created by the cutback in support from organized labor. As he wrote from Minneapolis in March 1929, "At the moment, my opinion is that we are going to find it increasingly difficult to get students to enroll at Brookwood who are members of the existing Unions." A prognosis that increasingly was shown to be more accurate as the year unfolded. Later, in

September 1929, he wrote in *Labor Age*, "The uncertainty of things, the insecurity of the job, create in the minds of most workers a subconscious cowardice when it comes to matters of organization. Yet, there is unrest. Something is happening in the minds of the workers. . . . There are varying numbers of militant workers in every section of the country. They are still hopeful. Those who have had the time and inclination to study economic changes to some extent are conscious of the significance of such changes." Golden earlier had referred to labor-saving machinery, efficiency schemes and the consequent unemployment while industry operated at full speed. "In the period of post-war reaction many of those who have been members of unions have been expelled on one pretext or another, others have been forced to cease being aggressive, and there are still many others who are working in company unionized or wholly unorganized industries. They are biding their time and awaiting a clarion call to intelligent realistic action. They do not expect that that call will come from present day leaders of A.F. of L. unions, nor do they cherish hope of it coming from the communists. They are fed up with unrealized extravagant promises from the one and empty revolutionary phrases from the other."

But Golden's optimism was tinged with despair; he was whistling his way past the graveyard of far too many hopes. "Our labor movement is growing old," he wrote earlier (*Labor Age*, June 1929). "The inflow of young blood so necessary to the life and vitality of an organization has almost ceased." After visits to Detroit and Milwaukee, he wrote in a letter to Muste, "The Socialist Party is without spirit or imagination." As for others sympathetic to the labor movement, "They are all fatigued radicals who are successful businessmen, lawyers or politicians and from their present comfortable circumstances (this was just before the 1929 crash), they look back over the past with considerable amusement and like to think that those of us who are at present carrying on the struggle are well meaning and sacrificing individuals who are deserving of sympathy and at least a little encouragement." Although he found a few bright spots, on the West Coast and in Butte, Montana, Golden concluded, "If I were to give an off-hand opinion as to my reactions to the whole movement, radical, conservative and otherwise . . . I would say the whole thing is politically, economically, morally and spiritually corrupt and bankrupt. It is just simply heartbreaking. . . ."

Golden, at forty-two, was approaching a crisis in his life. "For one whose entire life has been spent in the organized labor movement," he wrote in the September 1929 *Labor Age*, "it has been more painful than pleasant to have written these observations. It would have been pleasanter to have told of a growing, vigorous, achieving movement. But even radicals and the much despised plain progressives must sometimes pull their heads out of the sand and face realities." For all of his ardent advocacy of the CPLA, Golden was not convinced that it was headed altogether in the right direction. He wrote to Muste, early in 1929, "There is one point which we need to think about a good deal. And that refers to our personal feelings about the necessity for a Labor Party. When you get about as I have been and see that in nearly every locality where there is organization, efforts with varying degrees of success have been put forth to elect labor men and women to office and to use the potential strength of the organized workers to influence legislation in some fashion to secure political appointments, etc., and that as a result of all this, a good many people have been placed in office through the vehicle of the old parties, I just wonder if this in itself is not a pretty big handicap on any efforts to start a Labor Party. Outside of Minnesota, I will have to confess that I can count on my fingers the people I have seen who are really interested. I went into this matter pretty seriously with the folks in Tacoma yesterday. They admitted that this form of political activity which even they engage in extensively, gets them nowhere in particular, that nevertheless they have to 'do something.' But it seems to me that while they are also creating a psychology and a rather intangible political organization that will seriously interfere with their efforts at some future time to really build a real Labor Party."

Muste replied that "the Labor Party problem . . . is certainly a ticklish one. Nevertheless, I imagine that we are on the right line in continuing to push for a labor party. Anything else apparently only adds to the confusion already existing." The sudden collapse of the economy, the deepening depression that followed intensified Muste's development toward a more radical posture. His pursuit of the labor party chimera brought on a break with Brookwood, with all the faculty but Tom Tippett banding together to force Muste's resignation. In 1934 the CPLA became a radical sect, the American Workers Party. Golden remained on the executive committee of the CPLA to the end but he apparently did not join the AWP, though his close associate and long-time friend Jack Lever was a member of the group's executive committee.

In one of his last field reports to Muste, Golden wrote, "It is all very interesting, of course, but I will have to confess, rather bewildering, when one tries to think about a course of action that will fit the situation." He, too, was feeling the need for a change. He wanted to spend more time with his wife and his daughter. So in January 1931, he resigned his post at Brookwood. As he told a *Brookwood Review* reporter, "I have been in the labor movement for 30 years. In that time everything in industry has undergone a change. The organizations of the workers have not made any corresponding change; in many instances they have gone backward.

"The notion of having the labor movement support me in my advanced age makes no appeal to me. The idea of allowing myself to become a perpetual fixture, relying on the assistance of the movement because of my has-been role is not to my liking. I am still old-fashioned enough to think that I, and no one else, am responsible for the welfare of myself and my family."

Clint had decided to become a farmer. During the summer of 1929, he had visited Jack Lever, who, ailing, had retreated to the home of friends in Solebury, Pennsylvania, a Bucks County Quaker community, and had fallen in love with the area. Golden bought a colonial sandstone, built in 1740, with sixty-five (sixty-two tillable) acres at the headwaters of Honey Hollow Creek. If Dora, as Helen Norton Starr suggests, "suffered from Clint's rural desires," nothing was said, and the Goldens moved to their new home on the twentieth of February, 1931. The Starrs, who were among the first visitors, having stopped by on their honeymoon, recall the house as charming, "really old . . . with a spring in the basement with insets cut into the stone to cool the butter. They had two goats, chickens and what not." Behind the charm, however, was hard work, and the sorrow of leaving Brookwood. "Am getting to the point where I am only working 13 hours out of 24 instead of 18 as we did the first week," Clint wrote Muste. "Those last few days at Brookwood," he added, "were painful ones for us for we loved the place and all the things it stands for. Anything that was done while there was done as a matter of duty and of love. . . ."

Brookwood continued to call on Golden for help. He thought he would resign from the board of the Garland Fund, but Muste prevailed on him not to do so. As a member of its Workers Education Committee, he successfully urged, at Muste's prompting, funds to provide an education department for a progressive miners' union in West Virginia, and Tom Tippett became director. He also helped secure a grant to aid striking Patterson textile workers in 1931 and headed off a Communist attempt to cut out the CPLA and Brookwood from the Fund's largesse. Golden was one of the few who managed to remain on good terms with both sides after Muste was forced to resign. And in 1935, he was instrumental in getting the Garland Fund to release its grant of $5,000 to Brookwood. It was one of the last; Brookwood closed its doors in 1937.

The beginnings of the farming venture were not auspicious. "The grippe hit us rather hard," Clint wrote Muste in the spring, "and did not leave me in very good shape for the heavy work of plowing, harrowing and seeding but we are coming through after a fashion." Ernest Schliefer, an old friend who could "get no work at the machinists trade," was on hand to help out in exchange for his board. But financial difficulties undercut Clint's efforts from the first. "This business of starting life anew in a strange community," he remarked to Muste, "is made somewhat easier by establishing credit and paying one's obligations."

The Depression did not help, though there were deceptive moments when it seemed as if one could make a go of it. "I guess the bank will have to wait on me or else try to sell me out if they think that will do them any good," he wrote Muste in the fall of 1931. "In the meantime our chickens are giving us an additional increase in eggs every day and egg prices are going up while feed prices are coming down and I have just about completed arrangements for shipping about 40 quarts of milk daily to Philadelphia at a fair sort of price." But in January, he had to write to Muste, "we are hanging on." In February, the Goldens had to meet "about $600 in obligations." A year ago, he explained to Muste, "broiler prices February 1st to producers were about 45¢ per lb. At that figure we would have come thro in fine shape. However, they are now 20¢ with some possibility of a slight increase. At this figure we cannot hardly come thro." He asked if Muste "should hear of any organization that could use such services as I might be able to render and could pay enough to enable me to meet expenses while away from home plus a margin that I might be able to send home to help foot the bills, I would very much appreciate it if you would let me know." With some such work, Golden thought he could save the farm. "We have the foundation laid for self support," he wrote, "but if conditions do not improve in some small measure at least in the next few months I am afraid everything will be all over with us."

The Goldens held on. Golden wrote Jack Lever* in the spring of 1932, "We have cut every possible corner. Food purchases down to $6.00 per week for a family of 4. Have stopped feeding grain to cattle now that they are on pasture . . . Have all crops in excepting about a half acre of potatoes and 2,000 late tomato plants. . . . First planting of sweet corn up and been harrowed once. Winter wheat is all headed out. . . . Put in soy beans and soudan grass yesterday and last planting of sweet corn today." No matter, the farm could not be saved as agricultural prices plummeted. The Depression, Golden wrote to an old friend many years later, "wiped out our entire savings . . . I had debts of nearly $10,000. It took nearly ten years to pay off the debts and to get another home." A sheriff's sale foreclosed Clint's farming career.

* Lever was then living in New York City. He worked as a machinist, organized a CPLA, then an AWP, chapter. In 1931, he set up Co-operative Distributors, Inc., to provide office supplies and related goods to non-profit organizations on a co-operative basis. Golden was a member of its board along with economist Francis Henson, Lithographers' editor Justus Ebert, and IAM vice-president Robert Fechner, among others.

Mediator

TIME HUNG HEAVY on the hands of the steelworkers of Aliquippa in 1934. The country was slow in coming out of the depths of the Depression, and the men in the mills, it was said, were grateful for one or two days' work a week. Steelworkers were kept on part-time, sharing available work, so that they would not turn to charity for relief. As Myron C. Taylor, chairman of U.S. Steel's finance committee, declared, "Let it be said of the steel industry that none of its men was forced to call upon the public for help." "Staggering," however, and depleted savings, placed workers in debt at the company-owned stores and behind in rent for company-owned houses. At Aliquippa, Pennsylvania, on the south side of the Ohio River, some twenty miles below Pittsburgh, no one was allowed to forget that "J. & L.," Jones & Laughlin Steel Corporation, was *the* boss. The J. & L. whistle woke the town in the morning; the town's elected officials and its police danced to company tunes. J. & L. employed ten thousand of Aliquippa's thirty thousand people. It owned the streetcar line, buses, the water supply and 774 houses. "The company ought to have something to say about the way the town is run," a J. & L. official once declared. "The company owns pretty near everything in sight."

Just about the only place the men could call their own

were the street corners where they idled, falling silent when strangers passed by or when company or town police looked them over. They talked, as men will, of baseball, of the making of homemade brew and wine, of women and of the organizers who surreptitiously slipped into town across the bridge from Ambridge. They marveled at their courage, for even the governor's wife, Cornelia Bryce Pinchot, could not speak in Aliquippa. Some of the more daring of the Aliquippa men had heard her speak at a union-sponsored rally on August 28 in Ambridge. As they talked of such matters, whenever "the union" came up, someone would say, "Well, you know what happened to George, don't you?"

No one noticed the gaunt, shabbily-dressed, toothless bum who sidled up as they talked. Such panhandlers were all too common on the street corners of the country during those years to draw attention. So he was not missed when he ambled on, drifting through Aliquippa towards Ambridge. Once across the river, he straightened up, brushed off his clothes and hurried to a parked car where he sat and jotted down a few notes before driving off to Pittsburgh. As he drove, Clint Golden wondered what in God's name could have happened to George.

For Golden, the situation was nothing new. John S. Mayer, a fifty-one-year old organizer for the Amalgamated Association of Iron, Steel and Tin Workers of North America, AFL, had been beaten by thugs the year before in Aliquippa, then jailed and fined for "disorderly conduct." John Tefalski, who was sent to Aliquippa by the Amalgamated after Mayer had to leave, told Golden how union men were discharged, shadowed, beaten, and arrested, and union cards taken away by the police. But there had been no mention of a "George," and the flicker of fear running through that bunch on the street corner in Aliquippa had a strange quality; it was as if George had disappeared off the face of the earth. Golden had a new job with new powers and he was determined to find out what had happened to George.

Golden had done a good deal of traveling since the sheriff's sale at Solebury. The collapse of his farming hopes coincided with the economic collapse of the country into the trough of the 1930s depression. Dora went to Brookwood to work for her–and Olive's–room-and-board while Clint took a temporary assignment on the Amalgamated Clothing Workers' organizing staff. In February 1934, he was appointed a senior mediator for the Pennsylvania Department of Labor and Industry on the recommendation of the clothing union. Pennsylvania, New York and Wisconsin were among the states seeking a just resolution of labor strife. It was a new role for government, embodied nationally in Sections 7a and 7b of the National Industrial Recovery Act, which guaranteed, admittedly in a very general way, the right of workers to collective bargaining through representatives of their own choice and required of the President that he encourage "mutual agreements" between employers and employees on the "maximum hours of labor, minimum rates of pay, and other conditions of employment." A federal agency, the National Recovery Administration (NRA) was set up to administer the act. Acting within the spirit of this new–and evolving–public policy of encouraging collective bargaining, President Franklin D. Roosevelt created by executive order a National Steel Labor Relations Board on June 28, 1934.* Shortly thereafter, on

* The President acted on authority vested in him by a Public Resolution of the Seventy-third Congress, approved on June 19, 1934. The Steel Board consisted of Judge Walter P. Stacy, Chairman, Dr. James A. Mullenbach, and Admiral Henry A. Wiley, U.S. Navy, Ret.

The Board heard, investigated, and determined the merits of charges of interference, restraint, or coercion of employees in the exercise of their rights as defined in the National Industrial Recovery Act and the Code of Fair Competition for the Iron and Steel Industry. It heard complaints of discrimination against and discharge of employees in violation of their rights. It mediated disputes; ordered elections to nominate

September 12, the Board asked the Pennsylvania Department of Labor and Industry to investigate charges of alleged acts of intimidation and coercion by officers and agents of the Jones and Laughlin Steel Company at Aliquippa. Clint Golden was in charge.

With the assistance of Elizabeth S. Johnson, Golden uncovered a pattern of intimidation and harassment aimed at driving the union out of Aliquippa. The company maintained an extensive espionage system; practically every move and act of any one of its employees, whether at work or after working hours, was at once made known to company officials. "As an instance of this," Golden wrote in one of him many reports, "I saw a list of some 35 names of alleged stool pigeons in the employ of the company. Of this number 7 were Croations, 14 Serbians and the balance of various other nationalities. This would seem to indicate that it is the policy to plant informers among each racial or national group." In another memorandum Golden reported "a young fellow by the name of Reidel" passed himself off as a reporter from the Pittsburgh *Sun-Telegraph.* He bought drinks and lunches for workers who had crossed the river to visit the Ambridge headquarters of the union. Shortly after a union meeting at which a resolution was adopted asking the National Steel Labor Relations Board to conduct a hearing on union charges of intimidation and interference, Reidel asked Walter Payne and John Tefalski, union officers, if he might photograph the minutes for

---

employees to act as representatives in collective bargaining; supervised such elections; and in some cases obtained agreements whereby negotiations were carried on with employee committees without holding elections. During its existence the Board issued formal decisions in forty cases—fourteen of which were based upon petitions for elections, nineteen upon claims of discrimination, three upon allegations that collective bargaining rights had been denied, and four upon other grounds.

The President extended the Board on June 29, 1935, "until further order," but no cases involving formal action were heard after that date.

reproduction in an article he was writing for the *Sun-Telegraph.* The unsuspecting unionists agreed to let him do so. Golden's account continues, "Reidel then bought drinks for some 200 men who were about, [saying] 'this is on the Sun-Tele.'" When, later, Payne and Tefalski met Al Goff, a well-known *Sun-Telegraph* reporter, they asked of Reidel and were told that no such person worked for the paper. Further inquiries disclosed that Reidel worked for an Aliquippa biweekly with a pronounced J. & L. bias. As Golden's account closed, "Reidel came around to Union headquarters in Ambridge today and was unceremoniously ordered out."

The harassment of unionists was often ingenuous. Fiorindo DiGennari liked to make his own wine and had done so for many years. Shortly after he signed up with the union, two Borough policemen knocked on the door of his home and without speaking entered and went to the cellar where they found one hundred gallons of elderberry wine. DiGennari was told to report to the chief of police, who informed him that he was to pay a fine of $31.45. When he said he had no money to pay, the police returned to his home, and dumped the wine in the sewer. Other unionists so raided were by some strange coincidence always fined the exact amount due them that week in their paychecks. Intimidation, however, was not always so finely wrought. Joseph Latone had asked some friends to cross the river with him to hear Mrs. Pinchot speak on August 28. He was accosted by company police and told to stay away and when he ignored their advice, he was followed and watched throughout the meeting. The next day, Captain Harris and Lieutenant Kelly of the company police visited Latone and warned him "if he and the rest of the dagoes do not quit organizing the men, they will run all the c——s—— out of town and you rotten s—— of a b——s will be the first to go." J. & L., they added, "has been damn good to all their employees. Though the J. & L. has been feeding you s——b——s and that is the thanks you return to them." J. & L. thanked Latone by firing him; he was also told that if he worked with the company police as an informer, they would find work for his son.

On the day after Mrs. Pinchot's speech in Ambridge, Burgess Sohn of Aliquippa and a captain of the J. & L. police held their own rally in front of Tony Ferro's barber shop. Ferro's affidavit tells the story. "Captain Mauk began to speak and in a few minutes about 200 people gathered about him. His first words were, 'You black handed mothers and s——b——s, I am here to tell you if you don't soon try and bust this association of the Amalgamated we are going to bust you people up.' He also stated that no outside organization is 'worth while joining.' In the first place he further stated, 'they collect money off you people and after getting it they beat it.' In the second place he said, 'the J. & L. Co. does not like an outside Union and will close their plant before they will recognize them so get busy and drive these grafters out of town.' And further 'do you people know that that baldheaded organizer (Tefalski) at Ambridge is working hand in hand with those G——D—— reds that started the riot at Ambridge and you dagoes ought to be thankful that the J. & L. Co. allows you to remain in this town.' " To this account, Golden added, "At the above described 'meeting,' there were a considerable number of women and children present and regardless of this, Mauk used vile, obscene and profane language." It was an innocent time.

What happened to George Issoski was certainly unusual but it was also symbolic. Issoski, a hapless man, suffered a back injury in 1916 when a platform in the mill collapsed and he dropped twenty-five feet into a steel pit. He was never able to collect workmen's compensation, though the company gave him "light" work at reduced pay. In 1931, he was laid off and went on relief to support his family of seven children. When union organizers came to Aliquippa, Issoski was asked if he would sign up his acquaintances working at the mill. He agreed, and Golden tells what happened in a report. Issoski

> succeeded in getting a large number of signatures for them. Then a company policeman by the name of George Opsatnik began to follow him and threaten him, calling him vile names because he was "organizing for the Union." In the evening of September 11 he was accosted by Opsatnik who insisted on buying drinks for Issoski. He refused because he "knew he was a bad man and he was afraid of him." Again he was cursed and abused. Later a man by the name of John Kavki who had been a good friend in the past and who had signed a pledge card for the Union met him and asked him to have a drink. He took a drink of gin and followed it with a bottle of beer and then left the saloon to go home. As he approached the First National Bank at West Aliquippa he was seized by James Istock, a borough policeman, who said "give me those cards." The policeman then tore his shirt open and pulled it out of his trousers and hit him several times with his fist on each side of the face and took him to the local jail. He had had about 200 cards for delivery to the Union representatives but after being accosted by company policeman Opsatnik earlier in the evening, he had become afraid and had destroyed them. The borough policeman then found no cards on him.
>
> Upon arrival at the jail he was again beaten up and something was pointed at him that he thought was a gun and he was sure they were going to shoot him. The day following he was taken to the county jail in Beaver. His wife came there to see him but was told that he was "very crazy" and was not permitted to see him. She was then asked to sign some sort of a paper which she refused to

sign. Later a "lady and a man doctor" came to see him and asked him some questions and on September 19th 1934, he was brought to the State Hospital at Torrance.

Golden found him there and, after an interview, concluded, "Issoski is as sane as I am." He reported his discovery to Charlotte E. Carr, state secretary of labor, and got Mrs. Pinchot interested in the case. She prevailed upon her husband to have Issoski examined by a psychiatrist, Dr. Earl Bond of Philadelphia, who had no connection with the institution nor with Aliquippa. He reported that in his opinion that Issoski was sane and Governor Pinchot ordered Issoski's release. Meanwhile, Golden had convinced the governor that something had to be done to open up Aliquippa and restore civil liberties there. On his recommendation, the governor sent in the state police with instructions to protect workers' rights to hold meetings and organize without interference from J. & L. police. As Clint reported on October 18, 1934, to his superior, Clarence J. Moser, director of the Pennsylvania Bureau of Mediation, "There is a very noticeable change in the attitude of the people in Aliquippa generally this week and yesterday and today, at some temporary headquarters established in a worker's home by the Union, workers were coming in constantly to fill out application cards and make payments on same. While the state policemen have remained close to their headquarters in the hotel and have not patroled the streets at all, the fact that they are in town is known and has a healthy effect on the general situation."

On October 14, Cornelia Bryce Pinchot spoke at the first labor rally ever held in Aliquippa. There were four thousand people at the meeting. Soon some three thousand were signed up in the union. Hearings were held before the National Steel Labor Relations Board in November on union charges of intimidation, interference and coercion. The Board, however, decided against the union. As Golden wryly put it in a letter to AFL attorney Charlton Ogburn, "The only justification that the Board has so far as I can see is that, according to testimony, there was no coercion on *November 16 and 17th* when the Board was conducting the hearings."

Section 7a of the National Industrial Recovery Act turned out a weak reed despite John L. Lewis's insistence that it was a guarantee of collective bargaining. Within the steel industry, company unions flourished, protected by NRA Administrator Hugh S. Johnson's interpretations of the act, and employers, as J. & L. did in Aliquippa, kept up with discharges, discrimination, and evictions, using informers and hired thugs where necessary to break legitimate unionization.* Within the labor movement, the craft unions looked with suspicion at the new so-called "NRA unions," and, in steel in particular, those suspicions ran high, because the new local unions were the base of opposition to the entrenched leadership of the Amalgamated Association. With the NIRA on its way out—it was declared unconstitutional by the Supreme Court in 1935—the militants in steel were pushing for a general strike to force recognition on the steel companies. In *As Steel Goes*, Robert R. R. Brooks describes the activists who were at the heart of the sudden upsurge of the "NRA babies." "We were discovering," Brooks quotes a spokesman as saying, "that the government could not by itself guarantee the right to organization and collective bargaining. In the men's clothing, ladies' garment, and coal industries, the workers had the power to make their influence felt in the code authorities and to compel recognition. . . . In steel . . . [we] were given company unions, fake elections, legal delays, and the cold shoulder

* "Did you know," Golden wrote Ogburn on January 15, 1935, "that the union headquarters at Aliquippa had been entered and the charter and membership records stolen last month?" The AFL sought to reopen the Aliquippa case but got nowhere.

when it came to demands for recognition. That was what the rank-and-file movement was about. We were trying to force the thing back into Washington by demanding that the President use his power to bring the leaders of the Iron and Steel Institute and the Amalgamated Association together to settle in the public limelight instead of fighting it out with company police in the twilight of the Black Valley, the Mahoning, and the Monongahela."

Washington, it was thought, was worried about the possible consequences of strikes upon the recovery of the economy. An election year was coming up, the NIRA was declared unconstitutional, and the administration did not know which way to jump on the Wagner Labor Disputes Bill, which would provide for collective bargaining. So, as the rank-and-filer told R. R. Brooks, "What it came down to was that we were putting on a terrific publicity show, backed by the fact that thousands of steel workers were all set to strike—even though they were almost certain to lose." Such a prospect appalled the leaders of the Amalgamated, and such fears, of course, were intermingled with those of a takeover of the union by the militants.

Ogburn, in a letter to Golden, stated the other side of the case. "The idea of their winning a strike in the steel industry is absolutely absurd. They can call out their locals on strike, they might even force a strike vote throughout the entire Amalgamated, but the Amalgamated at this time, as you well know, is too weak to win such a strike; the industry is not organized and the unorganized steel workers will not join the strike. There are only two factors that make the situation any different today than what it has been for twenty or thirty years in the steel industry: one factor is the depression, which makes organization by strike methods all the more difficult to accomplish; the other factor, however, is in our favor, and that is the aid we can obtain from the Government. . . . Without the aid of the United States Government there is not the slightest hope of organizing the steel industry." Ogburn cited "the fine start" of the Steel Labor Board, pointing out that it had decided every case of any significance in labor's favor, except the J. & L case and the Acme Steel election case. Industry, he pointed out, was "eager enough to do away with these labor boards," leaving the unions without any protection. "Without the aid of the United States Government," Ogburn wrote, "there is not the slightest hope of organizing steel."

Golden agreed with Ogburn about the role of government, but he also recognized the new energies surfacing in the so-called rank-and-file movement. As he told Ogburn, "I do hope . . . that something can be done to harness this energy and direct it into constructive channels." As he reminded Ogburn, he knew men on both sides—rank-and-file rebels and officials of the Amalgamated. Elmer Cope, a Brookwood graduate, Muste protégé and CPLA activist, had organized in the Mahoning Valley much of the earlier opposition to the Amalgamated's established leadership. He had been expelled, in May 1933, from the Association for his CPLA connection but continued to have influence within the rank-and-file movement, though that lessened as he and his CPLA confederates increasingly concentrated their efforts on organizing unemployment leagues.* Though, technically, the faction fight with the Amalgamated was none of Golden's business as a state mediator, he was drawn in as a possible conciliator when the two groups were on the verge of a final break.

This break was precipitated by a change in the Communist Party line. It changed, in 1934, from the policy of organizing dual unions back to boring within non-Communist unions.

* Elmer F. Cope later joined the Steel Workers' Organizing Committee staff as an organizer and served the steel union for twenty-nine years. He was active in international affairs, serving in Europe as a CIO representative from 1947 to 1951. He was the first elected secretary-treasurer of the Ohio AFL–CIO.

The Communists disbanded the Steel and Metal Workers' Industrial Union and their members joined the rank-and-file movement within the Amalgamated at just about the time when the leadership seemed about to make their peace with the rebels. When the Amalgamated leaders got wind of the Communist infiltration, they counterattacked. When the rank-and-file group announced a proposed conference in Pittsburgh on February 3, 1935, the Amalgamated declared that all lodges sending delegates would be expelled.*

Golden became involved at this point. He did what he could to talk the rank-and-file leaders out of calling their conference. As he wrote Ogburn on January 30, 1935, "I am advised tonight that some of the leaders of this group feel that it should be called off while others stubbornly insist on going thro with it. I am hoping that the last letter [warning the lodges of possible expulsion] will have a sobering effect on the hot headed. . . ." He analyzed the rather confused situation for Ogburn's benefit—and through him, the AFL. "While I realize full well the strength of the opposition that the Amalgamated has had to contend with for a great many years from the steel mill owners, I feel, at the same time, that the organization could have been much more aggressive, especially so since the advent of the NRA. Because of this lack of aggressiveness I could understand how new members as yet lacking in experience in organization activities could become impatient. With the apparent inactivity of the administrative officials of the Amalgamated, I think I can understand how a small handful of communists could take advantage of the impatience of these new members and undertake to direct it into channels advantageous to the communist party interests. If anything of this sort should happen it would of

* The rank-and-file group included Clarence Irwin, L. A. Morris, Joseph J. Clair, William J. Spang, Albert Atallah, Harold J. Ruttenberg, Joseph Scanlon and John Harris.

course naturally follow that the Amalgamated leadership would undertake to purge the ranks of the Union of these elements. This might develop a new set of hatreds and loyalties and create all sorts of difficulties which would have to be met in some fashion if an organizing campaign in the steel industry would be undertaken by either the A.F. of L., itself or the Amalgamated or both.* It was out of a desire to prevent this sort of thing that I have taken as much interest as I have in the situation. I have been handicapped to some extent because of the position I hold. This has been particularly true since the new state administration took office. . . . And of course it is a highly questionable policy for representatives of a state government to project themselves into the shaping of trade union policies." Nonetheless, he advised Ogburn "it is important that the A.F. of L. should carefully look into the situation and try to work out some sort of plan jointly with the Amalgamated if at all possible, looking toward the organization of the steel industry."

Over the course of the next month, Clint met with representatives of the rank-and-file group, with officers of the Amalgamated, with AFL President William Green. His contacts with the rank-and-file group were circumspect, necessarily so. On March 12, he provided some background for journalist William P. Mangold, a contributor to *Labor Age* and *The New Republic*. Golden wrote:

* John L. Lewis and his supporters at the October 1934 AFL convention had pushed through a strong resolution urging that the Executive Council take action to organize steel. Lewis, at the time, was having trouble with the steel companies over the so-called "captive mines," coal mines owned by the steel companies. Gains won by the mine workers were threatened by the lower standards in steel. Lewis, too, was having trouble with progressive elements within the UMW so he had little sympathy with the rebels within the Amalgamated. Nonetheless, their activities in 1933 and 1934 encouraged his stand as well as the hopes that steel might be organized and so protect his nonunion flank and, incidentally, utimately undo his opposition within the UMW.

At the moment I do not know the exact number of Lodges of the Amalgamated whose charters have been revoked. Prior to any recent revocations there were a total of 122 Lodges chartered by that organization. Of this number 78 were represented at the so-called rank and file conference or convention in this city on February 3rd. Of the 78 represented, there were no Lodges which had agreements in any form with any of the steel or tin mills. All of them were so-called "NRA Lodges" because they came in to existence since the passage of the NIRA. The Amalgamated Association officials threatened to revoke the charter of *every* Lodge that participated in the banned conference. I am sure they have not carried out this threat fully largely because they did not *know* for certain, the numbers of *all* the Lodges participating. I judge charters have been revoked in about a dozen instances at the most up to the present time.

As to the number of members affected by this action and the percentage of the total membership that this represents—certain complications arise. To arrive at a conclusion about this we have to start from some sort of a definition as to what constitutes "membership" in the Amalgamated. From the point of view of constitution provisions as to requirements I think there are probably at the present moment not more than 7,000 members of the Amalgamated who have paid a *full* initiation fee and whose dues are *paid up to date*. On the other hand I think that perhaps 150,000 steel workers in the past 20 months have either signed so-called pledge cards authorizing the Amalgamated to act for them as a collective bargaining agency or representative, or have filled out an application for membership, or have paid a sum ranging from 25¢ to $2.00 on the application or initiation fee. Amalgamated officials will tell you with some degree of justification I think, that applicants who pay nothing at all or anything less than the amount provided by the constitution, are not members. The rows at the conventions last year revolved about this point and there is no doubt but what a lot of delegates were seated at the conventions as such, who either were not members in good standing or whose Lodges had not met the constitutional requirements regarding payment of taxes to the national organization. And roughly, it is this group which now constitutes the "rank and file."

I should say that this condition grows out of an antiquated constitution governing an organization officered by men utterly unable to adjust themselves to present day conditions. On the side of the "rank and file group" is the fact that in other than the tin mills, there has been practically no full time employment for the workers. Such employment as there has been has been staggered to give as many work as possible and in some cases that I am familiar with the total earnings thus secured were less than the relief allowances given in the communities in which these mills were located. Under these circumstances it is understandable that lots of mill workers who wanted to follow the normal procedure in becoming members of a Union were utterly unable to meet even the $2.00 application fee required and the modest sliding scale of dues based on earnings.

From a strict constitutional point of view the Amalgamated officials can say that the good standing membership of the Lodges whose charters have been revoked does not amount to a great number.

While it is undoubtedly true that the present officials of the Amalgamated are reactionary, incompetent and unimaginative (I am certain none of them are crooked or corrupt) and utterly unable to meet the situation in the industry as it exists today, it should also be pointed out that the leaders of the rank and file group have shown little intelligence or ability in handling the affairs of that group. Pages could be written on this phase of the situation.

I have not time to go into the situation further except to say that last night's papers here reported that Aaron Sapiro, a New York lawyer, addressed a meeting of rank and file delegates in Weirton Sunday at which about 300 were present, denouncing Green, Tighe and other leaders and that he has been retained as counsel for the rank and file group. I do not know anything about this other than the newspaper accounts—a copy of which I sent Dave Saposs last night. But I do know that Sapiro has had a great deal of success in years past organizing some of the large fruit growers cooperatives on the west coast, the dyeing and cleaning business in Chicago, etc.

In my judgment it is entirely possible that an astonishing result would come from a campaign of organization in the steel industry if directed by intelligent people and use made of modern methods of publicity and propaganda. If the situation were left solely in the hands of either the present Amalgamated leadership or the rank and file leadership, there would be little likelihood of a strike of any proportions in my judgment. If Sapiro is taking hold of the situation in earnest and has some resources with which to work, I should not be at all surprised to see a new independent union emerge that might shake the foundations not only of the steel industry but of the whole labor movement as represented by the AFL. I'll guess that the next 6 months is going to be an exciting period in the history of the labor movement.

So they would prove to be. Golden was appointed associate director of the Pittsburgh Regional Board by Francis Biddle, then chairman of the National Labor Relations Board, on April 1, 1935, at an annual salary of $4,500. The Pittsburgh NLRB office covered the Ohio-Pittsburgh steel area as well as the western half of Pennsylvania and northern West Virginia. The appointment came at a rather trying moment; the Wagner Bill was up for debate and the fate of the Board seemed uncertain. Golden, however, plunged immediately into his new task. Mostly he spent his days trying to secure the reinstatement of men fired because their activities, organizing, were considered "detrimental" to the interests of one steel company or other. Much of it was frustrated by lack of any real power to do anything, a situation that changed when the Wagner Bill became law in June 1935. (Golden was then appointed Director of the 6th Region of the NLRB.) Cases began to build up before the Board and the courts. In letters and memorandums, Clint made the same point, time and time again, about this steel town or that. "Some very effective organizing work might be done in Brackenridge," he wrote on June 28, 1935. "From what we can gather, the sentiment of the community is largely with [men discharged because of union activity]. I doubt, however, whether there is any organization capable or willing to undertake this work."

He was drawn once again into the internal confusions of the Amalgamated, which had expelled several lodges controlled by leaders of the rebel rank-and-file movement. He talked with AFL President Green, who told him that if unity could be established in the Association "it was entirely probable that an organization campaign in the steel industry could be undertaken after the Supreme Court had passed on the constitutionality of the Wagner act." Golden arranged for "a thoroughly reliable acquaintance" to see leaders of the expelled lodges to discover if they were sincere about their expressed wishes for reinstatement. "On the whole," he wrote Ogburn on July 9, the day of his meeting with Green, "it appears there is a sincere desire, although the sincerity of a few individuals can probably be questioned." Golden's man got the expelled leaders to waive a number of the ten demands they had originally made as a basis for reinstatement. As for the Association, it was under pressure from the courts to readmit the expelled units. So, over the summer a compromise was worked out involving back payment of dues. Reinstatement, however, did not set off the long-awaited organizing drive.

In his talk with Golden, AFL President Green raised the possibility of a test case coming out of the steel industry over the constitutionality of the recently enacted National Labor Relations Act, which became law on July 5, 1935. Albert Atallah, president of Amalgamated Lodge 200, Aliquippa, kept Golden informed of continued harassment of unionists by the J. & L. company police. When Lodge members filed aboard two buses to attend the rank-and-file Pittsburgh conference on February 3, 1935, company police watched them board and followed them to Pittsburgh. Some twenty-odd foremen gathered outside the Polish Hall in Aliquippa when the union held an "open meeting" on February 10, frightening off some of the more timid. Golden also obtained photostats of bills of sale of tear gas and Thompson submachine guns and equipment to J. & L. When J. & L. discharged ten workers known to have been active on behalf of the union, Lodge 200 filed a complaint with the NLRB. After investigation, conducted by Golden, and hearings, in which the company refused to participate on the grounds that the Wagner Act was unconstitutional, the NLRB ordered Jones and Laughlin to cease and desist from interfering with the self-organization of its employees and from discouraging union membership by discrimination. The discharged workers were to be rehired and paid their wage losses for the period between their discharge and their return to work.

J. & L. refused to comply with the NLRB order and the Board petitioned the courts for enforcement. The case was argued before the Supreme Court in February 1937, and the decision was handed down on April 12, 1937. The Court upheld the constitutionality of the Act and J. & L. was ordered to comply with the NLRB's cease and desist order. Socially and legally, as Elias Lieberman points out in his informative *Unions Before the Bar*, "the Supreme Court's thin majority decision in this case revolutionized industrial relations in the United States and climaxed more than a century of labor history. The court placed its stamp of approval not only on the legal status of organized labor and the law to protect the workers' right to organize, but also on the *duty* of employers to deal in good faith with the authorized representatives of the workers concerning wages, hours and other conditions of employment. There could no longer be any question of a union's right to exist. The very interference with its existence by an employer through unfair labor practices became outlawed."

By the time the high court rendered its decision, there was not much doubt as to what the public wanted—the resolution of industrial conflict peaceably. Franklin D. Roosevelt's 1936 reelection sweep was a mandate for the New Deal, including the recently enacted National Labor Relations Act. The build-up of support for collective bargaining as a solution for industrial strife entailed exposure of employer complicity in the creation of violence. Much of Clint Golden's work over the winter of 1935–1936 involved gathering information about industrial espionage and corporate strikebreaking. Heber Blankenhorn, a veteran reporter who had served as the secretary to the commission of the Interchurch World Movement investigating the 1919 steel strike, joined the NLRB as one of its industrial economists, serving in reality as a troubleshooter and investigator. On October 23, 1935, he wrote Golden, "Here I am going through a lot of files of data on undercover agencies, heading toward asking the NLRB to request Congress for an investigation of dicks as agencies to break the Wagner law. Will write you more of it shortly. Got a couple of resolutions on it through the [A. F. of L.] convention."

Golden was asked to provide a background memo on industrial espionage, and soon Blankenhorn was urging him on as "Chief Aide and Nestor of our dick hunt." He unearthed a prodigious amount of material that became grist for the first of the so-called La Follette hearings, held in Washington, D.C., over April 10 to 23, 1936. Senator La Follette chaired the subcommittee of the Senate Committee on Education and Labor charged by Congress to investigate "violations of the right of free speech and assembly and interference with the right of labor to organize and bargain collectively."

"It is not difficult to check up details," Golden wrote Blankenhorn, "once you have friends and acquaintances who believe in you and are willing to render service wherever possible." So it was throughout the "dick hunt." R. J. Davidson, a former Greyhound bus driver and an organizer for the Amalgamated Association of Street and Electric Railway and Motor Coach Employees, reported to Golden that a certain Harry Hill, a coach cleaner thought to be a "stool pigeon" by his fellow workers, "now openly states that he is employed by the Railway Audit and Inspection Company to report on the activities of the Greyhound employees in this region." Ernest Schliefer, a Machinist comrade in Boston, formerly a railroad shopman and now working in the Boston shipyard, wrote, "A better lead than any other I can think of at the moment is the American Legion, for in my last interest in this business of Labor Spys I found that ex-service men and members of the Legion were given preference for this work. This came to me by way of a complaint, as for a number of years I had a good contact with a police stool pigeon and exconvict who did much of this kind of work for the Railway Audit and Inspection Bureau."

James M. Duffy, president of the National Brotherhood of Operative Potters, wrote, "I took up with Mr. Frank Hull, our representative in charge of the Barberton [Ohio] strike situation, concerning guards employed at said place, as a means of determining whether or not said guards were supplied by any of the professional strike breaking guard companies. Brother Hull says that from the best information he has the sheriff has an arrangement with the company whereby he receives so much per guard and he in turn hires the guards at a price, in all probability leaving him a handsome profit. He further states that he understands most of the guards are ex-soldiers who for various reasons find themselves desperately in need of money and have readily accepted the opportunity for service." The head of the Better Business Bureau "confidentially" passed on a list of the directors and officers of the Employers' Association of Pittsburgh, whose business was "to maintain an open shop condition in the Pittsburgh district." Golden added in his report to Blankenhorn, "I am informed on good authority that they had a large number of undercover men working in the unions, but particularly in the metal trades industries. If necessary, Jerry McMunn, international board member of the Moulders Union, and Andrew T. McNamara, who was formerly Business Representative of the Machinists here, will testify to efforts made by E. W. Moreland, who was formerly the secretary-manager of the Association, to bribe them with monthly payments for advance information on the plans and activities of their respective organizations."

Through J. Alfred Wilner, a special deputy attorney general for Pennsylvania, Golden uncovered the unsavory backgrounds of four "detectives" who helped convict J. L. Anderson and six other cotton textile workers on charges of dynamiting at the Holt Plaid Mill in Burlington, North Carolina, during the 1934 textile strike. Wilner referred Golden to State Senator Anthony Calvacante, a Uniontown, Pennsylvania, attorney and a lawyer for the Mineworkers, who knew something of the activities of the four men during the 1933 Fayette County coal strike. Two were considered especially dangerous and were experts in the use of dynamite. One, an admitted perjurer who had been convicted of assault on a young girl and her escort, provoked a riot during a strike; the other fired into a group of sleeping pickets, seriously wounding one near the hip. All four were deputized during the Fayette coal strike, serving under the direction of the H. C. Frick Coal and Coke Company police.

Harry Lefker, a public accountant with offices in New York City and an old friend, provided Golden with reports from Dunn and Bradstreet on Federal Laboratories, Inc., and Railway Audit and Inspection, firms specializing in, respectively, "protective engineering" sources and "general inspection work." Federal Laboratories was a major manufacturer of tear gas and vomiting gas as well as a distributor of submachine guns. Railway Audit employed "300 accountants." Lefker also obtained the client list of the American Confidential Bureau, an outfit that specialized in investigating guards which claimed to have the records of fifty thousand employees together with their fingerprints. The Burns, Pinkerton and International Auxiliary Company sent representatives to see Lefker. "They all tell the same story and quite frankly," he wrote Golden. "They protect property *inside* and will not do any strike-breaking or scab work outside the plant's property. They will place men skilled in any particular industry in the plant. These men will join the Union if necessary, spy on other workers and do all the things you read and hear about. All this was told with a rather naive frankness. They can supply as many men as are necessary but must be given about a week's notice in advance. The compensation is $12.00 per day plus expenses—this latter being a very indefinite term. I could not ascertain their clients except that Burns worked in the Cushman strike at White Plains. There, they had men working as drivers and men in the plant as stooges who gave them all the data."

Golden also engaged in a little undercover work, helping John Edelman, research director for the American Federation of Full Fashioned Hosiery Workers, draft an advertisement to draw out secret operatives. In March 1936, during the Akron rubber strike, he reported to Blankenhorn: "Are you aware that an outfit known as the Cresswell Agency, offices Akron Savings and Loan Building, Akron, Ohio, is supplying operatives in the present rubber strike; also that Col. Joseph Johnson, who I understand is an agent for the Lake Erie Chemical Company, tear gas dispensers, represents another agency, name unknown, which is supplying operatives in the present Rubber Workers strike?" Steelworkers dropped in regularly to report various attempts at harassment. As a consequence, Golden was able to provide the first direct worker testimony about employer espionage for the La Follette committee.

John J. Mullen, a thirty-two-year-old coke worker at the Carnegie coke works in Clairton, Pennsylvania, "one of the better company towns," came in to see Clint on January 26, 1936. He was chairman of the Clairton Employee Representation Plan, active in the Democratic Party and had recently left the mill to work as a clerk of the County Bureau of Elections. He had been approached by a "big bruiser," who introduced himself as Walter Sears and said he represented a group of steel stockholders who were "very much aware that there was dissension among employees and a lack of harmony between management and employees" and wanted to rectify it. Sears wanted Mullen to meet his boss, a Mr. Henning, or as he turned out to be later, W. O. L. Hemingray, an employee of Railway Audit and Inspection. "They thought they were smart as hell," Mullen later recalled. "They lavished praise on me until I thought I was too good to be wholesome. I had been reading a summary of Levinson's *I Break Strikes* and I knew right away that they were finks."

They offered Mullen fifty dollars a month to supply reports of "favoritism by the bosses." Mullen was to rent a post office box, take the code name "Ben," and was later given telephone numbers where he could call "Henning" or Sears. Mullen, at first indignant, decided to play along. He had read about Golden and thought it "safe" to talk to him about the offer. "I told him about my experiences with these fellows and asked for advice as to whether I should go on or not. He told me that further information would be very useful to the La Follette Committee on Civil Liberties . . . but that it was up to me as a young married man with a family whether I should take a chance. He said that they would stop at nothing to prevent me from exposing them. On the other hand, he thought I might be able to discover the missing link between the spies and the interests which were supporting them." Mullen reported to his new employers every week. "Mr. Golden used to help me prepare my reports. He said give them good strong fictitious ones. He said they were paying for it and ought to get their money's worth." Mullen gave the money he was paid to Golden, who earmarked it and placed it in a safe.

Mullen—and others like him—were attempting to make the employee representative plans (ERPs) launched by their employers independent. At Carnegie-Illinois, George A. Patterson, a roll turner, had organized the Independent Steel Organization in rebellion against the company-sponsored employee representation plan. But Patterson also maintained contact with other rebels who were active in the corporation's employee representation groups. Sears and "Henning" visited Patterson in February with much the same pitch they made to Mullen, offering, however, more money, seventy-five dollars a month for information. As Patterson told Golden, when he made a visit to Pittsburgh to see Mullen on ERP business, he was upset and rejected the offer. "Sears became very insistent," Golden's account of Patterson's report continues, "It appears that Patterson has an invalid sister and [Sears] called this to Patterson's attention, advising him how much better medical attention he would be able to get for her if Patterson accepted the offer." While Patterson was in Pittsburgh, Golden and Mullen arranged Mullen's weekly visit with Sears and "Henning," and Patterson identified them as the same two men who had tried to recruit him as an informer. Patterson agreed to testify before the La Follette Committee.

Mullen continued to meet with his "employers," and in March, they decided to introduce him to the "big boss." "We arranged to have an observer in the vicinity," Golden wrote afterwards to Blankenhorn. The observer followed Mullen and Hemingray to the Keystone Hotel, where they were joined by a third person, "the chief" to "Henning," and "Mr. Macklin" of New York City to Mullen. They went to "Macklin's" hotel room. "He exchanged pleasantries with me," Mullen said of the meeting, "and then lay across the bed for fifteen or twenty minutes looking me over while I talked." Before the La Follette Committee, Mullen said of "Henning," "I would not want to meet him in a dark alley by myself. He was a bad-looking man . . . Mr. Macklin did not impress me as such a hard character, only he had a somewhat sanctimonious appearance."

After the meeting in the hotel room, Mullen and "Henning" left, then "Macklin" came out alone. Golden's man followed him to Donahoe's cafeteria, then to Murphy's 5 & 10 where he purchased a door handle, to a florist shop and then to the Frick Building Annex where he entered the elevator and left on the fifteenth floor, offices occupied by the H. C. Frick Coal and Coke Company. "Macklin," Golden discovered, was an ex-FBI agent, George Rauk, who headed Frick's notorious coal and coke police. During the Fayette County mine strike of 1932–1933, he tapped Governor Pinchot's telephone and overheard the governor ordering the National Guard into the county. Mullen had uncovered the link between his "finks" and "the interests employing them." When he and Patterson went to Washington to testify before the La Follette committee in April, they used the money the finks had paid them to cover their expenses. "We didn't want to use their blood money for personal gain," Mullen explained, "but we thought that we were justified in using it as we did, because otherwise we couldn't have made the trip."

Golden was increasingly drawn into the fast-developing steel situation. John L. Lewis's interest in organizing the industry deepened as his conflict with the AFL leadership intensified. After the 1935 AFL convention rebuffed his plea for a drive to organize the mass production industries on an industrial basis rather than by craft, he formed the Committee for Industrial Organization and resigned as an AFL vice-president. When the Federation executive council, meeting in January 1936, ordered the Committee dissolved, Lewis counterattacked in steel. In the spring, he told Heber Blankenhorn that the "deluge of invitations [to the CIO] from steel towns continues" and indicated that he would make a call to steel in a forthcoming speech to the miners at Greensburg, Pennsylvania, on April 1, "Miners' Day," 1936. When Blankenhorn wondered if the steel people were not egging on the anthracite operators to force a strike in order to detract Lewis from steel, Lewis laughed and told Blankenhorn a story, "typical Lewis, . . . not a brag, but an act."

"I met a man in the steel business at the New York negotiations the other day," Lewis said, "who wanted me to go to lunch, across the street, in the Chrysler Building. I asked him if that wasn't where Tom Girdler and his bunch lunched. He said, yes. I told him I couldn't lunch but he should take his message to Girdler: Tell him you saw John Lewis and Lewis says that he was bored with negotiating with a little bunch like the anthracite monopoly and Morgan's and was just waiting for the day when he could take on a man-sized negotiation with the steel people. Tell him also that the contract will be stiffer than the contracts he signed up for his coal mines."

Lewis signaled his intentions at Greensburg, where a rank-and-file group of steelworkers also appeared as guests. The CIO offered $500,000 to the Amalgamated Association for the organization of steel, provided that it was done on an industrial basis. Golden wrote to Patterson, "I shall be glad to hear from you following the meeting of the employee representatives . . . It appears that the C.I.O. has made some rather practical proposals for the organization of the industry, and I would be interested in knowing how your people feel about that."

John Brophy, a friend of long standing who had been on Brookwood's board of labor advisors, asked Golden to "put a little pressure on Leonard [secretary-treasurer of the Amalgamated] for action [on the CIO proposal]." Golden met with Leonard for over two hours on May 19, 1936. He gave the following report to Blankenhorn on the next day:

He claimed that Tighe, while an old man and feeble, still does his own thinking and permits no one to do any thinking for him. I laid a great deal of stress on the whole situation and pointed out that in my opinion the present is one of those crucial moments in the history of the labor movement when organizations must go forward or be swept aside. I tried to point out to him what an important role he could play by abandoning the present negative attitude and adopting one of a very positive nature. I will have to confess that I did not feel particularly confident that my talk with him would have any effect.

He did claim however that when board meetings were called, no opinions were expressed and there was no indication of initiative on the part of any of the board members. He claims that in part this influences Tighe's action. In other words, the failure of any of the board members to come forth with ideas and suggestions causes Mike to feel that everything is left on his shoulders. It seems that the only thing that came out of their board meeting Monday was action directing Leonard to notify all national and international unions of the action taken at the Canonsburg convention in adopting a resolution proposing the organization of the industry and asking for help in so doing.*

After talking to Leonard in the afternoon I had a talk with Miller [Edward W. Miller, a vice-president of the

* The Canonsburg convention was held at the end of April. The so-called rank-and-file group gained control of the convention but was unable to have its way entirely. It wanted to take up the CIO offer but the convention sent a committee to see Green and Lewis. What the AFL proposed was clearly not satisfactory to the delegates. Nonetheless, the resolution finally adopted was worded so as to allow the officers to canvass all the unions in the AFL for assistance before accepting the CIO offer.

Amalgamated] in the evening. He seems to feel that the adoption of the resolution by the convention was a great achievement. I pointed out to him that this had no significance unless it was translated into immediate action. I could not get much satisfaction out of him.

I pressed him to get what he expected to come out of their action in notifying all national and international unions of the adoption of the resolution. He was noncommittal on this point other than to say that they were obligated to inform other organizations of the action taken. I also pressed him as to how long they expected to await word from the unions to whom these communications had been sent. He replied they would "wait a week or so." In the meantime he says that Tighe has been invited by Green to come to Washington for a conference sometime this week.

I have passed this information on to Brophy and have said to him that in my judgment the only possible move that is left is for someone to sit down and to write out point by point the plans and procedure for a campaign providing the greatest possible amount of detail and then for someone to meet with the Amalgamated officers and take the matter up point by point with them, making such changes as may seem to be necessary in order to secure fairly immediate action. To expect them to take any initiative in formulating plans in getting the work under way is just simply expecting too much.

I have pointed out to both Leonard and Miller that in my judgment Lewis is in a position where he must either work with the Amalgamated in getting the industry organized, or in the event of that being impossible, he must

> launch out and give his aid in organizing the industry independently, in which case there is no doubt whatever that they would simply be swept aside by the momentum of such a campaign.

That is what happened to the Amalgamated Association.

The Association leaders accepted the CIO offer of $500,000 and agreed to the formation of a Steel Workers' Organizing Committee to be appointed by Lewis.* He named Philip Murray chairman, and David J. McDonald secretary-treasurer, as well as Patrick T. Fagin and Van A. Bittner, all from the United Mine Workers; Joseph K. Gaither and Thomas G. Gillis, vice-presidents of the Amalgamated; Julius Hochman, a vice-president of the ILGWU and a Brookwood graduate; Leo Kryzyki, a vice-president of the Amalgamated Clothing Workers, former secretary of the Socialist Party and an old acquaintance of Golden's; and John Brophy, who suggested Golden to Murray as a possible addition. "So I called Clint," Brophy recalled many years later. "I'd talked to Clint a day or two before, not with this thing in mind, but we'd had lunch together and we'd talked over some things, and we'd known each other over the years." On June 12, 1936, John L. Lewis sent the following letter to Clinton S. Golden, "I am enclosing a copy of the statement issued to the press today relating to the Steel Workers Organizing Committee, of which you have been made Regional Director for the Pittsburgh area. I suggest you work in cooperation with Chairman Murray and the Committee."

Golden assumed his new duties on June 15, 1936.

* The AFL responded to the formation of SWOC by suspending the CIO unions on charges of dual unionism. The final break came in late 1937 and the Committee became the Congress of Industrial Organizations the following year.

SWOC

THERE WAS NOT much time for reflection that summer. The tasks confronting the Steel Workers' Organizing Committee, at times, must have seemed insurmountable. The giant steel companies had quelled the worker rebellions of 1934 and 1935. Hundreds of thousands of steelworkers were enrolled in employee representation plans, the latest euphemism for company unions. Many workers were discouraged by the abortive attempts made at organization by the Amalgamated Association as well as the eruptions of leftwing fanaticism and factionalism. Still, the news that the CIO was organizing came as a welcoming breeze down sweltering steel-town streets all across industrial America.

There is an old union adage, "the best organizer for the union is a bad boss." The steel industry also proved to be the union's best herald. When John L. Lewis announced the CIO steel drive on June 12, 1936, he got a fair amount of newspaper and radio coverage but the drive was not exactly front-page news in the company-dominated towns where steel was produced. Neither the scope of the drive nor the case for unionization got the play it deserved in the news accounts of Lewisian flamboyancy. As Lewis, Murray and their staffs worried over the response of the steelworkers to the CIO call, the American Iron and Steel Institute prepared a mass advertising campaign.

On June 24th, the Institute placed full-page advertisements in 375 daily newspapers at a cost of close to a half-million dollars. In the advertisement, the employers charged the CIO with coercion and intimidation, damned it with seeking the closed shop, and declared that workers would be forced to pay tribute for the right to work. The industry claimed that it was bargaining collectively through the employee representation system and boasted that it paid the highest wages in the country. With righteous indignation, John L. Lewis took to the airwaves on July 6 to challenge the industry's claims. In stentorian tones, over a national network, Lewis cited hard facts: Hourly wages in March 1936, said Lewis, were 65.6 cents in steel; 79.3 in bituminous coal, 83.2 in anthracite, and 79.8 in building construction. Common labor in steel, he added, received 47.9 cents an hour. In weekly wages, the steel industry occupied twentieth place in a list of twenty-one industries. Lewis accepted the Steel Institute's advertisement as "a declaration of war"; "a momentous battle for democracy impends in America," he concluded.

The steel industry's flood of advertising created a wave of attention for the CIO's steel-organizing campaign far larger than its strength warranted at the time. As Edward Levinson reported in his account of the birth of the CIO, *Labor on the March*, "The campaign was placed on front pages and on the minds and tongues of all steelworkers; and the union organizers were satisfied." As well they might be, for the industry's attack was backfiring, working to CIO's advantage. The crux of industry's strategy was the company union; those employee representation plans that, in the words of Arthur H. Young, vice-president in charge of labor relations for U.S. Steel, provided the means for developing "sound and harmonious relationships between men and management [comparable to the] sound and harmonious relationship between man and wife." One can imagine the ribald comments this pronouncement raised in the mills among unregenerate steelworkers. Nonetheless, the companies had hold of a good thing in the employee representation plans, or so they believed. For one thing, as the courts interpreted the new labor law, if "independent," they were legal; management felt sure these plans would forestall "this outside union stuff," as one steel operator phrased it.

By 1936, steel managements realized something more. As a steel executive put it, "don't make the mistake of thinking that that's their only value to us now. We've gotten a real education out of our experience. We hadn't realized, as we grew bigger, how far away we had drifted from personal contact with the men in the plant. We . . . knew nothing of the men's feelings and grievances." The lesson was implemented nigh overnight. Within a year, the number of company unions in steel had increased from seven to ninety-three. The percentage of all steelworkers affected by employee representation plans rose from about 20 to 90 percent. Steel employers had discovered that such plans were superior to the paternalistic "drop in and tell us about it" nod from foreman and the use of stool pigeons, finks and the like, although the use of company spies would not disappear until well after the victory of the CIO in organizing the mass-production industries. As R. R. Brooks concluded in *As Steel Goes*, "There can be little question that this discovery was a gain not only to the management, but to the employees of those companies which did a thorough job of making the plans work." It was an education for both.

But at the time few realized the significance of the employee representative plans to the future of unionization and to the future of collective bargaining in the industry. Golden, however, and a handful of rebels within U.S. Steel's employee groups, including John Mullen and George Patterson, did. Mullen was among the first organizers, or field representatives, hired by Golden. His first assignment, working with Harold

Ruttenberg, later SWOC research director, and Clarence Irwin, was to seek out key people among the employee representation groups with SWOC or union sympathies. In Chicago, Van Bittner sent out like feelers. Within a matter of months, SWOC had an effective "caucus" within the employee representative groups with Elmer Maloy and John Kane at the Carnegie-Illinois Duquesne works, Bill Garrity from Braddock, Patterson at the South Chicago works, and Paul Fasser at the Farrel plant of Carnegie's sheet and tin division. The idea was to keep the employee representatives "biting at the heels of management." In *As Steel Goes*, R. R. Brooks summed up the consequence of this remarkable strategy: "First, the aggressiveness of employee representatives and the scope of their demands rapidly increased. Second, a split emerged between those representatives who became identified with the S. W. O. C. and those who remained loyal to management but who were willing to take every possible advantage for themselves or their constituencies of the company's defensive position. Third, Carnegie-Illinois was forced to make one concession after another with the result that the E. R. P. came more and more to approximate truly independent industrial unionism. Fourth, the S. W. O. C. was in the enviable strategic position of being able to point to every company concession as evidence of the power of the S. W. O. C. while describing every refusal as evidence of the weakness of the E. R. P. Fifth, the transference of loyalties from management to the union remained in part concealed until the climax of the campaign."

After SWOC's first great victory in steel, Cornelia Bryce Pinchot, on March 22, 1937, wrote to Golden: "Your strategy for winning over of the company Unions and the intensive campaign you put over was a magnificent achievement. Mr. Lewis and I were talking it over last night." But in the early days of the CIO drive, despite Golden's sure grasp of the situation and his command over the staff in the field, nothing was certain, not even the cautious cultivation of the more militant members of the employee representative groups. SWOC was not yet a union and, as a consequence, had to tread warily in a minefield laid with charges of "dual-unionism," "communist-controlled," or "outsiders." Still a member of the Machinists, Golden was brought up on charges of working for a "dual union." His rebuttal of these in early 1937 reflects a CIO still reluctant to sever ties with the AFL. "Since my appointment," he wrote in his defense, "I have repeatedly advised individuals and groups of machinists who appealed to the Steel Workers Organizing Committee for assistance in organizing into the Amalgamated Association that our organizing activities are confined to workers included in the jurisdiction of the Amalgamated Association and that machinists in other industries could not be accepted as members of the Amalgamated Association." Golden also assured the Machinist trial committee that SWOC staff were instructed "to assist workers in any industry other than steel to organize into the existing Unions having jurisdiction over such workers." He was, however, expelled from his old union.

The Communists, having once again changed their party line, were eager to push any and all workers into the CIO. When workers from all kinds of industries were seeking out the highly visible and dynamic CIO, such eagerness was something of an embarrassment to the CIO leadership. In part, it was a problem of limited resources as well as an unwillingness to offend other unions. As Golden wrote to Garfield Lewis, SWOC man in charge of eastern Pennsylvania at the time about a staff man close to the Communists, "I have been obliged to warn him that we do not want to disorganize any existing Federal or other labor unions or to expend any time to get these people to change their affiliations from the A. F. of L. to us . . . I have tried to make clear to him that we simply cannot expend our time in organizing every little mill and shop employing a handful of people when we still have the larger mills only in the process of organization." Writing to Jack Lever, who had been working as a volunteer organizing the Trenton plant of John A. Roebling and Sons, Golden characterized this same organizer, a hard-coal miner, as "well meaning" but "the type that Toohey and other communists think they could use." He added, "We are not interested in starting any fight with the communists, neither do we propose to have them running our affairs either out in the open or from behind the scenes."

Communists, however, were a minor irritant compared to the coercion exerted by the steel companies over their employees. "So strong were the forces of the steel corporation," Golden declared at a SWOC labor Chautauqua held in Portsmouth, Ohio, "that the very thought of a union not controlled by a company was treason." The companies, paradoxically, furthered the unionization of steel by their attempts to be "good employers." Encouraged behind the scenes by SWOC, the Carnegie-Illinois employee representative groups formulated a program that called for a five-dollar-a-day minimum wage and a forty-hour week. In July 1936, the industry announced that it would pay time-and-a-half for overtime *after* forty-eight hours a week. Phil Murray, speaking for SWOC, immediately denounced the move as a "trick to impose the forty-eight hour week on the industry," an increase over the forty-four-hour week that had prevailed under the NRA. An anti-SWOC employee representative remarked, "One hundred organizers for John L. Lewis could not have done as much good for an outside cause as this did." The company encouraged its "unions" to adopt anti-SWOC resolutions, a move that not only further publicized the CIO but enabled its partisans within the employee groups to make speeches discussing the relative merits of the ERP and "real" industrial unionism.

In November, after the electoral triumph of Franklin D. Roosevelt, when to many it appeared that the nation had voiced approval of the CIO, U.S. Steel announced an "average 10 percent" wage increase to be incorporated in a one-year contract with its employee representatives. Ordinarily, such an offer would have been a stunning blow to trade unionist hopes. But the company tied its offer to a cost-of-living formula designed to protect itself and its workers from wide swings in the price level over the term of the agreement. It was a new notion and SWOC, with considerable aplomb, convinced most steelworkers that "the sliding wage which United States Steel seeks to force on its workers would prevent workers from *ever* receiving better wages." In a way the claim was outrageous, but it succeeded in planting doubts, disrupting acceptance by the employee representation groups.

The ERP rebels met daily at SWOC headquarters, conferring with Murray, Golden and others on strategy. U.S. Steel decided to foster a central joint conference of all its employee representation groups. Flushed with their new-found generosity, company officials believed that ERP "conservatives," armed with the wage-contract offer, would carry the day and win all posts. But some clever political maneuvering by the rebels, especially Elmer Maloy and Paul Fasser, secured Maloy the chairmanship of the new group. While the "conservatives" made hasty plans to oust Maloy, he and George Patterson, at SWOC expense, hied themselves off to Washington in a blaze of publicity. They were going "to confer" with the head of the CIO, John L. Lewis. They did so, but in passing dropped in to see Secretary of Labor Perkins and secured her opinion that the employee-representation groups had no legal right to sign contracts. ERP was, to say the least, in a state of near-complete disarray. SWOC filed charged claiming that Carnegie-Illinois maintained a company union. The wage increases were granted to one and all whether or not a contract had been signed, making the fast dwindling band of company loyalists look doubly foolish.

To stimulate membership, SWOC suspended dues payments and application fees. As Golden wrote Jack Lever in the fall of 1936, "the demand for applications is greater than we can fill." Philip Murray announced that 82,315 steelworkers had signed membership cards through SWOC. The employee representatives from forty-two plants, most from Carnegie-Illinois, joined SWOC, re-forming into a SWOC unit, the CIO Representatives Council, the joint conference initiated by the employers. Though the tide was running towards SWOC, there were scary shoals and dangerous breakers to be skirted. When Golden put Jack Lever on staff on November 16, 1936 "at $8.00 per day plus expenses," he cautioned his old friend about employing any new people. Dues suspension had created a financial crisis. "We are discontinuing the services of several people on our staff," Golden informed Lever. "We are able to expand our activities only to a point where the total expenditures are not in excess of those now being made." Lever, who was assigned responsibility for a Pennsylvania district covering Lancaster, Coatsville, Pottstown, Philadelphia, Chester and Trenton, was urged "to develop committees to assist you and a few part time people" in organizing.

Something of the mood of those months comes through in a letter Golden sent to J. H. Bowman, vice-president of the American Steel Band Company in Pittsburgh. It is, obviously, a bit of propaganda as well as an attempt to educate employees—and employers—in the new ways of collective bargaining:

> A few weeks ago your employees went out on strike. They were not members of any Union at the time, nor had they been asked to join a Union.
>
> They came to this office seeking advice. They told us

how Mr. Spahr, your so-called efficiency expert, was paying them wages below even the U.S. Steel Corporation base rate, which, God knows, is low enough. How Mr. Spahr kept speeding them up and working them over time, Saturdays and Sundays for straight time. So they came out on strike in protest against Mr. Spahr's efficiency system.

We advised your employees who came to us to organize themselves into a Union. We expressed the opinion that either you or your company were affiliated with some employers organization such as the National Association of Manufacturers or the Chamber of Commerce and that you probably thought it benefited you in some way to be affiliated with such organizations. But we knew, and so advised your employees, that inasmuch as your business operated as the American Steel Band Company, you had probably organized a group of people, each of whom had some money, into a business corporation so that they could unite their money to do collectively, what none of your stockholders could do individually, or alone. Then we showed them how organized money, represented by you, placed your employees at a disadvantage when they undertook to bargain with you individually and without a Union. I am sure you realize, Mr. Bowman, that this is what is called "inequality of bargaining power," and some people say this is, in part, the cause of depressions and panics.

We did not take any money from employees, Mr. Bowman. The fact of the matter is that we found out how little you were paying them for their labor, we knew they could not afford to pay an application fee of only $1.00.

So we suggested they just sign an application for membership in the union, select a set of officers and a committee from among themselves, and we would try to help them settle the strike by getting some wage and other concessions from your company.

You know what happened after that. You had to raise their wages, agree to pay them time and one-half for overtime and agree to deal with the committee they had selected. We know you agreed to all this because we saw the letter you wrote to the government representative who used his good offices to bring a settlement.

Well your employees were kind of tickled because through organized action—sticking together you know—they got a wage increase and some other things they could never get from you before. So a majority of them paid a dollar for a month's dues into the Union. Now they have a charter for a Local Lodge—a Union—from the Amalgamated Association of Iron, Steel and Tin Workers. They have a set of officers for their Union which they themselves selected. And they are sort of proud of their Union, Mr. Bowman, like you are about your membership in some trade association, employers union, or perhaps the Chamber of Commerce.

Now when they agreed to return to work, and I am sure you remember they all stayed away from work for a couple of weeks until you settled with them, they did not insist on a closed shop. The fact of the matter is, Mr. Bowman, they did not want to embarrass you because they knew if you were obliged to sign a closed shop agreement, the other anti-Union employers in the steel and metal industry would be awfully mad at you, and they would probably call you a traitor and a turncoat. So they were satisfied, temporarily at least, that you agree to the principle of Unionism—collective bargaining, you know—dealing with your employees through a committee. The law says that this is what the employees can do whenever they want to.

Well you know after you agreed to raise wages, pay time and one-half for overtime and deal with a committee of your employees—and we don't want to kid you, Mr. Bowman, they all belong to the Union—your employees returned to work. They felt better after they got back to work because they felt more powerful you know.

Things went along pretty well, but that doggone efficiency expert of yours, Mr. Spahr, is kicking over the traces, just like an ordinary mule. It looks like he doesn't know what teamwork means. Then you write a letter to all your employees telling them your company "will never sign an agreement with the Union" and a lot of other things. Now, Mr. Bowman, "never" is a long, long time. And times really do change.

You know, Tom Girdler, President of Republic Steel Company, who gets $140,000 salary a year, once said he would hoe potatoes before he would sign an agreement with President John L. Lewis of the United Mine Workers. But he signed one just the same. So did Mr. Grace of Bethlehem Steel and the executives of a lot of other steel companies who don't like Unions but who do need coal for their steel mills. We'd advise against using the word "never" these days, Mr. Bowman, when so many workers are joining Unions.

Now a word about your efficiency expert, Mr. Spahr. Can't you get him to direct his energies into some really constructive channel, Mr. Bowman? We're afraid he is going to cause a lot of trouble and probably reduce your profits if he doesn't quit messing around with the Union. These "efficiency" and "personnel" experts as a rule are a terribly ignorant and a misguided lot of people. They don't seem to ever learn much about human nature, Mr. Bowman. They are pretty well described in the little ditty about the lightning bugs:

"Oh, the firefly is brilliant
 But he hasn't any mind;
He wanders thro creation
 With his headlight on behind."

Don't take our word for it when it comes to these "experts." Ask Mr. P. W. Litchfield, the President of the Goodyear Tire and Rubber Company, over in Akron, Ohio, what kind of a mess they got him into. Or Myron Taylor of the U.S. Steel Corporation about a fellow by the name of Arthur Young that his company hired for $75,000 a year, according to the newspapers, as a "labor relations expert." You no doubt recall that the late Judge E. H. Gary, Chairman of the Board of U.S. Steel, publicly stated that the Corporation would "never" deal with a Union.

This fellow Young came along and sold the idea of an "employee representation plan" or "company union," as the workers call the plan, to Judge Gary's successors in the Steel Corporation. Young guaranteed his company union plan to be the best possible insurance against the steel workers joining a real Union. But you see, Mr. Bowman, the Steel Corporation really bought a "pig in a poke," as they say down South, because the "employee representatives" under Young's company union plan are all joining a real industrial Union, the Amalgamated Association of Iron, Steel and Tin Workers, since we started this organizing drive.

We advise you to keep an eye on these so-called "experts," Mr. Bowman. It might be a good idea for you to tell your Mr. Spahr to quit advising your employees not to pay their Union dues and a lot of other things that will eventually get both you and him into trouble with your Union employees.

We are sorry that this has become such a long letter, Mr. Bowman, but we had a lot of things to tell you. One of these days, when we finish organizing the steel companies, we will be around to ask you to sign a real Union contract with a lot stiffer provisions in it than the temporary one you are operating under now. In the meantime, sort of keep your eye on your efficiency expert, Mr. Spahr.

If you ever get in the neighborhood of the Grant Building, drop in and pay us a visit. We have a nice respectable office on the thirty-sixth floor. Mr. Ernest T. Weir of the National Steel Corporation who calls himself "an economic royalist" and Attorney Earl Reed, the Chairman of the Liberty League's Kangaroo Court that passes on all New Deal legislation affecting labor, are neighbors of ours here in the Grant Building. If you should decide to pay us a visit, you need not be embarrassed because no one would think you are coming to our office. They would just naturally think you were going to see either Mr. Weir or Attorney Reed.

Late in the afternoon of March 1, 1937, a SWOC organizer called Philip Murray and said he had been hearing some pretty wild rumors. "A guy came in and said he heard over the radio that U.S. Steel was meeting with the CIO," the organizer told Murray. "I said he was crazy and kicked him out of the office."

"Well, you'd better call him back," said Murray. "It's true."

What the canny Scot miner did not tell the astonished organizer was that he was as damn-near surprised as anyone else in SWOC. Lewis had been meeting privately with Myron C. Taylor, chairman of U.S. Steel's board of directors. Taylor had come to the conclusion that if the corporation, or, rather, its affiliates, were willing to sign agreements with its employee representative groups, there was no reason, especially in the light of the failure of that strategy, not to sign one with SWOC. Taylor was much more reconciled to the New Deal than his colleagues in the industry and he recognized that the 1936 election signaled public approval of the Wagner Labor Act and all that it implied for industrial relations. He benefited, too, from the advice of Tom Moses, president of a U.S. Steel subsidiary, the H. C. Frick Coal Company, who had negotiated with Lewis and enjoyed a friendly relationship with the CIO leader. The NLRB case was not going well for Carnegie-Illinois and there was a growing possibility of a strike for recognition by SWOC. Recent sit-in strikes at General Motors made it clear that the cost of open combat with the CIO came high both in terms of money and public opinion. The La Follette Committee was looking into the purchases of tear gas and threatening to examine the labor espionage practices of the giant steel corporation. As for Taylor's hard-headed associates in the corporate board room, they were aware that Lord Runciman, president of the British Board of Trade, who was arranging for the purchase of steel for Great Britain's rearmament program, had, in effect, delivered an ultimatum. No contracts unless accompanied by a guarantee of uninterrupted production.

On Monday morning, March 2, 1937, Philip Murray lead a solemn parade of five men—himself, Golden, Van Bittner, David J. McDonald, SWOC secretary-treasurer, and Lee Pressman, SWOC's general counsel—to the Carnegie building in downtown Pittsburgh. "The doorman there," Pressman later recalled, "damn near dropped dead when he saw us." The five were ushered into the Carnegie-Illinois boardroom with proper solemnity. Benjamin F. Fairless, son of a coal miner and president of Carnegie-Illinois, rose from the head of a great long table to greet them. "There's a conversation between Murray and Fairless about Pittsburgh stogies that Ben Fairless smokes," Pressman's account of that historic meeting continues, "and a few more commonplaces were exchanged. Then Murray says, 'I guess we're ready to do some business.' Fairless says, 'Yes, I guess we are.' "

Lewis and Taylor had already spelled out the terms of a proposed agreement—recognition of SWOC, a five-to-ten-cent-an-hour wage increase, a five-dollar-a-day minimum, an eight-hour day and a forty-hour week, and time-and-a-half for overtime. More details were to be worked out through negotiations. As Murray explained to reporters, "We are going to select a committee of about seven or eight, probably the chairman of the SWOC will preside, and we expect to have a representative of the mill workers from each of the plants to meet with the executives of the SWOC sometime before the end of the week. This committee will attempt to work out with the executives of the Carnegie-Illinois Steel Corporation a suitable application of rates on a basis of equity." Murray expressed SWOC's "appreciation and gratitude" at the outcome of the conference with Carnegie-Illinois. "It paves the way for a maintenance of peace in the industry and is in accord with the announced policy of the CIO and SWOC to organize the employees of the steel industry for collective bargaining purposes without resorting to strike, violence or industrial disturbances."

In a written statement, Murray remarked that the SWOC-Carnegie steel conferences, which marked "an epoch in the history of industrial relations," were "mystifying to the casual observer." But to the steelworkers, he added, "they represent a realization by steel management that this is 1937 and not 1919 nor 1892." The outcome, he predicted, "will be constructive leadership and real industrial progress. We expect it will bring about complete unionization of the entire steel industry."

A reporter remarked to Golden, "You were a long time."

"No," he replied, "it takes time to break down the position of fifty years. Yes, fifty years, a half century, Steel's traditional opposition to unions. The Homestead riots. Deaths, battles, bloodshed—No, we were not long."

In a letter thanking Mrs. Pinchot for her congratulations on SWOC's success, Golden wrote, "The fact that since the inception of our organizing campaign we made use of new methods of organization served to completely upset the plans of the industrialists. We were able to put the steel magnates on the defensive, I think, for the first time and keep them there."

Mrs. Pinchot expressed her concern over a possible counter-drive on the part of industry. "It's clear," she wrote Golden, "that the Big Business strategy now is to make the country believe that the high cost of living is due to the wage increases which the Unions are winning. We are going to hear more of this new phrase—the Monopoly of Labor—used by Marriner Eccles, Chairman of the Reserve Board, before we are much older, I fear."

Mrs. Pinchot touched upon one of Golden's lifelong concerns, and his response was a declaration of his priorities at the time:

> It is undoubtedly true that the industry will pass on the present wage increases to consumers in the form of increased prices, and they will thereby pyramid their profits. This will present some very real problems, especially so as organization is vigorously pushed in other fields. It seems to me however that the problem of price control can be dealt with much more effectively if the workers are organized than is possible when they are unorganized and completely at the mercy of big business.
>
> I think forces have been set in motion that are going to profoundly influence the future economic life of our

country. Right now we have a gigantic task of administering the affairs of the Union in such a way as to put it on a permanent and constructive basis.

Golden was soon immersed in that task, made infinitely more complicated by the sudden growth of the union. The Carnegie-Illinois agreement "broke the dam," as SWOC publicity director, Vince Sweeney, later recalled, "and the action in the ensuing weeks was breathtaking. Smaller firms waged a hot race to sign." Within four feeks, forty-one companies negotiated contracts. Thirty-five thousand steel workers signed union cards in the ten days following March 2. The week of May 3 to May 8 broke all records, and Secretary-Treasurer David J. McDonald reported, with evident pleasure, that 37,048 more had joined the union. Murray announced that SWOC had 325,000 members, 600 new lodges and contracts with ninety companies, including all the subsidiaries of U.S. Steel and such independents as Wheeling Steel, Timken Roller Bearing, Caterpillar Tractor, and McKeesport Tin-Plate. Jones & Laughlin caved in after a thirty-six hour strike and agreed to an NLRB election, and on May 20, J. & L employees voted for the union, 13,028 to 7,207. The company signed a contract establishing SWOC as the exclusive bargaining agent for its workers.

While SWOC had some four hundred organizers in the field, it had little in the way of backup, the support structure necessary to organize a near-inchoate mass into a disciplined, effective trade union. "We have multiplied our obligations and responsibilities without at the same time having either the resources of money or trained men to meet these responsibilities," Golden wrote an old friend and associate of Brookwood days, Katherine Pollack Ellickson, now acting as research director for the CIO. "Right now," he added, "the future permanance of the Union is in grave danger because we have grown and expanded and assumed responsibilities clear out of proportion to our ability to properly direct and guide this huge army of the rawest kind of Union recruits."

No one, really, had much of an idea as to what kind of organization SWOC should be building. Industrial unionism was much more a slogan than, say, a table of organization. John L. Lewis governed the CIO with a firm hand, and of all the unions grouped within that paternal grip SWOC was held most closely. Lewis, to put it mildly, tended to view SWOC as an extension of his United Mine Workers. Even so, SWOC was growing so rapidly in a vastly more complicated industry that it could not, even if Lewis had demanded it, have remained a carbon-copy of the mine union. But exactly what shape it would take was scarcely known as steel organizers turned up at plant gates and steelworkers flocked to the raised banners of the CIO.

"When we started this organizing drive almost a year ago," Golden wrote Kitty Ellickson on June 3, 1937,

> I was under the impression we were going to organize the basic iron, steel, and tin producing industry, which includes: a) blast furnaces, bessemer converters and open hearth furnaces; b) wrought iron and malleable iron producing firms; and c) rolling mill producers and steel workers.
>
> Now then, a necessarily superficial (because of lack of time) analysis of the contracts which have been signed to date indicates that we have such contracts in not only the above mentioned industry but in some sixteen additional indirectly allied industries. By this I mean sixteen different competitive trade groups engaged in some form of metal working, manufacturing or fabricating.
>
> The alarming feature about all this—to me at least—is the fact that every time we enter one of these competi-

tive trade groups by organizing a single firm and putting that firm under contract, there is an implied assumption of responsibility on our part to organize and bring under a similar contract every other competing firm within that group. If we fail to do this, one of two things will eventually happen—either the firm we have organized and put under contract will have to go out of business because of being out of line in labor costs with his competitors; or the Local Union directly involved will evaporate because it cannot function except in a very limited way as an agency for the advancement of the interest of its members . . .

Only today Phil Murray has handed me correspondence from John Brophy relative to the SWOC absorbing an independent organization known as the National Die Casting Workers League. If we do, we have added one more to our variety of industries.

Well what to do about it all? We talked originally about a "Steel Workers Industrial Union." As I see the situation at present, we are away beyond that. If so, then what? It seems to me that whether we like it or not, we are headed in the direction of what must eventually be a *metal* workers industrial union. If this is true, must we not think and plan about a *departmentalized* industrial union? If so, someone ought to be given the job of blocking out the industries that are to be component parts thereof. The competitive and natural trade groups ought to be outlined, and we ought to have some sort of an outline of just where we propose to go and how we are to get there.

I am sure something of a similar character exists in other basic industries particularly. It leads me to believe that if we are to avoid becoming another hodge podge of all kinds of Unions a la A. F. L., someone ought to get hold of a copy of the old I. W. W. "Wheel of Fortune," as they called it, which was a graphic chart demonstrating their conception of industrial unions applied to our industrial set-up. This then ought to be reworked or revised in the light of present day developments in the industrial scene. If something of this sort could be done, I feel it would be enormously valuable to all of us . . .

As I see the situation ahead of us, we have got to adopt a policy of doing all we can to force these competitive trade groups to negotiate for the contracts next year on a trade group—not an individual firm—basis.* In other words, we, through organization of the workers, have got to provide the stimulus that the NRA tried to provide—to force the *employers to organize* for collective bargaining *with the union.* If this is so, is it not one more important reason why we should be making plans for a *departmentalized* Industrial Union of Metal Workers?

* Elsewhere in his letter Golden listed twenty-nine such trade groups:

1. metal toy mfg.
2. standard and narrow guage locomotives
3. grey iron foundry
4. steel castings
5. diesel engine
6. steam turbines
7. tin can fabricating
8. bed springs
9. building hardware
10. metal furniture
11. steel chain
12. air conditioning
13. cutlery
14. railway springs
15. stoves and ranges
16. steam fittings
17. cast iron pipe
18. seamless steel pipe
19. metal signs
20. rolling mill machinery
21. pole line hardware (for electrical power lines)
22. steel R.R. car building
23. oil well machinery
24. air compressors
25. mining machinery
26. steel wire
27. power driven conveyors
28. metal stamped enamelware
29. machine tool builders

Over the years there have been many changes but SWOC has developed into a metal workers industrial union, as Golden predicted, embracing aluminum, copper and many other metal trades organized into some sixteen separate industrial groups, or "conferences," for bargaining purposes.

SWOC's first contracts were simple documents indeed when compared with the agreements negotiated today by the United Steelworkers. Certain basic issues had to be recognized and established—union recognition, some sort of machinery for the adjustment of disputes, the principles of arbitration, the forty-hour week, time-and-a-half for overtime, and so on. "There has been no attempt—because there has been no time—to undertake anything like a scientific reclassification of rates of pay," as Golden wrote to Kitty Ellickson. "But we will surely have to face this problem in our next contracts. Well how?"

It was a question very much on Golden's mind during that hectic first year. "Found a company the other day," he wrote, "who had a number of men classified as 'apprentices to common laborers' so they could pay grown men 35¢ per hour." He had urged on Murray the need for a research director for SWOC. When Murray demurred, so goes an anecdote of the day, Golden let the matter drop. Soon after, Murray came into Golden's office and said, "You know, Clint, we ought to have someone around here to study and keep track of wages, employment, production costs, prices and that kind of thing in the steel industry."

Astonished, Golden blurted, "Why, Phil, I thought you didn't want a research director."

"Oh," said the imperturbable Murray, "is that what you meant by a research director? You know, when you brought it up before, I was thinking of the time, thirty years ago, when my local union got stuck by a traveling salesman with an encyclopedia. We put it in a glass enclosed bookcase and elected a 'research director' to look after it. When you proposed a research director, I didn't see any reason for getting stuck with an encyclopedia again."

Murray, as Golden once remarked, was no great reader of books. However, he evoked loyalty and deep affection from all who knew him. As Murray Kempton perceptively put it, his special quality was "to touch the love and not the fears of men." Softspoken, with a touch of a Scottish accent serving as a reminder of his ancestry, Murray had almost uncanny ability to analyze groups of figures at a glance and had quickly accumulated a vast knowledge of steel production and manufacture. A droll humor, patience and tact made him a superb negotiator. Though his hand was gentle, it was nevertheless firm and he governed the union with a sure grip that, in time, came to match John L. Lewis's over the Mine Workers and the CIO.

R. R. Brooks, who observed the early development of SWOC and described its emergence as a great industrial union in *As Steel Goes,* remarked on Murray's "ability to work with able subordinates who are anything but 'yes men' but who share in his general views and put them into practice with initiative and imagination." The United Mine Workers supplied much of the original field staff but Golden in the Northeast, Van Bittner in the West, and William A. Mitch in the South supplemented the original complement with men of their own choosing. District directors, too, hired their own staff as the budget permitted.

Murray had brought over from the mine union his former secretary, David J. McDonald, to serve as SWOC's secretary-treasurer. Lee Pressman, who, according to Kempton, "had eyes like a squirrel's after a nut and a manner which even a friend would occasionally find too near arrogance," was assigned by John L. Lewis to SWOC to serve as its general counsel. In time, he would become Philip Murray's closest advisor; from the beginning, he served as the quasi-official representative of the CIO's pro-Communist wing. (Pressman, by his own account, joined the Communist Party in 1933 and left in 1935; but he adhered to its political line throughout his entire career with the CIO.) J. B. S. Hardman, Golden's associate from the Conference for Progressive Labor Action days, was on loan from the Amalgamated Clothing Workers to edit SWOC's newspaper. When he returned to the Amalgamated after putting out the initial issues, Vincent Sweeney, a Pittsburgh newspaper reporter, was asked by Murray to become SWOC's publicity director. He served the union well, but as a devout Catholic was often a target of ridicule among CIO leftists.

As for the rest, it was Clint Golden's task to fashion a staff suitable for a modern, giant industrial union. McDonald, of course, recruited his own staff. Howard R. Hague and Thomas Murray (no relative of Philip) were persuaded to leave good jobs with Pittsburgh's financial institutions to serve the union. Tom Murray, a gentle accountant, found himself teaching horny-handed steelworkers how to keep union books. Research and education, however, were Golden's special interests, and Murray allowed him a free hand to create these services for the emerging steel union. Averell Harriman once asked Golden, "Where do you find these young people?" Golden responded, "Averell, they are in the mills; all you do is comb them out." He did just that in staffing his region—John Mullen was a subregional director for Clairton, Phil Clowes worked the Tarentum-Kiski Valley and Johnstown in the same capacity, and Clarence Irwin held that post for Sharon-Farrell. Martin "Mike" Walsh in New England, Jack Lever in Philadelphia, and Joseph Timko in Aliquippa, however, were worker organizers out of other industries—a seafarer, machinist and miner, respectively. Elmer Cope was working on his graduate degree when he got the call to go to work for Golden, organizing in the Steubenville, Ohio-Weirton, West Virginia area.

Harold Ruttenberg, the brash young intellectual of the rank-and-file-movement, was already on SWOC's staff when Clint asked him to become the union's research director. In

1933, Ruttenberg had been an interviewer for the Brookings study of the economic effects of the NRA code on the iron and steel industry, a research job that he turned into that of advisor to the rebel rank-and-file movement of 1934–35. As an ex-newspaper reporter and an ex-amateur heavyweight boxer, though still in his early twenties, he was, as a steelworker once put it, "a useful man to have around." Under Golden's guidance, Ruttenberg churned out a mass of statistics, analyzed their significance, and turned them into useful tools in the hands of union negotiators and organizers. Later, Clint wooed genial Joseph Scanlon away from his Mansfield, Ohio, local union to work for SWOC as its first industrial engineer. Meyer Bernstein hitched in from New York City to volunteer his services to the cause of organized labor. He had graduated from Cornell but a lack of funds ended his plans for a career in law. Golden, to put it mildly, was sceptical of this spunky young man's intentions, but he did send him to Aliquippa as a "volunteer." Bernstein began by mimeographing leaflets; four days later, he was arrested for distributing them. Joe Timko gave him food money whenever he was in pocket. After a while, the union began paying his expenses and when it was discovered he was something of a photographer, Bernstein was put on staff at twenty dollars a week. Later, Golden brought him to the national office, where Bernstein worked on National Labor Relations Board cases, becoming an early specialist in that field.

Ruttenberg's "brown-covered pamphlets"—pocket-sized booklets on collective bargaining procedures, union operations, etc.—were only the first in a long line of steelworkers publications. They were the raw material for a much-needed educational process. As Frank Fernbach, who had been asked by Golden to organize labor Chautauquas, later recalled those trying times, "We were electing presidents who didn't know how to preside at meetings and never had, and secretaries who didn't know how to write, and treasurers who didn't know how to count. Those are all a bit of overstatement, but we were actually electing thousands of people for the first time in their lives to positions of responsibility in the trade-union movement at the local level." So, every weekend, Frank Fernbach, sometimes accompanied by Golden or Ruttenberg or some other officer, would meet in steel-town hotel rooms with organizing staff and local union officers and go over trade-union basics, grievance procedure and contract administration. The Chautauquas lead to the union's first summer school, a two-week training course for union officers held in 1938 at an abandoned Civilian Conservation Corps camp near Meyersdale, Pennsylvania. Phil Clowes and his wife, Flossie, were hosts to that first school and many succeeding ones. I. W. Abel, then a local union vice-president, was a student at the second summer school, held at Raccoon Creek.

Although SWOC burgeoned in numbers, it was not yet a union. The initial wave of success that had followed the Carnegie-Illinois agreement washed out in the deepening recession over the summer of 1937. Republic, Bethlehem, Inland and Youngstown Sheet & Tube Corporation, the so-called Little Steel companies, rallied around Tom M. Girdler, president of Republic Steel, to block the further unionization of the industry. Under his leadership, the Little Steel companies rejected all overtures from SWOC for collective bargaining negotiations. By late May and early June, seventy thousand were out on strike. The bitterness of that struggle is highlighted by the Memorial Day Massacre. On May 30, 1937, as white clouds billowed across the blue sky south of Chicago, Republic strikers at a rally decided to cross an open field and picket the plant. Casually, even in a holiday mood—for hadn't the mayor asserted their right to picket?—the strikers with their families strolled in twos and threes and small groups toward the plant gates. The Chicago police were lined up across the street with drawn clubs and hands on revolvers. Spokesmen for the strikers spoke with police authorities. The strikers were ordered to disperse "in the name of the law." As the line of police advanced upon the crowd, it dispersed. The police fired a volley at fleeing backs. Seven were killed; ninety wounded. Three of the injured died later. "The police," the La Follette Senate Committee reported later, "dragged seriously wounded, unconscious men along the ground with no more care than would be employed by a common drunkard."

By fall, most of the strikers were back to work—without a signed contract. SWOC was crippled, though still fighting in the courts and by organizing whenever and wherever it could. Within a few short years, the Little Steel companies, compelled by law and worker persistence, would sign agreements with SWOC. In the interim, however, SWOC's future was uncertain. With its contracts due to expire on February 1, 1938, SWOC called a "wage and policy" convention to meet in Pittsburgh on December 14, 1937. Nine hundred and twenty-four delegates from all parts of the United States and Canada gathered to ponder the fate of unionization in their industry. As the Northeastern regional director, Golden reported to the convention on the gains scored within a territory that ran east from Indiana to Masachusetts and south to Maryland and whose mills produced 65 percent of the total ingot production of the steel industry within the United States. Well over half of the members of the union worked in the Northeastern region, belonged to 464 lodges and were protected by 211 contracts signed with an equal number of employers. "The granting of Union recognition in 9 industries with long-established traditions of hostility to Union organization," Golden said, "create serious problems of readjustment both for management representatives and the newly organized wage earners. As the old traditions of fear growing out of ironclad corporation and employer dictatorship are broken down, we find a new relationship evolving based on mutual respect, confidence in each other, and the beginning of a genuinely democratic and self-governing relationship."

Golden was assigned the task of chairing the crucial wage-scale and policy committee. Some 837 resolutions were submitted by local lodges for consideration by the committee and the convention. The resolutions varied in content, but Clint and Harold Ruttenberg broke them down into four major areas—wages, hours, other contract terms, and authorization empowering SWOC officers to negotiate new wage contracts. The majority of wage resolutions favored six dollars a day as the goal of up-coming negotiations, and the abolition of tonnage and piecework rates. Significantly, 15 resolutions called for the establishment of a guaranteed annual wage. Most called for a minimum guarantee of so many days' work a year. The staggered work week was widely condemned and a work week of five consecutive days was favored as an objective. Shorter hours—six a day and thirty a week—were proposed, and characterized by Golden as "the ultimate goal of all organized labor." There was widespread dissatisfaction with seniority provisions in existing contracts. Many resolutions pressed for the closed shop, the check-off of dues, or sole bargaining rights. "SWOC officers," Golden reported, "were conscious of the immense volume of false propaganda continually disseminated by anti-union forces. . . . In view of the long-established traditions of hostility to unionism in any effective form existing in the industry, it was considered both unwise and provocative of unnecessary difficulty to make such demands. . . . Your committee feels that a more cooperative attitude on the part of the employers will evolve, as confidence grows out of the collective bargaining relationships with the Union, and that the time will come when employers, fully recognizing the responsibility and discipline of the Union, will agree to a closer relationship that will enable the Union to function more efficiently in its sphere of operations."

Though Golden in his committee report presented for the consideration of the delegates the substance of the many resolutions submitted, he—and the committee—plumped for the adoption of one straightforward declaration: "We authorize and instruct the Steel Workers Organizing Committee to continue their services as representatives of our union, and as our collective bargaining agents, and that when meeting in conference with the representatives of our employers, that they will have full power to secure the best joint wage agreement possible."

The reasons for this were amply detailed in Golden's report. There were a quarter of a million steel and metal fabricating workers unemployed. Eighty-five thousand more steel workers faced unemployment because of technological displacement. "We do not know," Golden concluded, "whether the basic steel industry will still be in a depressed state two months hence, or whether it will be recovering from the current depression. We hope recovery will be the case. It, therefore, is necessary that the representatives of the SWOC in forthcoming contract negotiations have a free hand to meet any changed economic conditions that may arise in the meantime."

Workers' Tribune

GOLDEN had signed on with SWOC to oversee the organization of steelworkers in the Northeastern region, but increasingly he was called upon by Philip Murray to assume administrative responsibility for the national organization. This, of course, was a tribute to his talent and acknowledgment of his experience, but it was also true that he was the man on the spot. His region was headquartered in Pittsburgh. Van Bittner, who had the ability and experience to second Murray though not quite in the way Golden did, was based in Chicago. David McDonald, who had the necessary ambition and was personally close to Murray, as yet lacked the experience to cope with the administrative complexities of a fast-growing giant union nor could he command the loyalty of the men in the field as did both Golden and Van Bittner. Beyond that, Golden was the first to recognize that the National Labor Relations Act of 1935 had created something new in the history of American labor. The Lewises and Murrays were quick to seize the advantages of organization offered under that Act, but Golden saw changes in the making in labor-management relations, the potential for an industrial democracy based on union recognition by America's giant corporations and grasped the need for productivity to underwrite that potential.

Circumstances, as the song put it, would have it so. But

they were not opportune when Golden came before the 1940 SWOC convention to make his Wage and Policy Committee report. Continuing unemployment concentrated unionist minds on jobs, seniority, the need for union recognition. The heady confidence generated by the recognition granted by U.S. Steel and won through such strike victories as at Jones & Laughlin had been undercut by the losses of the Little Steel strike, the recession of 1937–1938 and troubles within the labor movement. CIO membership, for example, which had peaked at slightly over 4 million in 1938 was down to 3.6 million two years later. SWOC won most of its unfair-labor-practice cases before the NLRB and in the courts, but these legal victories were no guarantee of unionization. Workers in the mill had to be won over, signed up, organized. Representation elections had to be secured and won. All this took money and manpower, resources limited by the crisis within the CIO.

With the signing of the Hitler-Stalin pact of August, 1939, the Communists who had influence among CIO unions, launched bitter attacks on President Franklin D. Roosevelt, on the nation's foreign policy and on those trade-union leaders who, as Golden and Murray did, favored aid to the beleaguered anti-Axis nations. A fortnight before the 1940 presidential election, CIO president John L. Lewis over a nationwide radio hookup bitterly attacked President Roosevelt and endorsed Republican candidate Wendell Willkie. (Lewis had been angered by Roosevelt's quipping "A plague on both your houses" in 1937, when he felt the President ought to have thrown his support behind labor.) If Roosevelt were elected, Lewis thundered, "it will mean that the members of the Congress of Industrial Organizations have rejected my advice and recommendation. I will accept the result as being the equivalent of a vote of no confidence and I will retire as president of the Congress of Industrial Organizations in November."

A "draft Lewis" movement failed at the CIO convention and "retire" Lewis did, subsequently taking his mine union out of the CIO. Philip Murray was elected CIO president, which meant he could not longer devote full time to SWOC when that organization needed him the most. Mineworkers on loan to SWOC were recalled by Lewis. Forced to choose between returning to the UMW or staying on with SWOC many chose the latter course, which meant that the financially strained steel union had to pick up the tab for their salaries and expenses. SWOC also felt obligated to repay a UMW loan of $601,000 sooner than it might have done otherwise. Murray was expelled from the mineworkers' union and the emotional strain of his break with Lewis contributed to a heart attack, which laid him up over the summer and early fall of 1941.

Golden, who had been assuming additional administrative tasks to ease Murray's double-burden as head of SWOC and the CIO, was designated acting chairman of SWOC by Murray. Drew Pearson and Robert S. Allen, speculating in their "Washington Merry-Go-Round" column of September 6, 1941, reported shaggy-browed Lewis as "pulling wires behind the scenes to make one of his men the new SWOC president." Leading aspirants for the job, Pearson and Allen wrote, were Golden, McDonald and Van Bittner. "Messrs. Golden and McDonald," they added, "are strong anti-leftists and curbed radical elements with an iron hand in the SWOC. They also oppose Mr. Lewis' isolationism and support Mr. Roosevelt's foreign policies." Lewis, the columnists claimed, was supporting Van Bittner while "insiders are betting [on] . . . Mr. Golden, who is close to [Murray] and one of his ablest leaders in the CIO."

Such speculation was distasteful to Golden, who did not like to play politics within the labor movement. I. W. Abel recalls asking Golden what his "obligations" were at the time

Golden approached him about taking on a district directorship. "Clint hit the roof," Abel said, "and gave me a ten minute lecture on trade unionism." The Pearson-Allen speculations could not help but exacerbate the already touchy relations that existed between Golden and McDonald, Pressman and others within the union. John Mayo, whom Abel replaced as district director when Mayo returned to the Mine Workers, once advised Abel, "When you're in Pittsburgh make a point of seeing Dave when you are there on business with Clint, and vice-versa." When SWOC first retrenched, following the Little Steel strike loss, organizers on loan from the Mine Workers continued to get their UMW paychecks while others suffered pay cuts, a built-in discrimination that irritated some Steelworker staff members. Later, it was said that McDonald showed favoritism in the granting of allowances for expenses, a charge he denied in a acerbic memo to Golden. "My duties are not those of chief bookkeeper," he added, "as reportedly has been stated by some staff employees."

Such strains were minor and easily papered over when compared to the difficulties of organizing the Little Steel companies. The Bethlehem drive, in particular, was not going at all well, much to Golden's regret, for he had placed his old friend Jack Lever in charge. Lever, by all accounts, was a good organizer but not a good organization man. As an old-time Machinist, he had a somewhat different conception of unionization than that of the Mine Workers assigned to organize steel, who, as Elmer Maloy put it (describing Bittner), "believed that if you had to drive them in, drive them in and talk afterwards." Lever believed in what he called "pentrative organization instead of ballyhoo." As Lever explained, "we really taught them how to organize themselves, which is another way of doing it, you see, from the usual organizing effort, where somebody comes in from the outside and somehow manages to organize those people. But that's not building a real union. A real union has to be built from the bottom up by the people themselves, because they will need to gain the experience to operate the union on their own behalf." Lever pointed to a real difference between his approach and that of the Mine Workers. "An organizer from the anthracite was sent in [to Bethlehem] and he proceeded to ballyhoo the organization of the Steelworkers without backing from inside the plant at all. So he had himself a uniform made in the form of a union-all with the initials SWOC across his chest, and he organized a few cronies and they held a parade with signs and a blaring band and everything, marching through Third Street in Bethlehem. That was his way of organizing the Steelworkers and, of course, he got nowhere. The more of that kind of tactics they followed, the more they organized the workers against SWOC . . . And Clint Golden just dissolved that setup immediately." Lever, by contrast, built an "underground organization under Bethlehem's nose."

Lever, however, was not producing results fast enough to suit SWOC. Moreover, he could not refrain from getting into disputes with the SWOC leadership, in particular with Dave McDonald and his people on the staff, and he did not hesitate to air his differences before the union rank-and-file. This violated what CIO people considered CIO discipline. As Golden put it in a letter to Lever, "It is not expected that the staff member will . . . promote and foster destruction of confidence and lack of respect in and for the executive officers by airing his differences before the membership."* Lever, as

* The full text of the letter, dated January 29, 1941, is of interest, as it casts light on how Golden conceived of his role in SWOC:

Dear Jack:

Just so there will be but a minimum possibility of misunderstanding between us in our future association in the Steel Workers Organizing Committee, may I point out that:

another friend, Frank Fernbach, once described him, was "a devoted man of real competence, hard to get along with, a bachelor, and ex-World War I veteran with a bad belly, quickly irritated, but a fine man." So, there was nothing for

---

1. The executive officers of the SWOC were originally charged with the responsibility of building a union of steel workers. They accepted that responsibility and will continue to execute same until relieved by Convention or other action.

2. Among the responsibilities of the executive officers is that of engaging staff members, assigning them specific duties and seeing to it that they perform same. The execution of this particular responsibility is predicated upon the fact that they have a right to expect the staff members thus engaged to be loyal to the executive officers and follow closely the organization's policy however formulated.

3. If staff members have occasion to differ with the executive officers over methods of administration or interpretation of policy, it is expected that they will bring their differences and criticisms to the executive officers rather than to the rank and file membership. If the differences cannot be reconciled or adjusted on the basis of calm reasoning and discussion, the executive officers under the present set-up, then expect the staff member to dissociate himself from the staff of the organization. It is not expected that the staff member will then or at any other time promote and foster destruction of confidence and lack of respect in and for the executive officers by airing his differences before the membership.

This may seem to be a pretty blunt statement. Nevertheless, it is put just that way in an attempt to avoid misunderstanding. The SWOC is not as yet functioning on a wholly constitutional basis. Until it is placed on such a basis, the executive officers are prepared to discharge their full responsibilities.

Specifically, if you are to return to our staff, we expect you to be guided by the foregoing. We do not expect that in your capacity as a staff member, you will promote dissension among the members you come in contact with because of differences you may personally have, either with the executive officers or fellow staff members of the SWOC. It is also expected that you will accept such assignments as are given you and execute same to the best of your ability. If we understand each other in respect to these matters, I will appreciate hearing from you to that effect. I will then be able to give you an assignment.

it, but to resign, which Lever did. Meanwhile, SWOC had decided to concentrate on the biggest of the Little Steel companies, Bethlehem. The usual pattern of organizing, that is, making each regional director responsible for the mills in his territory, was changed. Van Bittner was brought in from Chicago to head up a special Bethlehem organizing drive and staff men were assigned to the huge mills in Lackawanna, New York, Sparrows Point, Maryland, and in Bethlehem and Johnstown, Pennsylvania. During the spring of 1941, strikes flared up at a half-dozen Bethlehem mills and an NLRB election was set for Lackawanna on May 15, 1941. Huge tents were erected off company property, and all day long until late into the night, workmen dropped their ballots into the boxes lined up for that purpose. When the count was in, they had voted union, 8,223 to 2,961. Elections followed at the other Bethlehem plants and at the other Little Steel companies, all resulting in resounding victories for the union. Negotiations followed, but the companies dragged their respective feet and, once the nation was at war, the matter was referred to the War Labor Board. SWOC's victory became the famous "Little Steel Formula," an award that served as the basis for wartime wage increases for all workers. The steelworkers won a 5½ cent-an-hour increase based on the decline in their real hourly wages since January 1, 1941. The WLB panel also awarded the union a maintenance-of-membership clause and the check-off, the deduction of union dues from wages by management was transferred to the union. As Golden wrote to his old friend Sumner Slichter at Harvard, "we can look forward to a greater measure of stability and security for our organization from now on."

Since Jack Lever was considered a "Golden man," his leaving was thought a setback for Clint by some within the union. But not by Murray, clearly, who continued to add to Golden's responsibilities, appointing him to serve as the CIO's man on the War Labor Board and as a member of the Management-

Labor Policy Committee of the War Manpower Commission. He was also asked to work on the constitution for the United Steelworkers, the union born of SWOC on May 19, 1943 in the Cleveland Auditorium. As the constitutional architect of the new union, it fell to Golden to defend the proposed constitution against charges of "dictatorship" raised in the floor debate over its adoption, and, in particular, over an amendment, subsequently defeated, proposing the election of organizers by referendum.

"If there is one subject I am a little sensitive about," Golden told the delegates, "it is these charges of dictatorship . . . hurled against the Chairman and some of his associates, including myself." Golden pointed out that the proposed constitution provided for the election of the union's top officers, its district directors who would make up the union's executive board, by referendum, a poll of the rank-and-file, which was surely democratic. If, however, he added, "we have got to begin right now after having gotten along this far in six years to have every last person who is to work for this Union selected on the basis of local votes, it seems to me we are going to be playing politics more of the time than we are going to be organizing and strengthening the position of our Union."

Golden, of course, was dedicated to that task. He was, however, one of the first trade unionists to realize that management had to be educated to the value of union recognition just as much as a green rank-and-file had to be educated as to the value of contract observance. One of the first educational ventures within Golden's Northeastern region had been a monthly symposium for workers and management people. Frank Fernbach conducted these monthly exchanges. As Golden explained their operation, "Some twenty steel companies from in and around this suburb of Pittsburgh sent representatives to thrash out common problems with leaders and active members of as many local union lodges. The discussion frequently makes for strange bedfellows. Management doesn't always agree, and sometimes union officers find themselves on different sides of the fence. But two results are certain. Everybody gets some new ideas; and has to think a little harder about his own."

The symposia petered out and were not repeated, but Golden began what amounted to a mission among the nation's employers, speaking most often on college campuses at a growing number of labor-relations seminars. Merlyn S. Pitzele, writing in the February 19, 1944 issue of *The Saturday Evening Post*, reported, "Golden is introduced to such blue-chip business groups as the United States Chamber of Commerce, the National Industrial Conference Board and the American Management Association as 'labor's ambassador to business,' and he gives off ideas that make his employer audiences want to run home and invite the local business agent in for dinner." No one, Pitzele, labor editor of prestigous *Business Week*, concluded "has yet equaled Golden's influence on union-management relations. . . . He has won acceptance for his ideas from sections of business which have traditionally felt that unionism was a kind of latterday demonology. As a unionist he pioneered in making organized labor see its common interests with industry, and when businessmen, hearing him, realized that not all labor leaders wore horns or breathed fire and brimstone, they were on their way to finding a pattern for living with the organizations which these men represented."

Golden's reactions to these encomiums were, as he wrote a friend, "mixed." Pitzele had cited his opposition to Communists within the labor movement, declared that Golden "picked the union business as a career as other people have chosen banking or teaching," and called him "virtual boss of the nation's second largest labor union." Golden did not much like being characterized as "1) A Union Boss, 2) A Union Careerist [and] 3) A one-man Dies Committee [a House un-

American activities committee chaired by Martin Dies from 1938 and 1944]. I have never thought of myself as being any one of these three." Nonetheless, there is not much doubt that Golden's contribution to industrial relations lies in his belief that if collective bargaining was to work both sides had something to learn from each other. At the same time, however, he was convinced that labor had learned the necessary lessons first. As he told the 1940 SWOC convention, "I thought for a long time that there was a conscious effort on the part of management officials to distort and misinterpret these contract provisions [those, in particular, covering the forty-hour week and work scheduling] with the idea in mind that the workers would become so disgusted and displeased with the way it worked out that they would give up the union in disgust. I think a tribute should be paid to the patience, the cooperation, the willingness of our people and committees, in the face of great annoyance and irritation and exasperation, that they have not lost their heads, and I think the net result has been to impress upon the management officials of the United States Steel Corporation that our union does have a sense of responsibility, that the members do exercise restraint and that they do take their jobs seriously, and they are not going to be stampeded into ill-advised action over the stupidity of local management officials."

Golden's faith in unionism was fundamental. As he told the delegates at that convention, "The remedy [for difficulties with management] is the spirit of unity and determination among the workers in the mills to see that their rights under the terms of the contract are fully protected and observed." His thinking was most often stimulated by concrete problems. For example, in 1940, as a consequence of layoffs brought on by technological change, he worked out a plan to "transfer the burden of the social cost of technological changes from the shoulders of the wage earners to those of industry." As spelled out to the 1940 SWOC meeting, his proposals cast light, not only on the issue of the day but also on the workings of Golden's mind. The convention's wage-scale policy committee, under Golden's guidance, recommended:

1. The workers to be displaced by technological changes should be re-absorbed in the regular labor turnover of the companies installing them.

2. The workers to be displaced should be notified at least six months in advance. From then until they are finally displaced, they should be given opportunities to learn how to do other jobs where openings develop periodically. Where necessary, expert vocational guidance and training should be provided for those workers who cannot easily adjust themselves to other jobs.

3. Those workers for whom there are no openings when they are finally displaced should be employed in some capacity until regular jobs open up for them. Wages paid these workers until they are placed on regular jobs should be charged to the original cost of the technological change.

4. Displaced workers who suffer a reduction of 10 or more per cent in their average daily earnings as a result of being absorbed on lower paying jobs than their original ones, should be paid a job compensation of 3 percent of their earnings while in the service of the company. The job compensation payments should be charged to the cost of the technological change.

5. The displaced workers who, for various reasons, cannot be re-absorbed in other jobs should be paid a dismissal wage of 10 per cent of their earnings for a ten-year period, but not less than $500.00 to those workers with less than ten years of service. The dismissal wages shall be charged to the cost of the technological change.

Philip Murray, in his book, *Organized Labor and Production* (coauthored at Clint's instigation with Morris Llewellyn Cooke, a liberal engineering consultant, and published in 1949), made the point that "when companies oppose unions, the unions elect as their leaders belligerent and willful men. No other type could survive. If, on the other hand, the company does not oppose the union with unlawful methods, the union is likely to choose for its leadership, men noted not for their fighting qualities, but for their ability as negotiators." Murray also insisted that "the rank and file is more concerned about pay and job security than about 'scraps.' A liberal seniority clause is more exciting than a soup kitchen. The point is that there are 'scraps' only because they are necessary to bring about certain gains . . . No artificial device is needed to keep up interest in the labor movement. The desire to enjoy a democratic, reasonably secure and comfortable economic life will always be the main source of rank and file interest in the labor movement." This is a view Golden would echo in countless speeches and would be embodied in his book, coauthored with Harold Ruttenberg, the steel union's research director. The book, provisionally titled *Paths to Industrial Peace*, was prompted by Clint's concern with the problem of union security. In March 1941, the month he and Ruttenberg signed their contract with Harper & Brothers calling for a $250 advance on delivery of a ninety-thousand-word manuscript, maintenance of membership and the dues check-off as well as recognition were, as we have noted, very much on the minds of the leaders of SWOC. *The Dynamics of Industrial Democracy* (as the book was eventually titled) may indeed be read as one long brief for the union shop as a vehicle of industrial peace.

The book, of course, was something more than that, as its subsequent history amply demonstrated. It found a ready audience in that new, fast-growing group of professionals spawned by the National Labor Relations Act of 1937—arbitrators, industrial relations counselors, mediators, negotiators on both sides of the bargaining table, professors of industrial relations and their students as well as an interested public. It became something of a bible for the new profession of industrial relations.

The book was well received, with a number of reviewers apparently astonished that union men were, as Bernard Ostrolenk wrote in the *New York Times Book Review*, "craftsmen in English, in diction, in description, in story-telling, and in argument." Ostrolenk also found the book "one of the most illuminating contributions yet made to labor literature," as did John A. Fitch, writing in *Survey Graphic*, who called it "the most informing and thought provoking of books . . . yet written in the field of labor relations." Thomas Russell Fisher, reviewer for the *Annals of the American Academy*, was more restrained, "The contention that co-operation with unions would benefit management is not a new one, but this book adds new evidence of the validity of the contention." Lewis Corey, in *The Nation*, saw the book as "an important expression of the new unionism," noting that the Golden-Ruttenberg "conception of union-management cooperation is much broader and more progressive than the one that prevailed in the 1920's. The older conception was largely an expression of union weakness; the new is an expression of union strength." The authors, Corey wrote, "use the term 'industrial democracy' in a narrower yet truer sense than the doctrinaire 'radicals,' to designate a constitutional democratic set-up in industry, where labor and its free unions have definite rights and powers in relation to management and government. It is not the metaphysical 'industrial democracy' of communism, which ends in bureaucratic totalitarian mastery over the workers. The Golden-Ruttenberg conception of industrial democracy—democratic relations and inalienable rights in the places where people must work to live—fits into any form of economic organization, from private enterprise to public enterprise and cooperatives." Solomon Barkin, in the *American Economic Review,* cautioned readers, noting that "the authors have not formulated a systematic and complete intellectual framework for labor's current philosophy," but added that "practical guides on specific problems of collective bargaining . . . such as this book presents would aid in advancing better understanding and serious consideration of the methods of establishing a democratic society in which the people's interests will predominate about the council tables dealing with economic, social and political problems."

Barkin's point is well taken. The book does not formulate a labor philosophy but rather a collective bargaining philosophy. Why, after all, should the public favor collective bargaining, as it did through the National Labor Relations Act of 1935? Law aside, why should management recognize unions? U.S. Steel, not to mention lesser steel companies, had got along for some fifty years without unions. The auto, rubber and other mass-production industries had flourished without unions. Conceivably, employee representation plans were a viable alternative to organized labor. During the 1937 crisis, it seemed likely that the new industrial unions would be contained, held to tenuous footholds at best in such giant firms as General Motors and U.S. Steel, or driven out of the mass-production industries altogether. Chaos seemed inevitable and so the country opted for a national labor relations policy that would assure industrial peace. But that was a static concept without a positive catalyst for change, for improvement, for progress. While Golden and Ruttenberg recognized the right to organize, the right to strike and the right to choose one's own representatives to bargain collectively as inalienable rights, they did not view them as sufficient. The concepts of a strike or a lockout, lasting until one side or the other caved in, clearly lacked something—a positive incentive for labor-management cooperation on matters of common concern. That incentive Golden and Ruttenberg located in productivity.

Productivity, then, is the *raison d'etre* for collective bargaining. Everyone benefits—society, management and employees. Increased productivity assures more for all, more profit for industry, higher wages for working people and lower prices and a greater range of goods for consumers. "Mass unemployment and scarcity production," the authors argued, are "a threat to the speedy prosecution of the war effort and the survival of democracy in the postwar era." Industrial democracy, they wrote, "is dynamic—an ever-changing, ever-growing way of life. Like its political counterpart it cannot become static, except at its peril. Inexorably it seeks to embrace everything that vitally affects the workingman in his work, community, and home. Personal happiness, family security, community integration, and a constantly rising plan of living are the fundamental objectives of industrial democracy. Their fulfillment depends on full production and employment on a sustained basis."

The literary critic Hugh Kenner once remarked that all American writing is how-to-do-it. Mark Twain taught us how to navigate the Mississippi by raft in *The Adventures of Huckleberry Finn,* Herman Melville, how to hunt whales in *Moby Dick* and Ernest Hemingway, how to catch a great fish in *The Old Man and the Sea.* Golden and Ruttenberg, in *The Dynamics of Industrial Democracy* offered a nation at war and already concerned about its aftermath a guide to achieving the industrial gains needed to guarantee progress. It was, among other things, a bid on behalf of the country's workers for a chance to help make industry more productive. Much of the book is given over to examples, drawn from Golden's and Ruttenberg's experiences with SWOC, to illustrate the basic "principles" of union-management relations.

Productivity was a goal common to labor and management, but its achievement rested on union recognition, union security. "The union shop is a necessary prerequisite for constructive union-management relations," Golden and Ruttenberg declared. Boiled down, their argument rests on a simple observation: The ever-present need of defending a union's very existence does not allow unionists to consider objectively the merits of employer proposals or employer problems.

"Management's assumption of sole responsibility for productive efficiency actually prevents the attainment of maximum output," was another Golden-Ruttenberg tenet. As an old-time craftsman and as the architect of SWOC's organizational fortunes, Golden was convinced that employers had not only failed to tap workers' resourcefulness but deliberately put them down. "The manager's brains are under the workman's cap," William D. (Big Bill) Haywood, the Wobbly leader, once observed. In describing a turn-of-the-century factory employing some five hundred to one thousand workmen, Frederick Winslow Taylor, the prophet of scientific management, wrote, "there will be found in many cases at least twenty to thirty different trades. The workmen in each of these trades have had their knowledge handed down to them by word of mouth . . . This mass of rule-of-thumb or traditional knowledge may be said to be the principle asset or possession of every tradesman . . . foremen and superintendents know, better than anyone else, that their own knowledge and personal skill falls short of the combined knowledge and dexterity of all the workmen under them . . . They recognize the task before them as that of inducing each workman to use his best endeavors, his hardest work, all his traditional knowledge, his skill, his ingenuity, and his good-will—in a word, his 'initiative,' so as to yield the largest possible return to his employer."

This fund of knowledge and skill, as Golden knew from his days on the railroad and as a machinist, was a source of power, a means of control exercised by the craftsmen over their jobs. Taylor found this inefficient, distasteful to his orderly mind. Scientific management, as historian David Montgomery has shown, went hand-in-glove with the open shop drive of the 1920s to transform, if not entirely destroy, the old ways, the workers' autonomy and job control. The stopwatch became the new industrial god. As Golden remarked in a memo to Joseph Scanlon (June 13, 1945), "Most . . . industrial engineers have a one-track mind. Most of their jobs and their reputations have been gained through a reduction in labor costs, rather than in overall improvement in production and engineering methods. So, finally, their major interest is seeing to it that every moment of a man's time is utilized to the fullest extent regardless of the type of equipment he may be forced to operate."

Job analysis through time-and-motion study coupled with systematic supervision and new forms of incentive payment brought on a transformation of industrial practices, a transformation Golden witnessed in his worklife, and created what Frederick Winslow Taylor called "*enforced* standardization of methods, *enforced* adoption of the best implements and working conditions, and *enforced* cooperation of all the employees under management's detailed direction." As a consequence, as Roethlisberger and Dickson discovered in their famous 1934 study of Western Electric's Hawthorne Works, the worker was placed "at the bottom level of a highly stratified organization" with his "established routines of work, his cultural traditions of craftsmanship, his personal interrelations" all "at the mercy of technical specialists."

Under such circumstances, the individual worker was compelled "to eat crow," as Golden liked to say, "when his boss jumped him, rightly or wrongly." Since the 1920s and the American Plan, however, workers discovered another answer.

"What they could no longer achieve as individuals, they found that they could do by joining together," Golden and Ruttenberg observed in their book. The strike expressed the workers' desire to "get even" and "crack back" at the boss. Such satisfactions, however were not long lasting. "Within a usually short period of time the desire to tell the boss 'to go to hell,' " they wrote, "grows into a positive, constructive desire for participation in making the vital decisions from which workers derive lasting satisfactions." On this observation, Golden and Ruttenberg crafted their notion of industrial democracy.

Collective bargaining, they held, "is the extension of the basic principles and practices of democracy into industry." It, therefore, followed: "Participation of workers, union representatives, and management at all levels is a prerequisite to the successful administration of a collective bargaining contract." This, in turn, called for "an effective system of communications for both management and the union, in bringing complaints from the bottom up and relaying decisions and policies from the top down." Workers, it must be recognized, "acquire a qualified property interest in their jobs" and will, therefore "strive for the kind of seniority rules which . . . will provide the greatest amount of job protection." Seniority, which eliminates favoritism and discrimination and allows for advancement and promotion, will not conflict with productive efficiency. "The prime objective of collective bargaining is the redistribution of the proceeds of production"; unions must participate with management in distributing the proceeds of each firm's production between owners and workers. "The proceeds of technological changes, labor saving machinery, and other factors contributing to lower unit costs or production should be shared equitably between owners and workers." Golden and Ruttenberg viewed the participation of organized workers in management as "a creative and cooperative undertaking." It would make management more efficient and unions more cost-conscious. "Union-management cooperation to reduce costs, eliminate wastes, increase productive efficiency, and improve quality represents a practical program that provides workers with effective direct participation in the creative phases of management."

Industrial democracy, in Golden's view, would once again free the worker from the dead hand of scientific management and allow for the creative use of those manager's brains beneath the worker's cap. Golden, however, was not starry-eyed about participation. "The policies and actions of unions are likely to reflect the policies and actions of management," was one of the thirty-seven principles of union-management relations set down by Golden and Ruttenberg. In their view, this meant that the attitudes and actions of management "largely determine" the degree of cooperativeness of union leadership, a point Phil Murray had made to Morris L. Cooke earlier. *The Dynamics of Industrial Democracy* addressed the point, repeatedly, speaking to the new men of management who would be responsible for labor relations within the giant corporations. "The leadership requirements and responsibilities of management increase under union-management relations," Golden and Ruttenberg observed.

Some of Golden's friends in the labor movement would come to believe that he put too much trust in sophisticated management. As Meyer Bernstein later remarked, "Phil Murray never trusted an employer. Clint had more respect for them as individuals. They regarded Clint as a person they could talk to, a man whose word would be respected, a person who would understand their problems . . . I think Clint went too far in one-direction and Murray did in the other. Murray remained a miner until his final days; he never trusted these people. Clint thought they were decent individuals who represented a point of view, an economic interest, and that it would be in their own interest to be rational. That wasn't always the case."

The Dynamics of Industrial Democracy rested on a faith in organized labor, not naive faith in the inherent goodness of the working class but a firm belief in the capability of workers to learn, and to take hold, and to participate in all matters affecting their lives. The authors insisted that their book "is about the dynamics, and not the economics, of industrial democracy. It is predicated upon the conviction that a free society is one of constant change, and that the increasing extension of democratic methods into industry will lead toward fuller production and employment and toward increasing the stature, well-being, dignity, and happiness of the individual worker." This conviction causes the authors to stress the importance of education, especially in the training for leadership. "Out of the process of change and adjustment during the last decade," they pointed out, "has come a rich fund of experience. Little of it finds its way into print. Most of it remains locked in the minds of the comparatively few people who participated in this process. We feel that this vast body of experience should be passed on to the next generation." They recognized that the immediate task was one of educating at the level of day-to-day union activity and collective bargaining. But more would be needed. "From a long-range viewpoint," they wrote, "the development of union leadership should be approached on a more fundamental basis. The newer unions need to face this problem realistically lest the passing of time ossify their leadership, as has happened, and is happening, in some of the older unions. Because not everyone shares our conviction that life is a constant process of change and adjustment, we are disturbed at times about the future of the great labor organizations that have meant so much to us and millions of others. We are fearful at times lest they become smug and complacent when they become secure. We want them to be always responsive to the interests of their members and the welfare of the nation. We want them to be democratic—to be agencies for the extension and implementation of the democratic process."

Prophetic and tough-minded, Golden and Ruttenberg insisted: "Workers and their unions cannot be exhorted into optimum productive efficiency; the way toward this goal is their participation on a democratic basis in the productive process, at the level both of the mines, mills, and factories and of industry-wide collective bargaining and national councils of government." They addressed the production problems of a nation engaged in a global war *and* those problems it would confront at the war's end. Successful reconversion and postwar prosperity, in their view, turned on the continued success of collective bargaining. The full participation of labor was necessary if the nation was to meet the harsh requirements of war, and so it would be to meet the new challenges of peace. The book closes with a plea for democratic planning. "Industrial democracy is characterized by the participation of labor," they wrote, "and this is no less true in the extension of democratic methods to our industrial economy as a whole." Moreover, "Organized labor is the one force that has the will and the independence to make its knowledge effective, which is so essential to national democratic planning."

The authors overestimated labor's commitment to national planning, taking up as a model the CIO's program for defense production, the "industry council." It was, essentially, a syndicalist notion modified by the experience of CIO unions with industry-wide bargaining. Later wartime experience soured many on the idea; it was viewed as a postwar palliative only and it was, for all practical consequences, dropped. Golden, however, remained convinced that the key to full employment, to prosperity, and to individual well-being, was in government, in democratic planning. He was aware, however, of the dangers of statism and, therefore, of the need for self-government on the part of all useful, functional groups in the community. "In a free society," Golden and Ruttenberg wrote, "private groups can fail to settle their problems in direct relationships only at the peril of their independent existence, because each unsettled social and economic problem eventually finds its way into the halls of Congress. And when the government assumes final responsibility for the solution of these problems, private groups must forfeit certain freedoms and powers. Government action in the field of social and economic matters should be in the form of assisting private groups in our economy toward a solution . . . The future of free America might well hinge on the extent to which industry will go in cooperation with organized labor, and government will go in encouraging it."

During the war, of course, government was very much involved in encouraging labor and management cooperation in production. At Phil Murray's behest, Golden was soon deep in such war work. Joseph Scanlon served as his assistant in Pittsburgh as Golden spent more of his time in Washington, rooming at the Carlton Hotel, where the chef was aware of his allergy to iodized salt, and shunting between offices at the War Production Board and the War Manpower Commission and at the CIO. He had little time for his family. Olive was enrolled at George School, a Quaker institution in Newton, Pennsylvania, and Dora joined him in Washington whenever possible. Otherwise, she waited at home for precious country weekends with her husband. Just before the war, Golden bought a thirty-five-acre farm in Solebury, "just up the road" from their old farm. He moved his family there as more of his work kept him in Washington and away from Pittsburgh. At Solebury, Clint refreshed himself, as he noted in his diary, on January 10, 1943: "Had my usual restful sleep at home. So different from restless nights spent in hotels and away from home. Spent the day in reading, smoking, visiting with Dora, a walk thro the woods and in general relaxation. Weather cold and brisk but no snow. Some would probably be helpful."

Such days were few during the war years. Golden, as someone said, was "the best hand-holder in the business." Phil Murray confided his concern over Van Bittner's performance as labor's man on the War Labor Board. Murray felt that Bittner was at times sacrificing principles for unanimity of decision and at other times was not altogether aware of implications of decisions. Whenever he was in town, Walter Reuther dropped in to propose one or another of his "plans" for increasing production. On one visit, he showed Golden a pressure-controlled rivetting gun developed by an auto worker, urging its adoption, as it would save countless thousands of man-hours in airplane construction. Golden promised to bring it up but noted in his diary, "I have my doubts as to its acceptance in as much as it came from a worker and not a 'recognized expert.' "

John Green, president of the CIO Shipbuilders, wanted advice about releasing to the newspapers charges of "labor hoarding" by a West Coast shipbuilder. H. L. Mitchell of the Southern Tenant Farmers Union sought help in heading off the importation of Bahamian labor to harvest vegetables in Florida, which meant a possible loss of jobs for farm workers and/or an undercutting of wages and work standards won by the union. Golden arranged a hearing for Mitchell before the War Manpower Commission and secured an agreement that Bahamians would not be brought in to work the fields unless domestic labor ran short and only if appropriate safeguards were enforced. R. Conrad Cooper, a steel executive and an industry representative on the Labor-Management Committee of the War Manpower Commission, complained that the WMC's Planning and Program Bureau, headed by William Haber, seemed "to think their function to be that of either changing policy formulated by our committee or of anticipating it and then getting out something that will reflect their views rather than those of the Committee."

Sumner Slichter wanted advice about Harvard's trade-union fellowship program. Joseph Schlossberg, the retired secretary-treasurer of the Amalgamated Clothing Workers, dropped in, expressed his unhappiness over his "lack of contact" with the labor movement, and remained for a long evening's discussion of the possible role of organized labor at peace conferences and in the postwar world. It was a rare evening, full, with the kind of discussion Golden most enjoyed. On another night, Golden "had a long talk with [Ruttenberg] about his apparent conceit and arrogance so evident to several people since his appointment to the Steel Division of the WPB as deputy chief. He denied being either conscious of this or of even knowing [the] meaning of either word. Claimed he thought many people were jealous of him because of his development and growth into his present position at 28 years of age. Tried to impress upon him the necessity for humility rather than arrogance. Before conversation was finished Walter Reuther came in for further discussion of plans for more effective labor contribution to war program." William Hart, a steel union district director, brought in a Mrs. Madden, "largely instrumental" in organizing the Pullman plant at Butler, seeking Golden's help in getting an appointment for her son at West Point.

Golden was generous, helped when he could, though he sometimes worked in mysterious ways. Meyer Bernstein recalls Golden as a private person, a man who talked easily about ideas but little, if at all, about himself. "Curiously," Bernstein recalled, "he was susceptible to scores of diseases, or at least thought he was. He wasn't a hypochondriac but he took a lot of medicine." He was a hearty eater and liked a drink on occasion. An avid reader, Golden read widely—

"biographies, but mostly economics books," Bernstein remembers. His favorite magazines, at the time, were the *New Republic, Nation, Fortune*, and *Business Week*. "He didn't care for the normal distractions of life," Bernstein added. "We lived together for many years and he didn't relax. He wouldn't read novels. I couldn't interest him in amusement in the ordinary sense. Music didn't inspire him. I once took him to Gilbert and Sullivan and he had no interest in that at all. Serious music wasn't his cup of tea either." Even Dora could not interest him in music. He once told an interviewer that while he enjoyed movies and plays, he did not go to the movies but once a year—"usually when my wife hauls me off to one." He added that he did listen to the radio a lot and depended on it for much of his entertainment. But he did not say what he listened to, only remarking in his diary on his distaste for "Colonel Stoopnagle type of humor." "My pipe, my family and my dog are the main things I live for." What he especially enjoyed was some sort of physical work; a day cutting brush in Solebury set him up fine for the weekly grind in Washington.

Golden liked to have around him people who could discuss ideas, and someone like Meyer Bernstein, who was something of a workaholic, with great intellectual capacity and a wide range of interests, was just the right sort. The two became very close, developing a friendship that approached a father-son relationship. And this perhaps explained something that puzzled Bernstein for years. "It was one time I didn't understand his reaction," Bernstein explained. "I was working on the settlement of the Little Steel strikes, the NLRB settlement, after the Supreme Court had acted on May of 1940. This involved 7,500 people, a big job, a full-time job for me. And during the course of that I got my draft notice, so I asked the draft board to give me a three months postponement to finish this and I said I'd be happy to go into the Army. Joe

Scanlon went with me. Well, the draft board finally said okay. I worked on it for three months and I finished it and I got my notice and I reported to duty at the time specified and they tell me, 'Oh no, you've been exempted.' 'Who's been exempted?' 'You've been exempted.' 'I didn't ask for any exemption.' Well, the draft board is flabbergasted. So they call up the Harrisburg headquarters and they discover that orders had come down from Washington that Bernstein is to be exempted as indispensable to the national security of the United States, or something. And I said, 'I don't ask for that. I don't want it. I said I would serve beginning in three months if I got postponement of induction to finish my job. The job is finished and I want to go.' 'You want to volunteer?' 'Sure.' So I did. So I signed a paper and I was inducted into the Army." (Bernstein served with the Thirty-seventh Infantry Division in the Solomon Islands.) "Clint never forgave me for that." He did, of course, later. "But he resented it; he showed it."

Bernstein, as a voluminous correspondence shows, served as a sounding board for Golden. In wartime Washington, he apparently had no such confidante. A tall man, actually six-foot-one, with an angular, ruddy-complexioned face, light brown eyes behind tortoise-rimmed glasses, a few strands of receding grayish hair swept over a balding pate above a high-domed forehead, Golden looked the scholar misplaced among burly trade unionists and paunchy government bureaucrats. He was something of an autodidact, according to Bernstein. "He had learned everything himself. This was obvious because he had a few words that he mispronounced that a college graduate wouldn't mispronounce—*adkate* for *adequate*, for example." Golden, however, exuded authority to bureaucrat, scholar and unionist alike. "Clint had injured his hand in his youth," Bernstein remarked, "and his handshake was therefore curious. But there was real strength in it. It didn't grasp your hand as a gorilla might but it was obvious that he was transmitting power when you shook his hand. It had a meaning far beyond that of an ordinary, cursory handshake."

If President Franklin D. Roosevelt had a failing, it was his habit of creating more than one agency to do one job, or closely related jobs. "Production for war is based on men and women —the human hands and brains which collectively we call Labor," he told Congress in his 1942 State of the Union Message. But the President acceded reluctantly to union demands for a larger voice in production decisions. Phil Murray, seconded by Walter Reuther, was pushing for joint labor-management committees for each industry and at all levels of the production effort. Early in the war, production responsibilities were assigned to the Office of Production Management with William S. Knudsen, an immigrant's son who had come up from the assembly line to become General Motors' production genius, and Sidney Hillman, an immigrant clothing worker who was a founder and president of the Amalgamated Clothing Workers, appointed production "czars,"—a newsman's phrase for what the President liked to think of as "a firm." When asked by reporters if Knudsen and Hillman would be equals, the President replied with a question of his own: "Is a firm equals?" Perhaps because of this uncertainty about how power was distributed, plus the symbolic nature of the men's respective origins—one from management, one from labor—the office of Production Management and its successor agency, the War Production Board, became a battleground where various factions (civilians and the military, labor and management, and so on) warred with one another over production goals and labor allocation. Hillman, ailing, and at odds with his former colleagues in the labor movement, was eased out and the President, in 1942, shifted all labor-supply functions from the WPB's labor division to the newly created War Manpower Commission and set up in the WPB a new Labor Production Division as a channel for labor information and ideas.

The consequences were positively Byzantine, with Washington warlords feuding every which way. Golden's skill at threading his way through the political maze as well as his dedication to the job of fitting labor into war-production needs made him a natural choice when the administration decided that there was a need to "bridge the gap" between the two agencies. He was named in June 1943 simultaneously to posts as vice-chairman of the War Production Board and vice-chairman of the War Manpower Commission. So as not to offend the American Federation of Labor, Joseph Keenan of the International Brotherhood of Electrical Workers was named also to serve as vice-chairman to the two agencies. As John Lord O'Brian, the able counsel of the WPB, said long after the war, "Both were very valuable men. As a matter of fact after their appointment they weren't particularly interested in anything but getting the work done. That is, they did not adhere very strictly to representing factions in labor." But that did not mean that they avoided all conflict. Donald Nelson, the then chairman of the WPB, tried to keep the peace but was unable to prevent the ongoing conflict between his staff and that of Charles E. ("GE Charley") Wilson, another of his vice-chairmen.

Golden tried not to allow the bureaucratic in-fighting interfere with his work. He vigorously promoted the idea of joint labor-management cooperation. He asked Phil Clowes of the Steelworkers to serve as his deputy at WPB and Charlotte Carr, his old friend and boss in the Pinchot administration, to join him as his executive assistant at the War Manpower Commission. On his appointment, Golden said, "I'm not down here representing just the Steelworkers, or the CIO, or any other groups affected, but I'm trying to do the best job I know for the government and for the country." Phil Murray was reported as telling Golden, "I want you to go over there and spend all the time you can, but I don't want you to get away from the union." The posts, incidentally, were unpaid and Golden was on Steelworkers salary all the time he was in Washington. He also had responsibilities to carry out for the union as an assistant to President Murray. Father Owen Rice recalled a wartime luncheon in Washington with Phil Murray and Golden when "some big decision" was in the offing. According to Father Rice's recollections, Golden said to Murray, "I'm representing the country as a whole rather than the movement." Murray, said Rice, "tore into him . . ."

Murray, uncharacteristically, was being a bit unfair. For Golden was directly up against a common attitude, a hostility to labor within wartime government circles that Murray felt, so to speak, at one remove. Labor was not only not allowed to serve as equal to management but denigrated further by an unspoken assumption that labor men were only capable of serving a special interest and not that of the country as a whole. As Golden put it in a memorandum about his government service, "I find it hard to understand why a person, who has been qualified to take a government post by practical experience on the side of labor, should be any less capable of discharging a public trust than one with a management background."

Clint earned respect because he was capable of discharging a public trust as well as of representing labor when such representation was called for. On January 7, 1943, Golden wrote in his diary that labor staff members of the WPB were "thoroughly frustrated" by their "inability to make any very real contribution to the war effort and program . . . It is perfectly clear that Donald Nelson [chairman of the WLB] and other high WPB officials either do not want Labor to play a real part or because of their inhibitions just cannot see how Labor can be permitted to make maximum contribution." As it turned out, Labor did make a significant contribution to the war effort. "Although manpower has been very tight and a number of critical bottlenecks appeared from time to time," Golden later reported, "no military operation has to my knowledge been held up by a lack of supplies due to a manpower shortage. On the contrary, production records have been broken even while military withdrawals cut deeper and deeper into the industrial labor force, and the reserves of manpower were used up in many areas."

Meanwhile, the pressures of work—the daily round of meetings in Washington, staff conferences in Pittsburgh, and speeches at Harvard, on the Town Meeting of the Air and elsewhere—exacted a toll of Golden's health. At fifty-eight, he worried about those intimations of mortality—the rumbling stomach, sleeplessness, the stiffness of one's joints on rising. A doctor advised rest, prescribed medicine to ease aches and smooth away tensions. But, though it seemed a touch of hypochondria to some or exhaustion from overwork to others, Clint was really sick. On Tuesday, August 10, 1943, he was admitted to Temple University Hospital for a gall bladder operation. Dr. Wayne Babcock, "one of Philadelphia's oldest and most skillful surgeons," operated with the assistance of Dr. John Hollander. Clint's diary records his experience:

> A spinal anesthetic was used and I was conscious throughout the 1½ hours. Dr. B. first removed the gall bladder which had stones in it and showed it to me. He then discovered that my appendix had ruptured and he removed that. He showed it to me and explained that it had previously ruptured—that adhesions had formed which closed the rupture which was lengthwise and at the same time they had formed crosswise to make a sort of partition or bulkhead within. One end had again ruptured. I stood the ordeal well thanks to skillful surgery and care of doctors, nurses, and the ever loyal and devoted good wife Dora. Olive had decided to a few weeks course in typing

at a business school in the neighborhood and she visited me daily which was a great comfort.

The day following the operation Dr. Morrison came to see me and advised that the hospital laboratory had found a small parasite in my appendix which had evidently been there a number of years living a life cycle reproducing etc. which in part at least was responsible for the inflammation and no doubt the recurring attacks of what I thought digestive trouble I have experienced for years.

Recovery was rapid; the doctors solemnly pronounced it "phenomenal," as well they might since this was before penicillin became available to civilians, and Clint returned to work on October 4. "I feel better than for many years," he recorded in his diary. "My two jobs in Washington have been difficult—at times discouraging, but always interesting. The war situation at least on the production front has changed profoundly. Production schedules and goals are being met in many cases and are in sight in others. This has caused cutbacks in production in some instances and caused new dislocations. The problem of reconversion of some war plants and industries is daily becoming more acute."

The issue of reconversion had cropped up earlier in the year. Bruce Catton in his informative account of the war years in Washington, *The War Lords of Washington,* wrote "It was useless to argue that every ounce of metal was vitally needed for war work when there were large-scale shutdowns of aluminum pot lines due to a surplus of aluminum. Manufacturers who learned, via the cancellation of their contracts, that they were no longer needed for war production, could not be kept from thinking that in such case they might as well use a bit of the surplus metal to make nonwar goods. Workers who had been laid off from war jobs were bound to feel that patriotism need not prevent them from working to produce goods for civilians." Golden and Joe Keenan expressed their concern about the effect of increasing military cutbacks in a December 1943 memorandum: "Shutdowns of mines, mills, and factories will reduce the rate of output of all operations by injuring the workers' morale; for the effort of all workers will be affected if they feel, rightly or wrongly, that the harder they work the sooner they will work themselves out of a job." The labor vice-chairmen, therefore, urged that the WPB ought to get busy on concrete plans for the production of civilian goods. They suggested that production of raw materials be continued at full blast, even though military needs were declining, with the surplus stockpiled both as a reserve for military emergencies—we had as yet to invade France—and as a resource for quick expansion of civilian production. They also called for an expanded program to readapt manufacturing facilities to civilian use so that any surplus of labor, of materials, or of manufacturing capacity could be put to work as fast as it appeared.

Early in January 1944 Golden attended a WPB staff meeting, chaired by WPB-head Donald Nelson, to discuss a proposed order on war-contract termination and reconversion. In his diary, he noted, "Consensus of opinion that military should participate of necessity in discussion and decisions on contract termination but decisions on reconversion should be made by civilian WPB." On the afternoon of January 17, 1944, top WPB staff discussed President Roosevelt's proposed National Service legislation, which was the military's answer to the problems of wartime reconversion manpower dislocations. Nelson, according to Golden, "pooled all vice chairmen as to whether they were for or against and to my astonishment *all* were firmly *against*." The next afternoon, Golden went with Charles—"GE Charley," to distinguish him from the head of General Motors, "Engine Charley"—Wilson, a WPB vice-chairman, to a meeting in Assistant Secretary of the Navy Ralph Bard's office to discuss the National Service question. "Under Secretary of War Robert Patterson," Golden recorded in his diary that night, "took over meeting. Highly emotional and irrational to say the least. Insisted 'Commander-in-Chief' had demanded such legislation and all present had obligation to support." At the meeting were Bard, Patterson, Larry Appley and William Haber of WMC, Wilson, Admiral Jerry Land and Golden, with some aides. "Little enthusiasm shown for such legislation," his diary account continued. "Patterson contended it was needed to boost soldier morale. Very much doubt if it can be passed." Golden decided that he would resign if the administration had its way in WPB. "Talked with Phil Murray on phone and he agreed with this position."

Congress remained cool to the National Service legislation proposed by the President, tabbed the "work or fight" law by the press because it called for the drafting of strikers as well as the direct allocation of men to war jobs where and when necessary. But the issue surfaced at a CIO board meeting at the end of January where Murray, according to Golden's diary jottings, "lectured Communist leaders of three unions—Bridges, Curran, and Merrill—on their public statements supporting National Service." The Communists were super-patriots during the war, but Murray's lecture was effective, for the CIO board reaffirmed a convention decision opposing such legislation. The issue faded in public discussion for a time but was revived when the Allies suffered a stunning reversal in their military fortunes just before Christmas 1944, in the Battle of the Bulge. At the urgings of the secretaries of War and Navy, President Roosevelt requested the measure not only on the grounds of mobilization but to assure our fighting men that the country was making a total effort to win and to convince the enemy that we meant what we said in demanding "unconditional surrender." Unionists, excepting those influenced by the Communists, remained unconvinced. As Golden put it in his diary, writing on December 29, "We have some military setbacks and it seems some people think they can be compensated for by imposing regimentation upon all civilians. Where they are to get the manpower to administer such legislation in the face of their claims of a manpower shortage is beyond me. I am afraid our governmental bureaucrats have no faith in our people and our democratic system. One day the workers and management of industry are lauded for having created a 'miracle of production' and the next we are told compulsory national service legislation is necessary because some 300,000 additional workers are needed on urgent production programs. To say that a civilian labor force of 53 million must be regimented because of a shortage of 300,000 seems to me irrational and illogical."

As the war drew to its inevitable end, Golden entertained hopes that the labor-management cooperation fostered by the patriotism of the war effort would continue and contribute to postwar recovery. But there was cause for pessimism as well: Charles Wilson of General Electric, an able administrator and management advocate, had wrested effective control of the WPB away from Donald Nelson, who was sympathetic to labor's claims for participation. Wilson controlled the powerful Production Executive Committee of the WPB, which excluded labor from its deliberations. In an undated memorandum drafted sometime in 1944, in response to this and addressed to the problems of reconversion, Golden declared:

> The question is whether the reconversion period will be planned for full production and employment, and if so whether the WPB will play any large part in the planning. If the answer to this question is "No," then there is no point in making any special effort to get effective labor participation in the WPB. If there is to be any planning, the WPB is the logical place for it to be done. The WPB

will plan reconversion or there won't be any real planning, because the WPB is the agency which has (1) the machinery for production planning . . . and (2) the industry organizations to administer a production program industry by industry.

Whether or not reconversion is planned will mean the difference between employment and unemployment. The immediate goal of labor participation in the WPB is to fight for policies of reconversion planning.

At the present time there are no accepted plans. Even the NAM [National Association of Manufacturers] has objected to the lack of planning. WPB is in one of its crucial stages similar to the period before its creation when the old OPM failed to curtail civilian production. At that time, those in the OPM who saw ahead and talked and argued for curtailment and conversion proved to be right and took the lead. Later on, the WPB faced another issue over the type of controls to be established. Once again those who saw the necessity in advance of a controlled materials plan proved to be ahead of the game and took the lead.

Today the issue revolves about planning. The military will not take the lead because their primary responsibility is for military production. Business is holding back because it cannot decide between the continuation of government controls and the desire to be rid of all controls. The stage is set for someone to take the lead. Labor has a natural interest in planning to adjust civilian production to military cutback.

How is the fight for planning to be made? It is in the first instance a question of an idea, the emphasis upon a point of view. It is not necessary to work out all of the blue-print details of a reconversion plan. It is enough now to make the necessity for planning a constant and repeated theme in all meetings of top WPB officials. It is a theme for outside speeches and education. The general theory of the planning can be stated. It is (1) to find out what materials and facilities and manpower are released by military cutbacks and (2) to determine and promote the civilian production goals which will take up the released materials, facilities and manpower. The technique for doing this twofold job is pretty well under control. The WPB has perfected the machinery for taking a list of articles and breaking them down into the materials, facilities, component parts and to a degree, the manpower involved. This technique can be used to provide an overall picture and to work out a specific program within each industry.

This machinery can be used to carry out a planning program having for its objectives full production and full employment.

When Golden resigned from the War Production Board and the War Manpower Commission on October 15, 1945, he made the point again:

If our minds are bold and imaginative, we can see how to use these techniques, not to fix restrictive quotas, but to indicate levels of production and employment that are necessary to maintain an economy of abundance. The use of these techniques, even though in connection with estimates and guesses of production demands instead of firm demands in the form of government orders, will give us a basis for fixing voluntary production goals in the basic industries . . . In the past, the demands for production have come from the military who wanted war supplies to defeat our enemies. In the transition period, the demands for production will be associated with pools of unemployed workers. In the future, it will come from workers who want production for jobs to give them a livelihood and to produce the goods and services needed by the American people and by world-wide reconstruction.

The mood of the country, however, was changing and while Golden was undoubtedly right about the possible application of wartime production experiences to postwar planning, his views were not the dominant ones in the country at large. Phil Murray appointed him as a delegate to the postwar Labor-Management Conference called by President Harry S Truman in the fall of 1945. It met in Washington from November 5 to November 30, and there was widespread agreement on a number of matters, one of the positive results of wartime cooperation. The conferees agreed that grievances under existing contracts should be settled by voluntary arbitration rather than by strikes or lockouts; that the United States Conciliation Service should be strengthened; that during initial bargaining for contracts strikes should be postponed until all peaceful procedures had been exhausted; that there should be not discrimination because of race, color, creed, or sex in dealings between management and union; and that joint meetings of top labor and management officials should be continued in the hope that better understanding would be achieved. Nonetheless, the conference was a disappointment, for it failed to reach an agreement on machinery to avoid or minimize strikes in the reconversion period.

In his diary, Golden observed, "Had the conference been held at a time when there were less tensions—economic and political—and had it lasted longer, a much greater measure of achievement might well have resulted. John L. Lewis and some of the reactionary extremists of the N. A. M. succeeded in keeping the embers of suspicion and distrust alive." But other factors intruded. Strikes were in the offing as the restless giants of industry sought to shake loose from wartime controls.

Golden tried, but did not succeed in pushing his view that cooperation and not conflict was the way to follow in the difficult years ahead. He left Washington a saddened, weary man. He could, however, leave with some pride. As Bruce Catton wrote in *The War Lords of Washington*, "From first to last . . . the one steady and unavailing fight for an adequate, democratic approach to reconversion, an approach that would rest on confidence in the people rather than on distrust, was made, significantly enough by three men–by Maverick, the unrepentant New Dealer from Texas, and by Joe Keenan and Clint Golden, the two labor leaders who had been given vice-chairmanships in WPB." As Catton added, "They knew . . . what the fight was all about," and that is no small thing.

Causes of Industrial Peace

On July 1, 1946, Clinton S. Golden resigned as vice-president of the United Steelworkers, giving ill health as reason for doing so. Though the loose folds of flesh beneath his jaw indicated that he had not quite fully recovered from recent bouts of illness, his resignation came as a surprise to his associates. He confided in no one except Phil Murray, with whom he discussed the question some two months earlier, even though he had been thinking of quitting union work for some time. As he wrote in his diary on February 8, 1944, "Things do not go as well as I wish. Sometimes I feel strongly I should seek other means of livelihood and that a change of environment and new interests would be stimulating." Six months earlier, the Goldens had sold their Solebury farm, retaining about seventeen acres as a site for a house to be built during 1946. "Should like to have our home and garden here in the country," Golden's December 26, 1945 diary entry reads, "and do some speaking and writing. The problem is to retire with assurance of enough income to live modestly."

Golden, in truth, was "tired and frustrated" as he remarked to Joe Scanlon at the time, rather than seriously ill. "For all his qualities of leadership," Golden commented in his diary on

June 16, 1946, "Phil Murray is not a good administrator." This was a constant source of irritation and worry for Golden. During the war, he managed to arrange an afternoon session with Murray and the union's headquarters staff and, as he jotted in his diary for March 10, 1943, "Phil outlined their respective duties and responsibilities and made it clear [that] each department head is to report henceforth to him." But the arrangements made did not hold firm. On January 1, 1946, Golden noted that on Murray's return from a "brief but deserved and needed vacation," he hoped that Murray would "see the desirability of outlining my functions and responsibilities more clearly." Nothing happened, however, and Golden's closest associates became discouraged and decided to leave. Harold Ruttenberg left to take an executive post with the Portsmouth (Ohio) Steel Corporation, a firm largely owned by the Kaiser-Frazer Corporation. Joe Scanlon, whose loss Golden felt deeply, departed in September of 1946 to the Massachusetts Institute of Technology to become a lecturer and advisor to the faculty on industrial relations.

"Morale about the office," Golden later wrote Scanlon, "seemed to be pretty low. Evidently there are two research departments–Cope being one and working with McDonald as his right hand man and the other consisting of Meyer [Bernstein], Otis [Brubaker] and the others having no participation or feeling that their help or services were either desired or needed." This reflected the various pressures on Murray at the time–Lee Pressman doing his best to prevent Murray from coming out openly against the Communists within the CIO; Dave McDonald seeking to build his influence with the Steelworkers through his personal closeness to Murray; and Golden loath to participate in the internecine conflicts building up within the union. "No one," he noted in his diary on June 16, 1946, "has any clear outline of the duties he is expected to perform nor the measure of responsibility and authority delegated to him. To work under such circumstances is most difficult."

Golden, too, was discouraged by the immediate course of postwar collective bargaining. "It seems that most of the effort Joe Scanlon and I particularly have put forth to both advocate and to build cooperative relationships has been undone by our associates." It was this feeling, expressed in his diary on May 5, 1946 that precipitated Golden's decision to resign. Earlier, he had been much more optimistic. Though unions and managements were deadlocked over the question as to whether or not wage increases could be granted without price "relief," that is, increases, the government appeared to agree with the unions that wages could go up and prices be held firm. Some two hundred thousand General Motors workers had gone out on strike on November 21, 1945, asserting that the company could grant a 30 percent wage hike without any increase in automobile prices. Walter P. Reuther, then head of the union's GM division, called upon the companies "to open their books" to prove or disprove the union's contention. A presidential panel held mid-strike, in January 1946, asserted that an hourly increase of 19½ cents was well within the corporation's ability to pay without price increases. This meant that, in effect, the union was on strike for a *public* demand.

For a time it appeared that the steel companies would accede to presidential pressures, something Golden devoutly hoped for. On the evening of January 7, 1946, just a week before a steel strike deadline, he and Van Bittner met Ben Fairless of U.S. Steel in the Carlton lobby. They chatted about strike prospects and Fairless said, according to Golden's notes of the conversation, "it was up to O. P. A.," [the Office of Price Administration] which still retained wartime powers to set prices. Fairless was in good humor and told the union chiefs, "If I owned U.S. Steel, I'd give you what you're asking for."

Golden concluded from this exchange, "Begins to look like a 'break' in the situation."

But that was a momentary hope. A few days later Golden recorded in his diary, "Alarming reports coming in from the field re Bethlehem's rejection of offer to cooperate in seeing that plants are protected against damage and deterioration [in the event of a strike]. Looks as if they want a show-down fight." Industry could afford to stand pat, an unintended benefit of recent tax legislation. Corporations that lost money during reconversion could get returns on excess-profits taxes paid during the war. As the November 1946 issue of *Fortune* pointed out: "A variety of factors makes strikes fairly cheap, in the short-range view, for some corporations. The excess-profits tax was in force until December 31, 1945; in the first eight months of the year the big war contractors had already made about as much money as they could hope to clear for the whole year; in some cases it was actually more profitable in terms of the 1945 balance sheet to shut down toward the end of the year rather than pay higher wages in advance of price relief." But whatever the short-run advantages of "taking a strike," it was the long-run gain corporations sought. Simply put, they wanted an end to price controls. That made a steel strike inevitable.

Golden described in his diary the bargaining that took place just before the walkout began. Writing on January 12:

> Had conferences with Pres. Fairless of U.S. Steel and his associates in New York on the afternoons of the 10th and 11th. Initial offer was 12½¢ and subsequently raised to 15¢ after we had dropped from 25¢ to 20¢. Fairless is a quick tempered man and on one occasion indicated unless we accepted his offer he would cancel our contract and we would "have a real fight." With great restraint and

calmness Phil told him we were not required to accept his (Fairless') unilateral decisions and if he wanted a fight he would be accommodated. After Fairless left to keep an appointment, Roger Blaugh made a sort of an apology saying Fairless was under a great strain, etc. Fairless claims the industry needs $7.00 per ton increase in prices on finished steel products to make up past losses. O.P.A. offered him $2.50 but John Snyder, OWMR [Office of War Mobilization and Reconversion] director, was willing to offer $4.00 when Fairless dropped from $7.00 to $5.00. There seems to be some contradictions in their position. They claim 12½¢ per increase would increase their costs by $3.00 per ton. Yet they stated that a ton of finished steel products requires about 20 hours of labor. If they first stated that previous increased costs required $7.00 per ton, finally accepted $4.00 and then offered $1.00 a day wage increase which would allegedly increase costs by $3.00 per ton their argument is surely less than logical.

When they were convinced we were adamant in not accepting less than 19½¢ Fairless in a private talk with Phil offered 3¢ additional or a total of 18¢ if Phil would agree to have the 3¢ accepted as a settlement of a WLB directive in Jan 1944 setting up 5¢ per employee per hour as a fund to eliminate inequities. Phil insisted on an additional 2¢ and an assurance that the industry would accept this. Fairless claimed he could not assure this whereupon we broke off in a deadlock. When word of this reached Washington, President Truman requested that the parties come to Washington to meet with him.

At noon it was requested that only Phil and Fairless come at 2 P.M. which they did. It now appears that Fairless finally agreed to go along if given a week to convince the industry to go along with the settlement. On this basis instructions went out to postpone strike call for one week.

It is my fervent hope that a settlement can be effectuated without a strike.

And, again on January 13:

This experience adds to the belief that government will never act until forced by a crisis. Government officials and newspapers now claim production is all important and to achieve it, it is O.K. to advance both wages and prices where necessary. Judging by fact-finding boards reports in oil and autos together with probable settlement of steel the pattern of wage increases will run from 17% to 20%. Once the cycle of adjustment is well completed it ought to allay unrest and help create climate conducive to uninterrupted production. If so, then it would seem our union task would be to devise constructive policy directed toward securing equitable distribution of results of increased productivity.

Murray and Fairless met with President Truman again on the 16th of January. Golden jotted down the results in his diary the next day:

Phil spent nearly 8 hours—from 2 P.M. until 10 P.M. with a short period out for supper—at the White House with Ben Fairless and government officials trying to reach agreement which would settle wage dispute and prevent a strike. No progress was made. Fairless standing on a 15¢ per hour offer which is 3¢ less than he tentatively proposed in New York. He says the industry will not agree to a higher figure. Says he does not want to argue, but he won't move beyond his offer. Before leaving the White House last night the president told both that if they failed to reach an agreement he "would make a proposal today that neither would like."

On January 17, he wrote:

> Phil went to White House again at 2:00 P.M. When he and Fairless could not agree the President called them in and told them a rate of 18½¢ per increase was in order. Phil accepted subject to Policy Committee approval, while Fairless would not. The President gave him until noon tomorrow to decide, in meantime withholding publicity. If agreed to by the industry there won't be a strike and wages will be increased $1.48 per day of 8 hrs. If industry refuses, a strike will no doubt take place and then in support of government. I hope this will not be necessary.
>
> On the 18th Fairless refused the President's proposal for a settlement of the wage dispute. In the afternoon Phil had a largely attended press conference at which he announced the strike would become effective at 12:01 a.m. on the 21st. On the 19th Henry Kaiser settled for his company and ridiculed the refusal of the industry—to permit a strike over the difference of 3½¢ per hr. or 2%.

On the 19th, Golden and his wife left Washington for Pittsburgh; the weather was cold and clear, the roads perfect. "A most enjoyable trip," Golden confided to his diary. On the 26th, the day the steel strike began, Golden recorded:

> The strike is 100% effective. No attempts thus far to operate. No excitement such as usually accompanies strikes. Management according to reports is "cooperating"! To the extent in some instances of providing shelter for the pickets and coke or coal for their "salamanders" or heating contrivances that the pickets use to keep warm. We have had meetings of the U.S. Steel Negotiating Committee, the Int. Union Executive Board and the National Wage Policy Committee. Full reports have been submitted and unanimous votes of approval and confidence given the officers. Morale is high. The President has taken a firm

position that the industry should accept his recommendations for settlement. Phil has made a nationwide broadcast that brought in hundreds of letters of approval. I know because I have been answering them for him. No positive action by government has thus far been taken. The penalizing effect of the strike daily becomes more evident. Ford has begun laying men off because of lack of steel. Mines are closing down and railroads are curtailing operations. What a pity the issues could not be resolved without this show of strength by both sides. We are preparing for a long struggle. Relief machinery is being set up. Today I authorized McDonald to withhold my entire salary as a contribution. No one can say that I continued to accept my good salary while strikers received no wages. Many complaints are coming in from small firms who feel they should have individual treatment and special consideration. We have adopted the policy of settling with firms on the basis of application of the President's recommendations. To date about 30 settlements have been made with small firms. I hope before another week passes a settlement on an industry-wide basis can be had. In the main it seems that public opinion is largely on our side.

It is a great comfort to have Dora with me. Her counsel and company at the end of each hectic day is a great help. Her good breakfasts before starting work help get one started right. Joe and Meyer have enjoyed eating with us this week each morning.

On February 2, Golden took time off from his duties to drop Jack Lever a note about moving into an apartment in Solebury until the new house was finished. About the strike, he wrote, "as near as I can make out, the industry and Government are engaging in collective bargaining over prices." On the twentieth day of the strike, Golden noted in his diary that "Lines are firm—but there is evident uneasiness among both workers and management of the smaller companies." He also described the bargaining over prices and its consequences on industry-union bargaining:

> All during the week Phil and Pressman had conferences with U.S. Steel representatives. They were willing to put the 18½¢ increase into effect but were unwilling to make it effective as of Jan 1 which President Truman had recommended. They wanted to extend the present agreements which expire on Oct 10/46 to May 1, 47. This we felt unwise because of uncertainties of attempts to control inflation. We offered to extend to Feb 15/47. They wanted declarations favoring increased production; against unauthorized strikes and agreement as to the exact amount of the inequities settlement ordered by the WLB. All of these matters could no doubt be agreed upon if the Corp. would agree to make the raise effective of Jan 1/46. My own opinion is that they are playing for time and position. The government has evidently told the Corp. prices relief will not be granted until a wage agreement is reached. The Corp. representatives seem to want the price relief spelled out in a directive before they reach agreement.

In a subsequent entry, Golden remarked: "Government seems unable to evolve a wage-price formula that may serve to ease us over the bumps in this transition from a war to a peace economy."

The steel strike ended after thirty days with the 18½-cent wage increase suggested by President Truman. U.S. Steel was assured a five-dollar a-ton increase, and price controls were finally lifted on June 30. The price increase, according to the *Chicago-Sun*, netted the steel companies $435 million additional income at a cost of only $185 million in wage boosts. The smaller fabricating plants, however, were not granted the price relief given basic steel and they resisted the union's imposition of the pattern. As a consequence, the union's wage policy committee called what amounted to a general strike of steel fabricators. It was a decision that Golden did not think was wise. As he wrote in his diary on May 5:

> While I had my own doubts as to the desireability of engaging in a strike so general in nature before it took place, subsequent events have demonstrated to me at least the unwisdom of this policy. The decision to engage in so general a strike was based largely on so-called "expert" advice that no fabricating plants could operate much more than a week because of practically no inventories of unfinished or semi-finished materials. Under our kind of an industrial society there is no one–not even a government agency–that can accurately predict the character and size of inventories in so wide an area of fabrication of metals. To have differed with the "expert" publicly before a policy committee or our executive board would have indicated a split or cleavage among the top and this would have had a bad effect on the morale and unity of our membership. As matters stand today there have been numerous and devious departures from policy in making settlements that have created ill feeling among our directors and much harm to our relationship with many firms. Phil has told me privately that we will lose about 40,000 members as a result of the strike. This, I think, could have been avoided if we had not called out the fabricating firms. It should serve as a lesson for the future.

Clearly, the conduct of the fabricating strikes left Golden feeling out of sorts over the course of union events and union leadership. He was much happier with those settlements, such as ones with Kaiser Steel and SKF Corporation of Philadelphia, in which "reason rather than emotion prevailed." As

Golden indicated in a speech at a joint conference of SKF shop stewards and foremen, he believed in "restraint" and had faith that successful negotiations created

> a climate conducive to cooperative effort and endeavor. . . . The stockholders, the management, or the workers alone and by themselves can [not] operate the works. It is only when all three groups join together their resources, technical and production skills and know how, plus the application of energy that raw and semifinished materials are transformed into useful products that fill human needs and requirements. It is through the continuing efficient, economical production and sale of these products at fair prices that all of you can be assured of regular employment at good wages and salaries.
>
> I doubt very much if there is a manufacturing enterprise in America in which there is not room for a great deal of improvement in management methods and in production techniques. The responsibility of management for the planning and direction of operations and the work force is clearly recognized by our union. We have no desire to encroach upon management's functions. We are prepared, however, once we have become adjusted to a new and friendlier relationship, to join with management, if it so desires, in establishing labor-management or joint production committees.
>
> It has been our experience that where the relationships between our union and management are on a sound and friendly basis, such committees are capable of doing many things that tend to make work more congenial, creative, and productive. Such committees, operating separately and apart from the grievance committee or stewards, are usually able to bring to the attention of management valuable ideas and suggestions from the individual workers

as to possible improvements in work methods and production processes.

Murray did not differ substantively with Golden over the need for "mutual respect and confidence" in labor-management relations but he was readier to resort to a strike, or strike threats, than Golden thought sensible, especially in view of the public reaction to "big labor" then building up in the press. Congress was exploring possibilities for compulsory arbitration, which was anathema to organized labor. In an attempt to curb "labor abuses," it adopted the Taft-Hartley Act of 1948, which imposed various restrictions on collective bargaining. Labor, Golden argued in a speech shortly after his retirement,

> is one of the most powerful and influential organized groups in our society. The conduct and behavior of its leaders and representatives at every level, the nature of its wage and other policies, the way its contractual obligations are met and administered affect in varying degrees almost everyone in our society. We must ever be aware that we are living in the present—not in the past. Our unions, after years of unremitting struggle, have won both extensive recognition and growing acceptance as legitimate and, indeed, necessary social institutions. As such, and in the language of those who are usually entrusted with the task of drafting legislation, they are today in contrast to an earlier period, "affected with a public interest." They cannot isolate themselves from other social groups and institutions, neither can they put themselves beyond or above the widely accepted moral and ethical standards prevailing in society today.
>
> Unions today are something more than instruments of protest against exploitation and unacceptable conditions of employment. They are instruments of representation

of the largest segment of our population—the wage and, indeed, increasingly, the salary earners.

Unions are large property owners and some have major financial investments. They have heavy contractual obligations and responsibilities. Their officers occupy positions of what amounts to public trust. For historical and other reasons, they should be more concerned with the well being of people than with the accumulation of profits or excessively large treasuries. . . .

In the heat of the earlier struggle to become established and gain recognition, it was perfectly natural that they would assume those who were not aligned with them in this effort were against them. If this attitude ever had any validity, it no longer exists. The unions have become well established, they have gained recognition, and a very large measure of institutional security.

It is evident to many that the time has arrived when they need to evaluate their own conduct, behavior and administration in the light of the realities of present-day conditions rather than in the light of historical conditions.

It is more important now perhaps than ever in the past that they be able to devise methods and programs designed to stimulate and make possible ever wider and more responsible participation by the members in their own union affairs. Programs designed to develop a wider understanding of the role of unions in a complex, interdependent industrial society are today of great necessity. There is a need for a wider realization and consciousness on the part of the officers and the members of the effect of union policies as a whole.

There is need, likewise, to evaluate current relations with management especially in the more recently organized manufacturing industries, and determine what can be done by the unions to improve the climate of relationships and to acquire a more positive and constructive role rather than continue to be a party of unrelenting opposition to all management proposals, practices and policies.

Golden's rather mild and inferential criticism of his former colleagues created a touch of frostiness in his relationship with Murray. At first, his resignation brought the two closer than they had been in the recent past. Murray urged him not to retire, talked about "the youth" of the union and the lack of experienced people to take Golden's place. No one on the executive board, he said, would do. Golden reminded him, as he noted in his diary entry of June 15, "one gets experience by doing—and making mistakes—and that was the way he and I had acquired our experience." Golden suggested West Coast director James Thimmes as a possible successor, saying that there were no doubt "scores of men in a union of 800,000 members who either were or could become competent." Golden offered to remain with the union on a part-time basis for a year, taking care of committee work and other nonadministrative activities. "Murray was most generous," Golden wrote in his diary, "insisting that my regular salary be continued for a year." Later, he insisted on providing Golden with an office.

Golden's resignation was not submitted until after the 1946 steel-union convention. Back in Solebury after the convention, he wrote in his diary on June 16:

> Our convention was the largest—too large—thus far held. 2700 delegates are just too many to constitute a deliberative assembly. But it provided a demonstration of the size which our union has attained and a forum for formulation of policies. It no doubt had a stimulating effect on the delegates and gave them a sense of power and strength.
>
> For the third time I acted as chairman of the Committee

on Constitutions. A number of important changes were recommended and adopted. My title was changed from assistant to the President to that of Vice President.

He was pleased by the change in his title, but that did not prevent him from handing in his resignation, over Murray's objections, at the July executive board meeting. Thimmes was named as his successor.

Murray was under considerable strain. That fall, Joe Germano, the powerful director of the steel union's Indiana-Illinois district, introduced a statement at the union's executive board that said, in effect, to paraphrase Golden, who wrote Joe Scanlon about the incident, that since there were people in the CIO who did not appreciate Murray, while there was no wish to tell him what to do, it was the steelworkers' feeling that he ought to devote more time to the steel union. In a private conversation with Golden, Murray indicated that he was indeed "pretty filled up" with the CIO presidency and intended to give it up. "No other man," *Business Week* reported on September 28, 1946, "has preserved anywhere near Murray's impartiality in the C.I.O.'s basic and bitter left-wing, right-wing fight." With the end of the war, the Communist line had changed from a superpatriotic united front to an anti-American, supermilitant antiemployer posture. Trade-union leaders who refused to conform were subjected to increasingly nasty attacks of all kinds. Murray, so far, had been exempted from leftwing criticism but he was feeling the strain. At the steel union board meeting, Murray declared his dislike of the Communists, but requested that no publicity be given to his statement.

Word of Murray's mood, however, did leak out. *Business Week*, among other publications reported that Murray was considering retirement from his CIO post. He told Golden that his (Golden's) resignation had brought home to him the necessity of taking things easier. Allan Haywood and Golden were cited in a *Business Week* story as possible CIO successors to Murray. Haywood was described as "fond of creature comforts," puckish and without great ambition. "As president of the CIO," the magazine's account continued, "he would be overshadowed by the larger, stronger personalities found in the leadership of some of the CIO's international unions." Golden, despite his retirement, was considered by *Business Week* to be the more serious replacement possibility. The magazine, however added, "he would not, on his own initiative, make a bid for the Murray job." Nothing in Golden's diary or in his voluminous correspondence indicates that he ever gave the question a moment's thought. As for Murray, he did not think long on it, apparently, and, indeed, seems to have been irritated at the rumors circulated in labor circles and leaked to the newspapers. Golden was given no opportunity to talk with Murray at the union's wage policy committee meeting in December. "In fact," Golden wrote Scanlon, "I only shook hands at the first day's meeting. He was pretty well shepherded by Pressman and McDonald." And perhaps sensitive to Communist-left criticism of American labor leaders' class collaboration, Murray went out of his way to direct his remarks at the meeting to Golden, saying that he [Murray] "was not among those who believed that any substantial part of management wanted to get along peacefully with the Union." Murray wound up with a heated peroration, declaring, "I do not want peace at any price." ("As if anyone had suggested that he did!" exclaimed Golden in a letter to Scanlon.)

The estrangement was seemingly temporary, for Murray kept Golden busy with a variety of assignments. He was asked to explore the possibility of industry-wide bargaining with various trade associations, to prepare a resolution on health and hospitalization for the 1946 CIO convention, and to continue serving on several governmental committees—the Federal Committee on Apprentice Training, the Labor-Management Advisory Committee to the U.S. Conciliation Service, and on the Advisory Committee to the Civil Service Commission. Golden also served on the CIO's Veterans Committee, addressed several Steelworker district conferences and filled speaking engagements before the American Hospital Association, the Conference of Business Economists and at Columbia University.

Though, as he phrased it, "I just lazed around," during the first few months following his retirement, Golden and Dora drove Olive to Antioch for the start of her sophomore term, visited the Scanlons in Mansfield, Ohio, on the way back, stopped in Pittsburgh for a while, driving to Conneault Lake for District Director John Grajciar's convention, and then back home to Solebury, where he finished up his share of a book he was writing with a neighbor, a Quaker farmer, P. Alston Waring.

The Goldens and Warings were neighbors in Solebury, and had been drawn together by a common interest in farming and in cooperatives. Mrs. Waring's family had farmed the area ever since the Quakers had first moved up the Delaware from Philadelphia back in the 1700s. Alston and Clint had worked together in organizing distributive cooperatives in the troubled thirties. Alston Waring also had been instrumental in organizing the Honey Hollow watershed into one of the nation's first soil-conservation areas, taking advantage of programs developed by the New Deal Agricultural Administration. Golden and Waring decided to write a book because they believed "that many wage earners in cities do not know a great deal about farmers and their problems, and that most farmers are unaware of the life of people whose income is in a pay envelope." Golden undertook the task of explaining the workers to farmers; Waring, that of explaining farmers to workers.

Together, they hoped to "build a more interdependent, coordinated and cohesive community in America" by bridging the gap between farmers and wage earners. "As we become involved in the social and cultural wreckage of war," they wrote, "and in the spiritual chaos of our times, there is for us the sustaining thought that new birth and life can come and will come from the ordinary people whose lives are rooted in America's struggle for a just and decent social order."

Soil and Steel reflects a number of Golden's major concerns —cooperative rather than adversary relationships, full employment as essential to abundance, and productivity as the key to progress. To do something about these concerns, Golden became increasingly active in the National Planning Association, a nonprofit, private organization headquartered in Washington, D.C. Founded in 1934 by a group of businessmen, farm experts and labor leaders, the association employed a staff of twenty-three to do the legwork for NPA's membership brain trust, a prestigious group that included H. Christian Sonne, NPA board chairman and president of Amsinck, Sonne and Company; Fowler McCormick, chairman of the board of International Harvester Company; Charles J. Symington of Symington-Gould Corporation; Beardsley Ruml, director of R. H. Macy & Company; pollster Elmer Roper; Allan B. Kline, president of the American Farm Bureau; CIO President Philip Murray and other business and labor leaders. Charlton Ogburn served as NPA's general counsel. As Golden jotted in his diary, "It [NPA] brings me into pleasant contact with other labor people and some of our more farsighted industrialists. It exercises a wholesome influence on the thinking of some of our leaders." Planning, a NPA statement declared, "is as necessary to a nation as to an individual or a business. But let national planning be the concern of all Americans rather than government alone."

This Golden firmly believed and he was convinced that

successful labor-management relations contributed to a fundamental involvement of the American people in the process of planning. Indeed, it was, for him, the very heart of democratic planning. Golden had observed over the years that newspapers headlined strikes but reported little of the day-to-day give-and-take between unions and management. He became convinced that if one wanted to know how to make collective bargaining work one must look at its successes and not its breakdowns. At the semiannual meeting of NPA trustees, on June 4, 1946, he proposed a study, one that would have far-reaching consequences for industrial relations in the United States over the succeeding decades. There was a need, he told the trustees, for a new approach to labor-management problems. "About every seven or eight years since 1876," he said, "the government through Congressional committees or presidentially appointed commissions, has been making inquiries into the causes of industrial conflict and strike. In my opinion, the time has come when, instead of looking into the causes of conflict that we know and hear so much about, we ought to try to discover how much peace there is and what makes peace.

"Conflict in industrial relationships," he continued, "is not a *normal* condition. Even in the present period I believe there are far, far more people producing than there are on strike. I suggest the desirability of launching an inquiry into the causes of industrial peace. I think a plan should be developed having for its objectives:

> First: the discovery and identification of a number of firms with reputedly good records of industrial relationships, and high productivity;
> Second: a study designed to reveal publicly 'how they got that way' or 'what makes such firms tick.'

"I think the NPA, composed as it is of industrialists, representatives of organized labor and agriculture, is the logical nongovernmental agency to launch and conduct such an inquiry.

"By an impartial, objective examination of the 'facts of life' surrounding the operation of even a few firms having what are believed to be outstanding records of good relationships with their organized employees, together with a record of high productivity, I am convinced much can be discovered and subsequently publicized, that will contribute to better relationships between labor and management generally and thereby a genuinely valuable service can be rendered by NPA to our nation."

In August 1946, at a two-day meeting in Princeton, New Jersey, the NPA Executive Committee, composed of H. Christian Sonne, Marion H. Hedges, Frank Altschul, Clinton S. Golden, Beardsley Ruml, Theodore W. Schultz, Thomas Roy Jones, William L. Batt, Robert Heller, Fowler McCormick, Elmer Roper and Charles E. Wilson, authorized exploratory work. A number of conferences were held by Golden and the NPA staff and, by December, they were confident that such a study would be of great and immediate value and that it would not duplicate work being done any other place in the country. The project was outlined by Golden to the full NPA Trustee and Committee membership at their annual joint meeting in Washington in December 1946, and received the unanimous endorsement of the association. The project was carried out under the direction of two special committees composed of both NPA members and nonmembers. The first was a Sponsorship Committee composed of forty national business and labor leaders. This committee was responsible for the broad policy questions raised by the study. A Technical Advisory Committee to oversee research, composed of twenty-six specialists in the field of labor-management relations, worked under the chairmanship of Golden. Charles R. Walker (director of research in Technology and Industrial Relations, Labor and Management Center, Yale University) and Joseph Scanlon (Industrial Relations Department of the Massachusetts Institute of Technology) served as co-directors of the project's staff.

Some five thousand key individuals in the labor-management field nominated nine hundred or so firms. Fourteen of these were chosen for intensive study, including Crown Zellerbach Corporation, the Pacific Coast pulp and paper industry, Libbey-Owens-Ford Glass Company, Hickey-Freeman Company, and Sharon Steel Corporation. The John Hay Whitney Foundation donated $60,000 for labor-peace research and the project was officially launched on June 18, 1947. The subsequent reports were widely used, especially for classroom work in industrial-relations courses, and became "models" for others to follow. What *Business Week* termed a "labor-peace pattern" threaded the various studies into a useful whole. Father Benjamin L. Masse, industrial relations editor of the Jesuit weekly *America*, in a review of the committee's work seven years and thirty studies later, spelled out the pattern. It was remarkably close to what Golden had always envisioned.

1. *Management fully accepted collective bargaining and the union as an institution.* This was not a negative attitude. Management let it be known that it considered the union an asset to the company. Though it did not always agree to a union shop, it invariably made the union feel secure. It scrupulously avoided any interference with the union's internal affairs.

2. *The union fully accepted private ownership of the business and the role of management in administering it.* In every case the union recognized that the welfare of its members was dependent on the efficient and profitable operation of the firm.

3. *The mutual relations of the union and the employer were characterized by trust and confidence.* There were no ideological differences between them. In their dealings with one another, they studiously avoided a legalistic approach. There were no theoretical discussions about "rights"—either about the right of management to manage or the right of the union to job-control. Both parties were conscious of their rights but preferred to deal with specific problems in the concrete as they arose.

4. *Labor-management consultation and sharing of information were highly developed.* This went on both informally on a day-to-day basis and through formal means such as joint committees empowered to deal with a wide range of subjects. Management regularly conferred with the union before announcing changes, even though, under the contract, it had the right to make the changes unilaterally.

5. *Grievances were settled speedily on a flexible and informal basis.* The grievance machinery was used creatively, to ward off future gripes as well as to settle present ones. It became an informal vehicle for the friendly discussion of all sorts of questions.

6. *The union was strong, responsible and democratic.* It did not function either as a "protest" organization or as a "partner" of management. Rather it envisaged its role as one of "policing" the company in the interests of its members.

7. *Management recognized the difference between a trade union and a business organization.* It recognized, that is, the "political" character of the relationship between union leaders and the rank and file. This saved it from many disillusionments.

8. *Management placed great stress on personnel administration.* It rated the personnel department on the

same level as production and finance. In its dealings with workers it showed a concern for their welfare and a recognition of their needs and aspirations.

At the end of 1946, Golden confided to his diary, "I am disturbed by the conduct of some of our labor organizations and their leaders. They are using their newly acquired but vast power no more wisely than have some of our industrialists in the past. Unless they learn to use it wisely they will, I fear, weaken if not destroy their organizations." Increasingly, he placed his hopes on education. As he wrote in *The Dynamics of Industrial Democracy*, "Speculate for a moment on the effect of unions sending a certain number of their officers and staff members to a resident university for a school year, say, of eight months. Think of the effect of corporations sending their industrial-relations and operating officials to the same place. Here both could exchange experiences and ideas in an environment of inquiry; they could listen to talks by theoreticians and practical men in industry and labor. The union leaders and management officials would be reinvigorated by the change in environment and inspired by the new associations. The younger generation would learn from association with the older. The people who have a vast store of knowledge and experience stored in their heads could come here and unfold it. Such an undertaking, which admittedly is urgently needed, might play an important role in opening an entirely new era of American prosperity and democracy."

Much of labor education is, as it needs be, practical, a range of "how-to-do-its" from conduct of a meeting to grievance-handling and contract interpretation. Some labor history, a little cultural activity, a bit of current economic thought and a ladling of union policy, and there you have the average trade-union education program. Golden thought this inadequate, as he made plain to a group of adult educators at a

Philadelphia conference in mid-1946. He expressed his agreement with philosopher Alfred North Whitehead, who said, " 'There can be no adequate technical education which is not liberal and no liberal education which is not technical.' I should like to point out that in the field of management more and more attention is being given to what is generally referred to as liberal arts education. Management is evidently becoming aware of the inadequacies of too extensive specialized education of its own personnel. It has been quite natural that up to the present a great deal of the workers' educational programs and effort has been directed toward improving the quality of leadership and administration of the unions. But in this field, too, there can be such a thing as too much emphasis on specialization. I think that in many areas of endeavor the time has come when there can be a judicious intermingling of the cultural with the technical and vocational."

On his retirement, Golden had been offered part-time or full-time positions at both M.I.T. and Harvard. "At my time of life," he wrote in his diary on May 5, 1946, "when the desire to take things easier becomes more insistent, these offers tend to make me feel there is a field of usefulness which I can engage in that may help in some small way to show how men can live and work together with a minimum of conflict." Golden chose Harvard, in part out of a fear of overshadowing his former colleague and close friend, Joe Scanlon, who taught at M.I.T., and in part because his old friend Sumner Slichter had succeeded in establishing a Trade Union Program there as an "opposite number" to Harvard's famed Advance Management Program, which offered highly concentrated courses for younger executives who had demonstrated potential for future advancement in their careers. Golden had helped Slichter secure trade-union support for fellowships at the Harvard graduate school and had consulted with him on the kind of program best suited for young unionists who had shown signs of developing into labor leaders of the future. In the fall of 1946, he joined the Harvard Graduate School of Business faculty as a visiting lecturer on labor problems.

The former mine-boy had indeed come a long way. He was now a national figure, not a household name perhaps, but nonetheless of that cluster of men and women whose activities and thinking were of great consequence. He was urged to support a variety of causes. As he remarked in a letter to A. J. Muste, "I've tried to be good natured about serving on various committees. . . . [But] It has got me into no end of difficulties and misunderstandings." Nonetheless, he did join Muste's 1946 appeal for a "Christmas Amnesty" for World War II conscientious objectors. He also joined Governor Herbert Lehman and Clarence E. Pickett, among others, in urging President Truman to increase food shipments to famine-stricken areas around the world, implementing a program shaped by Professors John D. Black of Harvard and Theodore W. Schultz of Chicago. He became a sponsor of the National Council Against Conscription, co-chaired by Mordecai W. Johnson and Alonzo F. Myers. At Harvard, Golden hoped to find a haven where he might work quietly for fruitful labor-management cooperation, the necessary foundation for postwar peace and prosperity. Soon, however, he would receive a call from his government to serve freedom overseas by helping our war-torn allies. There was a new mission in Golden's life.

Mission to Greece

AT THE CLOSE of World War II, Clint Golden was asked if he would become a labor advisor to the American military government in either Germany or Japan. He turned the offer down, largely for the same reason he later gave for his retirement from the United Steelworkers—ill health. He was consulted, however, on the selection of others for the task. As he wrote Reinhold Niebuhr, the noted theologian, then a vice-chairman of the American Association for a Democratic Germany, "I have been assisting others in trying to get some civilian labor advisors placed in key positions with the American Military Government in Germany with the expectation that they can be helpful in influencing the Military Occupation authorities to encourage the emergence of leadership for a democratic labor movement in Germany." When Varian Fry, Secretary of the American Labor Conference on International Affairs, reported that German trade union and Social Democratic survivors were having difficulty in communicating with comrades in exile and desperately needed links with friends in the labor movements of Great Britain and the United States, Golden reassured Fry that Joseph Keenan, David Saposs and Paul Porter, who were all enroute to Germany to serve in the American military government as labor advisors, "had contact with some German refugees in this country who were identified with the labor movement in pre-Hitler days." In discussions with all three, Golden added, "the thoughts I expressed and which were readily accepted by those going over were very much in line with your memorandum."

In their efforts to help European workers reorganize their unions, which were destroyed by the Fascists and Nazis, the Americans soon ran up against Soviet-dominated Communists seeking to control worker organizations. United States policy-makers recognized the importance of trade-union assistance in the democratic development of European unions. David Morse, a graduate of Rutgers and of Harvard Law School and general counsel to the National Labor Relations Board and later director-general of the International Labor Organization (ILO), joined the Labor Department as assistant secretary of labor for international affairs. On December 12, 1946, he created a Trade Union Advisory Committee on International Labor Questions.* It was, as Morse later noted, the only place at the time where the various factions in American labor could meet officially in a joint undertaking.

Great Britain announced that it would no longer be able to meet her financial commitments in Greece. On the verge of economic collapse, that country was threatened by Communist guerrillas. To head off Communist totalitarianism, the United States devised an aid program in which civilians—the tax expert from Chicago, the agriculturalist from Texas, the public-health doctor from Washington—would work directly with Greek counterparts to develop democratic institutions in troubled Greece. That aid program would become the model for the European recovery program that followed. Secretary of State Dean Acheson gave a succinct account of the state of

* The committee was composed of: David Dubinsky, George Meany, Robert J. Watt, and Matthew Woll of the AFL; James Carey, Clinton Golden, Frank Rosenblum and Michael Ross of the CIO; Thomas J. Harkens of the Railroad Brotherhoods; and A. E. Lyon of the Railway Labor Executives Association.

affairs in Greece to the Trade Union Advisory Committee at its meeting of March 18: Greece was only about six weeks from total economic collapse, Acheson told the unionists. A memorandum from Michael Ross to CIO president Murray summed it up:

> [Acheson] stated that Greek military forces were insufficient to maintain order; that her financial and economic position was deteriorating; that her governmental administration was demoralized and breaking down. If help is not given, civil war would increase and the Communists, as the only strongly organized opposition group, would emerge in control. If Greece falls into the Soviet orbit, Turkey must follow. If Greece and Turkey go, the whole Middle East and on to the Far East will be endangered.
>
> Therefore, the United States should extend three types of aid.
>
> (1) Arms and Surplus Military Stores.
>
> (2) Loans for Economic Reconstruction.
>
> (3) Personnel to supervise the above and to reorganize the governmental apparatus.
>
> He stated that the internal Greek problem was not one that the United Nations could deal with. They were handling the border incidents which the Charter requires them to do.
>
> The AFL members of the committee all expressed unqualified approval, basing themselves on the need to oppose Soviet Russia and suppress Communists. Mr. Golden expressed himself as impressed by Mr. Acheson's exposition and on the need to help the Greek people. Mr. Carey agreed and went on to suggest that the Greek people should be offered something other than Communism or Royalist-Fascism—that is, they should have a

chance at democracy. He cited the position of the British TUC [Trade Union Congress] as a reason to believe that the Greek government should be liberalized (on this last point he was supported by the AFL).

Mr. Ross reiterated the above arguments and gave as a further example of the trade union point of view the fact that at the last ILO Conference in Montreal in September 1946, the Workers Group unanimously rejected the Greek workers' delegate because he was a government-picked man and not a workers' representative.

In conclusion (though there was, of course, no organizational commitment) the three CIO representatives agreed that speedy help should be extended to Greece and at the same time, that the advice given and policies and procedures advocated by the United States personnel sent in should be such as to encourage the development of democratic freedom, including the reconstruction of the free Greek Trade Union movement as Greek economic recovery takes place.

At the March meeting, Golden announced that he was resigning to accept a position at Harvard. Meanwhile, the government proceeded with the organization of the mission to Greece. It was to be small, with technicians in the fields of agriculture, finance, reconstruction, and labor. In addition to the labor technicians, however, it was felt that there should be a labor advisor solely responsible to the chief of the mission, Dwight Griswold. There was some discussion at a May 13 meeting of the Trade Union Advisory Committee and general agreement that Golden was the right man for the job. Acheson thought the choice excellent and Secretary of Commerce Averell Harriman, who had known Golden for many years and greatly respected his ability, was asked to approach him.

Golden declined at first, saying he did not like the idea of leaving Harvard. Harriman, however, called a second time, telling Golden that he was the only person acceptable to both the AFL and the CIO and that if he did not take the post his refusal would probably foreclose opportunities of other unionists to serve their country abroad in the future. Harriman also said that he had talked with Dean Donald K. David of the Harvard Business School who said that Golden would be granted a leave of absence if he accepted the appointment. After further conversations with Griswold and Thomas Holland of the Department of State, Golden said he would accept if his commitment was for no longer than six months and if he could have as his assistant a younger man with whom he had worked on the War Production Board, Alan Strachan. Born in England in 1903, a toolmaker who emigrated to the United States in 1926, Strachan had been active in the organization of the United Auto Workers and a leader in the anti-Communist caucus of the union. After serving with the government during the war, where he first met Golden, the former auto worker became Washington representative of his union.

"Frankly," Golden later told Margaret Mary Davies, secretary to the two trade unionists in Greece, "I did not expect that these conditions would be met, but to my surprise they were." Golden went to Washington for briefing but discovered that there was very little information available aside from some data from the general political reporting of the embassy in Athens. Dr. Kyriakos Varvaressos of the International Bank for Reconstruction and Development, however, was most helpful. He urged Golden to meet and talk with the rank-and-file as well as with contenders of office in the about-to-be-organized General Confederation of Greek Labor. Shortly after his arrival in Greece, Golden summarized the goals of the labor program for a visiting congressional committee:

The labor division is directed toward:

1. Aiding in the development of conditions favorable to orderly collective bargaining and the establishment of machinery designed to aid in promoting sound, peaceful and constructive labor-management relations;

2. Aiding in the development of a sound wage and salary structure designed to promote industrial efficiency and equitable wage-price relationships;

3. Assisting in the development of training programs designed to improve the quality of labor organization administration as well as the skills necessary for the reconstruction and expansion of the Greek economy;

4. Improving management and administration of the extensive social insurance and labor legislation now incorporated in Greek law.

Before sailing from New York to Piraeus with Dora and Olive on August 15, 1947, on the S.S. New Hellas, Golden wrote Meyer Bernstein, "Took the last of the inoculations yesterday. I have reacted pretty violently to them but they have not bothered Dora or Olive. After all this I expect to be puncture proof even against left wing bullets." At sea, he reported smooth sailing. "Dora however had some difficulty for a few days as did Olive, but they have gotten over it now. I have had no difficulties." Theodore Sinadinos, a Greek journalist with impressive credentials as president of the Society of Playwrights and general manager of the National Opera, interviewed Golden through an interpreter for feature articles in the Greek newspapers. The New Hellas had to anchor in the bay, for the piers and docks at Piraeus were still "bombed out." The Goldens were put up at the Acropole Palace, and the first person they saw at a reception given by the labor attaché was Golden's old friend, Mrs. Gifford Pinchot. She told the Goldens that she had reservations at the Acropole but was told that she could not have them "because of the expected arrival of a very important American—a Mr. Golden."

Golden's first letter from Greece to Meyer Bernstein inaugurated an extensive correspondence, excerpted below, that gives an inside picture of the trade-union mission.

Acropole Palace Hotel, Athens
Saturday P.M. *September 5, 1947*

DEAR MEYER:

No. 4. Churchill street is a huge building made available by the Greeks for our use. I am temporarily tucked away behind an UNRRA [United Nations Relief and Rehabilitation Administration.] desk fashioned out of packing box lumber in the legal department! I have a fine woman secretary from Seattle by the name of Margaret Davies who was previously in Greece with the Plebiscite Commission. . . .

I have met most of the top leaders in the Greek Confederation of Labor. They are an interesting and picturesque lot but some of them I suspect are pretty slippery politicians. One of them—Lascaris—of the Railwaymens Union, is trying to get a visa to leave for the States to attend some meeting of the Railroad organizations there. He has a Van Dyke beard, handle bar mustachios and is one of the old Socialist leaders in the labor movement here. But what a movement! Prior to the Metaxas dictatorship there were 600 known Unions. This number grew to 1400 in 1940 and to presently about 2200 completely automonous local unions. But the total membership is no greater than when they were 600 unions! During one of the many governments they have had since the liberation they had a communist Minister of Labor. (Incidently there are only 40 separate Ministeries in the government.) This genius discovered a forgotten law that permitted any 7 persons regardless of occupational similarity to apply to the government for a charter for a Union. The result is that scores of Unions of orphan children, blood donors, retired dancing instructors, retired railroad workers, postmen and pensioners of various sorts were formed at first by the Commies in order to gain votes in the national conventions of the Greek Confederation of Labor (GSEE). To this was added a process of fragmentation of the larger unions. To illustrate a Union of 500 members in a meat packing plant would be broken down into 10 unions of 50 members each. In this way 10 votes would be gained in the convention against 1 for a Union of 500 members.

When these tactics of the communists became apparent then the "rights" or non-communists used the same methods and tactics to fight the communists. Another result is that there are 44 Unions of dock workers alone in Salonika and I am told even more in Piraeus! Presently all these "unions" are identified with some sort of a political party of which there must be at least a dozen varieties ranging from the avowed communists to the extreme rightists. Another Greek law permits any disgruntled member to file a petition with the Ministry of Labor alleging corruption, inefficiency or some other malpractice whereupon the Ministery intervenes into the internal affairs of the Union with the result that the Courts usually throw out the elected officers and appoint "provisional officers" while the Ministery of Labor is so completely occupied with "interventions" that it has no time for mediation, concilliation or carrying on training or other functions. And don't overlook the fact that I am charged by the State Department in the U.S. with the responsibility for "establishing a free and democratic labor movement in Greece concerned primarily with the attainment of economic objectives!" Even tho your prayers go no higher than the ceiling of your apartment, please pray for me at least twice daily. And this after only a week here! Now for some less serious news.

Mrs. Pinchot is here with Dr. Evelyn (?) Burns a professor

at Columbia and, if I am not mistaken, an authority on social security legislation. Mrs. P——— is determined to go into the mountains to the north and look over the guerillas! . . .

AMAG. 4, W. Churchill Street
Athens, Greece
September 14, 1947

DEAR MEYER:

Today our newspaper publisher friends, the Bartolis, accompanied by an interpreter called for us in their Chrysler and drove us out into the country about 27 kilometers to the small village of Marcopoulo with a population of about 5,000 in the center of the vineyards and Olive groves north of Athens. The peasants were gathering their grapes and on burro backs, in carts and an occasional truck were bringing them to the wine presses. We saw them tramped upon by barefooted men with their trousers rolled up to their thighs. The grapes piled high in a sort of marble tank. As they were tramped upon the juice ran down into other marble vats below the floor. From these it was pumped out into casks which in turn were transported either by truck, cart or donkey back to the winery where the fermentation process began.

News of our presence spread rapidly throughout the community and we were shortly invited to visit the local cooperative winery and electric power generating station the latter being the only one in Greece owned and operatively cooperatively. A weatherbeaten peasant showed up who seemed to live in the most modern house in the community and whose name was Harry Orphan. He had worked for the Corn Products Refining Co., near Chicago for 12 years prior to World War I. He had gone into the army during the war and had fought in France. After the war he returned to Greece and when the soldiers bonus was paid he used the money he told us to build the best house in town. At any rate he could speak English very well and he was to be our guide. He first explained how he acquired the name of "Orphan." It seems that one of his ancestors who was a widower participated in a battle at the Acropolis 100 years or more ago. He had two sons. When he lay dying of wounds he asked another soldier to take care of the two boys. This they did but they came to be known as "the Orphans" when they were taken to Marcopoulo. All their male decendents have been known by that name. The cooperative winery proved to be a modern and completely mechanized plant where human hand or foot never came in contact with the grapes or wine once they were unloaded. Harry explained that in 1912 a "professor" had come to the village to expound the philosophy of co-operation. His efforts met with success because 90% of the people were poor. The winery has started with a small hand press and a cask. It was a clean and most impressive plant which had not only helped the peasants but had also made possible the building of electric generating and distributing cooperative. Every tiny peasants' cottage evidently had electric lights altho as I examined the wiring, I am sure it would never have met the building code requirements of Pittsburgh for instance! But then there is lots of stone and marble and practically no wood that can be used for lumber. All the cottages are made of stone, cement, bricks or marble with walls incredibly thick with little danger of fire. This serves to keep out the intense dry summer heat. Incidently they have had no rain in this village since last February and do not expect any until December.

In the office of the coop we were shown a picture of the "professor" founder along with a medal given him at an exposition at Salonika, a wallet with a few drachma that he had when he died 6 months ago. This constituted almost a "shrine" as Harry Orphan reverently described it. There was a modern, up to date laboratory spotlessly clean where the chemist analyzed the wine, the water and whatever else chemists do in that sort of a community. We were told that the Germans had a division camped in the vicinity which were trained and then sent to Africa. They did no damage we were told for two reasons; one was that the general was a man named Bausch of the Bausch-Lomb family who was billited at Harry Orphans modern home and who privately told Harry that he hated Hitler and all that warlords stood for and was in general a "gentleman" and secondly; the diesel engine and power generating machinery were built by Siemens of Germany with their name prominently displayed on all the castings and housings and the Germans were told that the equipment of the coop belonged still to Siemens!

After the tour of the coops and the village we were invited to a peasants home for the noon meal. We were treated to roast pork roasted in a huge brick oven in the yard and also pork en casserole both of which were delicious. French fried potatoes fried in a skillet half filled with olive oil and heated over a fire of twigs in a hearth or fireplace. For desert we had a delicious cheese made from sheep's milk, a pudding made from the juice of grapes, flour and pistachio nuts, wonderful grapes and ripe figs picked off the nearby trees and of course the inevitable coffee.

It was a great day for us and a fine opportunity to see how the great mass of common people live in this poor country with abundances only of sunshine and stone and wonderful mountain views. All work in the stony, dry field, men, women and children. The donkey is the most valued means of transport. Their only complaint was the fear of the guerillas and the threat of ever recurring wars. . . .

Will you try to get in touch with someone at the Cooperative League of America in New York preferably E. R. Bowen who I think is the secretary and see if they have not got some literature preferably illustrated with pictures that could be sent to Harry Orphan, Marcopoulo, Greece? He told me they were completely out of touch with the coop movement and it would mean so much to them. He can speak and read but cannot write English. . . .

AMAG
September 23, 1947

DEAR MEYER:

As you can see almost every sort of an antiquated car here as well as the latest models. Jordens, Peerless and the first Model A Fords still going strong along with Austins and other foreign makes. Gas is 55¢ legal rate but is rationed to 2 gallons per week. You can get it on the black market for $4.00 a gallon. Figuring finance here makes you dizzy. I received an expense check for $88.25 the other day which I had to convert into drachma. I received 441,000 drachma mostly in 20,000 notes. If I had converted it in the black market (which we are forbidden under penalty of dismissal to do) it would have been 30% more! If there is one thing the Greeks *don't* believe in it is *their currency* and I don't blame them much. The bus and street car conductors and newsboys carry their change in a satchel. There are no metal coins whatever. I saw a fellow carrying one of these "get weighed for a penny" scales the other day. Because there are no coins available he solicits customers by bringing the scale to them and is paid in paper money. You can give the enclosed 1,000 drachma note to Mike Kallas and tell him that it is the price of a glass of darn good Greek beer produced by a Bavarian turned Greek whose name is Mr. Fix. Mrs. Pinchot and Dr. Evelyn Burns are giving the Mission and military authorities constant headaches by their excursions into dangerous and sometimes forbidden territory in a jeep. Mrs. P——— seems to think the military are a bunch of "sissies." She thinks the government ought to arm the peasants and she is sure if they did so they would make short work of the commie guerillas. I suspect the reason the government does not follow her advice is that they expect once the peasants disposed of the guerillas they would train their muskets on the government!

AMAG
September 30, 1947

DEAR JOE [Scanlon]:

The labor movement here came into being as a result of legislation and almost ever since its inception in 1914 has been primarily concerned with achieving its objectives through politics and legislation. There are elaborate labor laws and social legislation which an improverished country like this can hardly afford at this time. Much of the legislation is ignored and little is enforced. There is an appalling lack of confidence in government and of course an almost psychopathic fear of the communists, guerilla, Russians and the countries to the north. Almost half of the national budget is allocated to the military and naval establishment and the budget is terribly out of balance—to the tune of something like 1½ *trillion* drachmas. There are about 90,000 people on the government payroll and 40,000 would be too many if they worked at 50% of efficiency. You cannot get anything done without securing at least the signatures of a dozen out of the 44 "Ministers" that make up the "government."

Most of the people are wretchedly poor but a few thousand of the very wealthy display their wealth with an arrogant disregard even of the consequences to themselves. The workers and peasants are the most warm hearted, hospitable and generous people I ever met. They ask for so very, very little and are so patient in the face of the most irritating and difficult circumstances.

When I first arrived I was visited by a delegation representing the "Union of Short Military Boot Makers." They were a picturesque group led by an old patriarch with huge mustachios. Before 1940 the Greek army boots were made by hand and this gave employment to 3,000. The Bank of Greece would purchase the hides and distribute them to the little handicraft cooperatives. The members of such would gather in some sort of a building and there cut and sew by hand according to standard design. The Bank assumed the responsibility for financing, quality and delivery to the army. This work was discontinued in 1940 because they could buy machine made boots cheaper. They have had no work since where they could use their skills. The Industrial Revolution you see had caught up with even Greece. These poor people eke out some sort of an existence by begging, selling cigarettes, grapes or peddling something or other. But they want to preserve and use their ancient skills.

I set to work on the theory that they should be employed at productive even tho uneconomic labor. If they were the communist propaganda would have much less appeal and they could regain some measure of their self respect while efforts were being made to develop other employment opportunities. Luckily R. E. Gilmor, president of Sperry Gyroscope an old friend of mine, showed up to serve as director of the industry division. He readily agreed with me that it was better to have these people at work than starving or being on meager relief. We then got a General Booth who arrived and who was one of Jimmy Doolittle's raiders interested in working out an arrangement with the Greek Army to take at least a part of the boots these folks could make. I was beginning to feel we were going to get something going until tonight when a tired and weary General came in to report that during the day while rumaging about the docks and warehouses, he had stumbled upon *one million*, four hundred thousand pairs of military boots and shoes which had been forgotten after they were unloaded from UNRRA ships two years or so ago. We have no where near typewriters enough and had sent a man to see if some could not be rounded up among army surplus in Germany. Booth discovered 2500 new Royals in one of the warehouses this afternoon that no one knew were there. Sometime ago, 23,400 large size horse collars and 11,000 sets of heavy duty harnesses were found. And about the biggest critter they have here is a poor little old donkey! These were also UNRRA supplies!

I was asked to prepare a section of a speech the Prime Minister is going to make shortly and which will deal with the labor situation here. I was rather happily surprised to learn tonight that he has accepted it and it will be incorporated in his talk. I wish I could understand Greek and listen to it when he makes it over the radio . . .

Alan Strachan is proving to be a very useful assistant. He is putting in a good deal of time in helping to develop a training program. No skilled workers have been developed here in the past 7 years and it is essential that the process not be delayed longer. . . .

AMAG
October 10, 1947

DEAR JACK [Lever]:

. . . We operate on a pretty primitive basis. No stenographer, an ancient typewriter held together with wires and a hairpin or two. A freeze has been placed on additional personnel and the Labor Division consists of two men and a woman clerk-secretary! Today we are advised that the Greek Confederation of Labor will call a general strike between the 14th and the 21st unless some positive action is taken on their wage demands which have been pending for months. I am having a hell of a time trying to convince Griswold and others both in the Mission and in government that action is necessary and that they can never stabalize their currency unless they have a national wage-price policy geared to it. . . .

So far I do not feel that I have been able to contribute very much here. These poor devils need some leadership which the government ought to but does not, provide. They need a well thought out long range program with some attainable goals outlined and dramatized in such a manner as to provide some inspiration and show them how to regain their self respect. But it is an awful job to get really at the job of doing this. Governmental bureaucracies whether Greek or American just are not geared to get necessary things done. . . .

AMAG
October 11, 1947

DEAR DAVE [Morse]:

. . . In the meantime the situation is further aggravated by the fact that our public administration experts have insisted on the discharge of 15,000 civil servants without much chance of their getting other employment. The same experts just before my arrival made an "adjustment" of the civil servants wage demands by granting what is supposed to be a 20% increase but at the same time insisted on increasing the hours of work from about 30 to 40, eliminating all overtime and other extras that helped to add up needed take home pay. Now, according to the Union representatives of this group after they have received their first pay under the new arrangement they are allegedly receiving some 20% less than the pre "adjustment" pay or "take home."

What is to me indicated as necessary is an examination of prevailing "free" or black market wage payment practices.

These exist because according to Greek law which no one observes, there is supposed to be both "legal" minimum and maximum rates of pay. These have no relation whatever to the realities. Employers are aware of the absurdities of the "legal rates" and one prominent employer told me the workers could by no means exist on the legal rates and therefore he granted them "loans" each week that mounted to triple the "legal" rate and periodically wrote off the loans as "bad debts"!

If an examination of the actual wage payment practice is made the results should be examined in relation to the best obtainable information as to living costs. On the basis of this a new level of wages should be established and a wage-price policy announced that would in effect stabilize both at a certain level and then permit wage increases only as a result of collective bargaining over the distribution of increased productivity. Informally leaders of the Confederation of Labor and the Federation of Greek Industries which by the way is *not* a counterpart of the NAM, agree in principle as to the desireability of this approach altho they differ in some slight but not irreconciable extent as to detail. I have been doing my utmost for weeks to try to get Griswold to put the pressure on the Greek government to take the leadership in using this approach. Because of the curious position he and the Mission is in with relation both to the American Embassy and the Greek Government he was unwilling until yesterday and then under the threat of a general strike to take any action. . . .

Last night, however, he persuaded the Prime Minister to appoint a committee consisting of the Ministers of Coordination, National Economy, Finance, Labor and Transport to meet with Eugene Clay our Economic Advisor, R. E. Gilmor, chief of the Industry Division and myself on Monday next (the 13th) to explore the possibilities of "doing something"! Between the inertia of the Greek governmental leaders and functionaries and the unwillingness of our chief to move into the situation and provide some leadership it is pretty discouraging to say the least. . . .

The officers of the Confederation of Labor are a decent crowd I find and most cooperative. They even asked that I act as a mediator in the present situation and promised to do anything I asked or suggested! They are classified by our politically minded Embassy "experts" as "moderate reformists" or "right wingers" but to me they are decent, down to earth trade unionists anxious to work increasingly in the economic field and be freed of the judicial and governmental controls under which they are now operating . . .

AMAG
October 12, 1947

DEAR MEYER:

. . . We had a chance to see at pretty close range (the guerillas engaged in an action only 10 miles from here a few nights ago) how their foreign policy works out in a country like this and there has been a tremendous shift in sentiment against them and all their works here in recent weeks.

One of our agricultural division people had been up north last week. When he returned he reported how a unit of the "democratic" (communist) military had come into a peasant village one day with a plentiful supply of gold sovereigns and bought up all the peasants crops at generous margins above what they could get elsewhere. The peasants were happy and put on a festival to celebrate their good fortune. The guerillas danced with the girls, etc. The next day they came back heavily armed and forcibly took 17 young men from the village to put in their ranks. The day following they made these recruits attack a nearby village where they were known, shoot some of the peasants, burn the houses etc., in order that they could be charged with crime and rebellion and thus keep them in the "democratic army" because fear of punishment if they left. This diabolical practice is used extensively and of course creates terrible social discord, enmities and hatreds and even tears families apart. . . .

Our Labor Division is destined I fear to consist of only two men and a woman. An awful lot of things that we were told in Washington have proved to me just not so and the matter of modestly enlarging our staff is one of them. Right now the personnel of the Mission consists of about 275 Americans all told and about 380 Greeks and we are told a *freeze* has been placed on new hirings and some of the Greeks will be laid off. . . .

The Army Engineers have completely taken over this hotel —the Acropole Palace and we have been notified to get out. All the other Mission people have already left but they graciously permitted us to remain until November 1. We think we have rented a place—an apartment—for $360.00 per month plus $60.00 for the two servants we are required to take over plus another $60.00 for electricity, water, heat, etc. But the dear old State Department will have to pay the bill for that is what they promised to do and they either do it or provide us with return passage in a hurry! We will be able to get our food at the commissary at prices lower than in the States but life for Americans in Greece is by no means too pleasant. . . .

October 28, 1947

DEAR MEYER:

. . . I am kept very busy with work mainly of trying to formulate something that can be called a "national wage policy." There has been great pressure for wage increases since the first of the year. The Unions have been put off first by the government telling them to wait until the Porter Mission came and then when nothing happened, they were told to wait until AMAG arrived. The least little report or rumor of an unfavorable nature will cause prices here to rise. Our budget balances as bookkeepers had a vision of any wage increase at all interfering with their efforts to balance the Greek budget. And in the main they are such advanced (?) thinkers that they believe the *only* thing that causes prices to rise *is wages!*

In the chaos and confusion that has reigned here since the beginning of the war, no reliable statistics or economic data has been accumulated. The Bank of Greece, a state institution and a bank of issue similar to our Federal Reserve, by some methods of calculation, claims that the cost of living has increased 213 times over pre war. It so happens that during the Metaxas dictatorship Unions and employers were literally compelled to enter into collective agreements. Such were published and appear to be the only thing in the past that can be referred to in formulating decisions relating to wages. In those days the dictatorship established a minimum of 58 drachmas daily for common unskilled labor and a minimum of 130 drachmas for the highest paid workers with gradations of course at about 5 drachmas each between. No maximums for any category were set.

Under the threat of a general strike to be called no later than October 21 a national wage policy committee was set up following a speech by the Prime Minister on October 14 which included a few paragraphs that I wrote. The committee consisted of representatives of the Ministery of Labor, the Federation of Greek Industries and the Greek Confederation of Labor with R. E. Gilmore, chief of our Industry Division (in private life, president of the Sperry Gyroscope Co., and an old friend) and I acting as technical advisors.

Some time during one of the several inflations that have taken place a governmental order placed the 5 Dr. prewar minimum wage at 5,000 Dr. It did not set any other minimums above that figure. Prices have gone up so much that very few employers actually paid the "legal" minimum of 5,000 but resorted to all sorts of subterfuges to get around it. . . .

At the present time by an annual ministerial decree, the workers are given the equivalent of 25 days pay at Xmas and 15 days pay at Easter. This practice has begun since liberation and did not exist prior to the war. In trying to devise "multipliers" for the pre-war wage categories, we have to make allowance for the fact that they get now 40 days pay which are not worked. At any rate I think we will come up with something in the shape of a national policy that will provide some adjustments; will give both labor and employers some measure of participation into the formulation of economic policies; perhaps get the essentials embodied into a national collective agreement; have an extended rationing and some sort of a price control plan limited perhaps to the basic necessities of life and a few other things that will begin to put the labor-industry-government relations on a different basis and pave the way for a new day in democratic industrial practices. . . .

Alan Strachan is doing a good job. He is handling the job of getting translations of the social insurance and labor laws, advising the AMAG contractors on wage rates and making himself very useful indeed. So for a "two man and one woman" department we manage to be both busy and useful . . .

The guerilla situation I think is worse than when we came. Nothing of a very permanent or lasting nature can be accomplished in my judgment until there is internal peace thro the ending of the civil war. That cannot come until the northern borders are sealed or the communists give up. Here great hopes are placed on actions of the UN. But unless the Russians change their tactics it will take more than resolutions and debates to bring peace to this poor country . . .

AMAG
November 9, 1947

DEAR MEYER:

. . . After a lot of hard work we have made some very significant progress here in the labor field the past week. Out of the efforts of our National Wage Policy Committee* have come the first national collective agreements freely negotiated since the pre-Metaxas dictatorship period. One covers what they describe here as "workers" which roughly means other than permanent employees and the other covers salaried "employees." New minimum wage and salary classifications are set forth and assurance is provided that price increases will not result therefore. There has been some complaint about the 15% differential for the provinces outside Athens-Piraeus (Arrica) and Salonika and not everyone was happy that the minimum was set 11,000 drachma for common labor but most people think it is a very significant advance in the labor and industrial relations field . . .

I have written a rather long letter to both Phil and Bill Green about the significance of these agreements and asked them to cable congratulations and encouragement to the Greek Confederation of Labor. If they do it will mean much because they feel so out of touch with the labor movements of other countries . . .

I have also persuaded the government to consult with the leaders of the labor movement "on all economic problems of direct concern to the workers." To begin with this has been

* Members of the tripartite wage policy committee were: Chr. Katsambas, a textile manufacturer, Elias Eliopoulos, Director of the Federation of Greek Industries, representing employers; John Patsantzis, general secretary of the Greek Confederation of Labor; John Kalomiros, a member of the confederation's secretariat, who represented labor; and Director-General Pavlakis, Malestas and Apostolakis, permanent civil servants of the Ministery of Labor, who represented government. Pavlakis served as presiding officer.

translated into the first action ever taken by the government in formally requesting the advice of the Greek Confederation of Labor on plans for price control and rationing of the basic food elements which are olive oil, bread, flour products, beans, peas, lentils and other dried vegetables, fuel, etc. They will also be consulted by the Currency Control Committee which consists of American and British representatives along with the Greeks and which has control over the issuance of credit and currency. They are all quite elated over this recognition and new status but I am a bit afraid they are rather bewildered by it all. I shall try to provide them with some guidance and I think they will respond and measure up very well . . .

R. E. Gilmor the chief of our industry division, has worked closely with me in all this effort. He has been with me 100% all thro this and has been of inestimable aid in getting the employers to give their full cooperation. I think he and I work together more closely than do any other members of the Mission. We are what is known here as the "Golden-Gilmor Front" and I rather feel that we are beginning to gain a few adherents to our viewpoints on the situation here. We seem to have won the respect of Greek employers and most of the cabinet ministers with whom we have come in contact and we in turn have found them increasingly responsive to our suggestions and most cooperative in our relationships with them . . .

AMAG
November 23, 1947

DEAR MEYER:

. . . Things are going along very well as far as the Labor Division is concerned. I expect we are making more progress toward achieving the goals set for us than is any other division. But I am afraid it will not be of a lasting nature unless progress is made in several other directions as well. The military-civil war situation *is not* improving and I think the guerilla forces are stronger today than when we arrived. The winter weather in the north is severe and this may handicap them somewhat. But the number of refugees plus those who have been evacuated from their homes total now 350,000. They are trying to move the peasants from their homes in the country and in the smaller villages into the larger towns both for their own safety and to prevent forcible recruiting of the young men by the guerillas. But they do not have adequate shelter and accommodations for them and frequently not enough food, clothing and shoes. This also prevents the planting of fall crops and winter wheat and that will show up next year in diminished domestic food supplies. So permanent and substantial economic progress cannot be expected while the civil war continues and the social and economic life of the country is so disorganized and chaotic . . .

Now that we have the process of negotiating collective agreements under way and the idea increasingly accepted that the Unions and management have the responsibility for negotiating wages and salaries instead of having the government issue decrees establishing wage and salary standards, many groups are concerning themselves with wage negotiations. The railway men have completed their agreements and by joint conference and negotiation have distributed 10.2 billion drachma for the 10 month period ensuing from September 1, among the various wage and salary classifications. The principle of retroactive adjustments has been accepted at my urging. In the case of the railroad men, their adjustments agreed upon a week ago are retroactive from September 1. Their total overall average increase amounted to 19.2% and they are quite happy about it. So happy in fact, that the Missus, Olive and I must go to a dinner in Piraeus Tuesday night to celebrate their achievement. They have *adopted me* and refer to me as "their representative"! Unless you have partaken of Greek hospitability in *Greece*, you have no idea of what such a dinner really is! . . .

. . . the wage and salary adjustments of the civil servants, the workers and employees of private enterprises and the railway employees have been reached through conference and negotiation, the next in line for consideration are the employees of the Public Utilities and Banks. The idea of a Tripartite Committee such as the National Wage Policy Committee which made possible the collective agreements for privately owned and managed enterprises, has taken hold. Tsaldaris, the deputy Prime Minister, summoned me to a meeting with the Ministers of Communication, Transport, Finance, Public Works and Labor Thursday night and asked for advice about handling the wage adjustment problem for the public utility people. I suggested a tripartite committee with equal representation from the government, labor and industry. Old Helmis, the Finance Minister, loudly objected but he was over ruled by Tsaldaris and the others. The Committee was setup Friday and the first meeting held last night (Saturday) in the Board room of the Bank of Greece.

Aristedes Protopapadakis, the Minister of Labor, presided. He was flanked on his right by Gilmor and I with our Greek interpreter, John Litsas, in between us. The Union representatives of the Bank Employees and the Public Utilities were there as were representatives of the banks and the management of the utilities. I have never witnessed better decorum or more intelligent presentation of viewpoints. The management people presented charts with wage curves, nominators, denominators, co-efficients, conversion factors, etc., that would have delighted the heart of Joe Scanlon and all the professors. The workers had theirs too. Together they created such a rarified mathematical atmosphere that I nearly succombed. At one point Gilmor was certain that the Deputy Governor of the Bank of Greece (read Federal Reserve Bank) was representing the Union of Bank Employees!

Protopapadakis (I am told that his name literally translated means "son of the first little priest") is a fine young man from the island of Noxos. He is an engineer by training and now speaks pretty good English because of his associations with us and other English speaking people. He is certainly no slouch when it comes to mathematics either! In order to be a Minister here you must be first elected a member of Parliment. He has been re-elected five times but he is the first full time Minister of Labor that they have had and only since last June! He takes his job seriously and works at it intelligently. Politically, he is a Populist but he is very liberal in his outlook. He presided with a dignity that was easy, but most impressive. He is in his early forties and the youngest of the 21 Ministers. I am very much impressed with him and he and I have become warm friends. He is taking his job and responsibilities very seriously and is doing a good job particularly since he gets some encouragement and inspiration from Gilmor and I. I predict he will be one of the future important leaders of this country.

The usual statements from each side were made for the record. Not all the facts were available as to the probable need for tariff adjustments if the Union proposals were accepted. The participants agreed on the specific information they wanted and arrangements were made to secure it for consideration at a later session. The Deputy Governor of the Bank of Greece nearly floored us by stating that there had been an unfair distribution of wealth in the last decade, that the workers had suffered as a result, that new tax and other measures were needed to correct this imbalance, that the present wage and salary structure of bank employees needed overhauling and that the best way to do it was by the application of a cost of living index number that could, he hoped, be agreed upon. The Minister of Labor told me that he never expected to hear a Bank of Greece director talking in this manner.

It was a most interesting and hopeful development. Future meetings will be held and I am confident, agreement will be reached on the adjustments and terms of new collective agreements. . . .

AMAG
November 30, 1947

DEAR MEYER:

. . . I shall be particularly interested hearing about Jim Carey's visit to the WFTU [World Federation of Trade Unions]. The GC of L [Greek Confederation of Labor] would like to be affiliated with an International Labor organization as I think is true of the other European labor movements. But in view of their experiences with the commies, they just cannot see the desireability of being with the WFTU in view of the role which they think the commies play therein. After all, more than 135 of the more promising younger leaders of the Unions here were executed by the communists in the early days of liberation when the communists were in positions of authority. You can evidently subject the Greeks to a lot of abuse and pushing around, but when you *kill* one it is *never forgotten or forgiven.* And that is what makes the guerilla situation so terrible. Man is set again man, people are murdered and their relatives swear personal vengence and according to the "law of the mountains" which evidently cannot be repealed by legislation, the murderers must pay with their lives. Vengence must be had in a very personal sense . . .

I am keeping a bit too busy for comfort. The Banks and Public Utilities Wage Committee held daily (or rather nightly) sessions here for nearly a week. They would meet at 5:30 P.M. and never adjourned before 10:30 and on two nights continued until 5:00 A.M.! The banks situation had to be separated from the utilities and dealt with separately. Due to the lack of confidence in the currency, as I have indicated before, there are few bank deposits and savings. The banks are therefore unable to function as they normally would. We have "severance pay" with a vengence here. When anyone is discharged or layed off they have to pay them so much that they prefer to keep them. If an employee has a protracted illness they have to continue his salary. The employees who are drafted into the army only get the equivilant of 3¢ per day but their dependents receive their *full salary*. So the banks have a lot of ill employees and others in the armed forces which they must not only pay but must also engage others to do the work the regular employee would normally do. Because of all these and many other reasons, they claimed they could not agree to any increase in salaries without some new sources of revenue. So it was decided to have the Wage Committee petition the government to review the whole banking and currency situation and try to devise some means for making what they call a "provisional salary adjustment." There was general recognition and agreement as to the need—altho the extent was not agreed upon—but evidently not the resources to permit the adjustments.

On the utility employees, the committee was directed to make adjustments that a) would not be reflected in price and tariff increases; and b) that as far as possible, would embody the wage curve provided for in the collective agreements for private enterprise. This curve gave an average increase of from 25–30% for the workers in private enterprise. Applying it to the utilities it would have meant varing amounts ranging from about 65% for the tramway employees to 25% for others whose wage and salary rates were higher. Because the Unions of Bank and Public Utility Employees (there are only 26 of them!) follow the leadership of Fotis Makris, a Populist member of parliament who, in my judgment, is a jackass, and he in turn is a political antagonist of the other leaders of the G. C. of L., they must of course have *more* than the Followers of Patsantzis, Kalomiros, etc. (Something familiar about this it seems!) The management of the various companies whose tariffs of course are set by the State, contended they could not make *any* adjustments without a corresponding increase in rates, charges and tariffs. (That sounds familiar too!) Not being able to reach any unanimous agreement, it was finally decided to send a report to the Ministers who had created the Wage Committee and authorized it to act, stating that agreement could *not be reached* so the Committee recommended that the wage adjustment curve embodied the collective agreements for private enterprise be applied to the pre-war schedules of the utility employees. The Union representatives refused to sign this report. In effect the Committee has passed the buck back to the government with a recommendation for *a* wage and salary *increase* that is *not* acceptable to the Union and given the government the unpleasant task of either approving it and granting or denying the companies an increase in tariffs.

Other than the language difficulties, the problems of Union-Employer relationships, wage adjustments, etc., are pretty much the same as back home!

Now in addition to the problems I have described in this and previous letters, the *two* men and *a* lady who constitute the Labor Division are squarely in the middle of another set. These grow out of the very complex system of social insurance. First, we have what is translated as the "Institution for Social Insurance." This is a State organization and is concerned with Death benefits. Workmen's Compensation and Unemployment and Retirement insurance. Because the latter is meager, various homogenous industrial groups are permitted to form supplementary retirement insurance organizations. There are scores of these and one, the Seamens, has been in existence since 1826!

Both employers and workers contribute to these funds and the payments made to those eligible plus those from the ISI or "EKA" as the Greeks call it, total from 85% to 100% of their wages or salaries.

Up to the Metaxas dictatorship, some of the funds had built up tremendous reserve funds that enabled them to meet their obligations fully. But Metaxas needed money for other purposes. So he either "persuaded" the Trustees of these funds to "loan" the State their reserves or he "appropriated" their funds for other purposes. But in order to enable them presumably to meet their obligations, he authorized the levying of special or what is known as "third party taxes" or "contributions." To illustrate: There are many motor powered public conveyances such as busses and taxicabs here. They need tires for instance. They have to be imported. When they arrive there is a customs duty or tax which must be paid by the purchaser. He pays it but before he gets the tires, he must go to the Bank of Greece and make a "contribution" equal to some percentage of this customs tax, to the Public Conveyance Drivers Pension Fund! He gets some sort of a receipt and then returns to the customs house, surrenders it and gets his tires. There are hundreds of these "taxes" and no one apparently knows how much is collected and who actually gets the tax money or how it is used by those who do get it. Added together they must constitute a tremendous sum.

Enter AMAG's "public finance division experts." They are trying to balance the Greek budget, a quite impossible task at a swoop in my humble judgment. They seek new sources of revenue. Why not consolidate all tax revenue payments and channel them into the Minister of Finance. They have a bill prepared providing that all such payments must be so made and introduced into parliament. Nothing is said about this to the Labor Division. Then the labor people and God knows who else, descends upon me to protest against this. Why? They have not forgotten their experiences under the Metaxas dictatorship and they think the Minister of Finance (Helmis by name and a most unpopular character by the way) is the custodian of a bottomless pit known as the Greek treasury. If the social insurance "taxes" or "contributions" are channeled into Helmis coffers, the only way the various organizations can get them back into their own treasuries in order to meet their pension obligations is to "petition" Helmis to return them! And they are sure their petitions will all land in his spacious waste baskets. The communists and other demogogues pick this up as evidence of the unholy alliance between the "monarcho-fascist" government and the "American imperialists." Politician Makris picks it up to show the perfidy of his fellow officers in the Confederation of Labor and *I have a problem!*

Well what to do? The ILO has had a Mission here for several weeks studying the social insurance and labor legislation at the invitation of the government. They are preparing their report and recommendations. I propose that the social insurance taxes or "contributions" other than those made by *workers* and *employers* which by the way are *not* included in the proposed legislation, be exempted from coverage by this legislation. In the meantime, we await the report of the ILO Commission and send for a team of social security administrative and operational experts from the U.S. to come over and examine the situation separately with a view of improving and rationalizing the administration of the system. What will happen? I'll be damned if I know! But it illustrates what happens when Americans get into a foreign country without any background of experience and with a determination to "clean things up" and "show the foreigners how to run their affairs efficiently" . . .

To add to all the other activities during the past week, we had Thanksgiving and an unexpected visit from the British

Undersecretary of Labor, Sir Gildhuame Myrrdon-Evans. In true Greek fashion, this called for a round of luncheons, dinners, etc. The Greek Federation of Industries gave a luncheon for him at the Yacht Club in Piraeus on Friday. I was invited and by some section of the Book of Protocol was placed next to that fabulous successor to Sir Basil Zarahoff, the eminent "Greek from Turkey" industrialist and munitions maker Bodosaki. He is an amazing character but seemingly much less sinister than Zarahoff. Everything he touches seems to turn to money. He has extensive interests in textiles, chemicals, rubber, and among many other things, he told me he owned a shipyard in San Pedro, Cal.! He talks a little English and I asked him what he would do if the government decided to nationalize all his holdings. With an air of resignation and helplessness such as only the Greeks can express, he replied "Let them take them all. It will relieve me of all responsibility." Then after a pause and a seeming inspiration he added, "Anyhow, after two years they will sell them back to me at 25% of their value!" So here was a risk taking, free enterpriser that would delight the hearts of his American counterparts!

December 6, 1947
Personal

TO: THOMAS W. HOLLAND
Acting Chief
Division of International Labor,
Social and Health Affairs
Department of State

DEAR TOM:

. . . My experience here has impressed me with the importance of enlisting the active interest and practical assistance of the labor movement in international affairs. The need for this is especially urgent if the so-called "cold war" of ideologies is to continue as now seems likely. A more active concern on the part of the American labor movement about preserving and safeguarding human rights, individual freedoms and democratic institutions, in the remaining democratic countries would give great encouragement and inspiration to the leaders in those countries who share the same ideals and convictions. . . .

Now to some other matters while I am writing. I regret that I have not been able to send formal reports from time to time. The fact is, that we have been so handicapped by lack of available shorthand stenographic assistance, that most of the writing has to be done either in long hand and then given to a typist for copying, or doing it oneself. The Reports Section of the Mission, seems to be well staffed and their people attend every staff and committee meeting and circulate through the Division offices in search of material for their weekly, monthly and other reports. I have, under the circumstances, left the formal report writing to them. I have concerned myself with personally typing letters to Dave Morse, yourself and other friends chiefly in the labor movement. Because we have so much to do during regular working hours, these letters have to be taken care of on Saturday afternoons or Sundays as a rule.

The Labor Division has made more progress toward achieving the objectives outlined for it than has any other division. That is not stated as a boast, in any sense of the word. I think anyone here who is familiar with our work and that of the other divisions will agree with the statement. The psychological climate of the labor movement is more healthy than anytime since the beginning of the Metaxas dictatorship, more than a decade ago. The climate of relationship between the officers of the Confederation of Labor and those of the most influential employers organizations, is vastly improved. The first collective agreements covering wages in private enterprises which were freely negotiated but a month ago, have had a most encouraging and stimulating effect. New negotiations are started almost daily with new groups. The tripartite wage committee is being followed in the negotiations of the railway workers, bank employees, public utility workers, petroleum pool employees, seamen, dock workers, longshoremen and others.

To make progress in the labor field without corresponding progress in related fields, means that much has been achieved by the Labor division will sooner or later be nullified. Our people have not been able to show the Greek government how to control prices and the cost of living; how to keep up the flow of imports of raw and semi-finished materials upon which factory and production and employment depends; how to prevent speculation in the English gold sovereign or how to stabilize the currency; although at the moment there seems to be some new developments in this direction.

They have driven me nearly mad with their frantic efforts to balance the budget, something that has never been achieved in the entire history of the Greek Nation. In these efforts they have insisted on the discharge of 15,000 civil servants, reduction in pension allowances, elimination of funds for necessary public works projects here in Athens that gave useful employment to 1,000 workers. But there have not been expanding employment opportunities which could absorb these people. Up until a few days ago the total number of people employed by the Mission's American and Greek contractors amounted to 2,800 Greeks and slightly more than 300 Americans!

In my judgment the general military situation is much worse than when I arrived a little over three months ago. The economic situation is deteriorating daily. I think the morale of the Mission personnel is at the lowest ebb. The atmosphere of fear and uncertainty that engulfed the Greek people prior to our arrival and was dissipated temporarily by our presence and promise of improvement up until perhaps a month ago, is again enveloping them.

I try not to be an alarmist but I certainly cannot help but be concerned about the turn of events. I am not blaming anyone. Our lack of experience in this field and lack of preparation before entering it is the probable cause in large part, for the present situation.

Too many of our colleagues in my judgment, have assumed that the Greeks are sly, cunning creatures, hell bent on making fools of the Americans. They distrust them, do not try to understand them. In some instances they are downright arrogant and contemptuous in their attitudes toward them. I suppose the psychiatrists would say that this is evidence of their own lack of confidence in themselves. Whatever the explanation, much harm has been done and the task made more difficult.

The experience of Alan and I has been quite different. On the labor, employer and government front, we have treated the Greeks with the same respect we expect them to accord us. We have assumed they were honest patriotic and competent until actual experience proved otherwise. As a result, we have not been fooled; we have learned much and found them most responsible to our suggestions and eager to learn from us. Meeting and working with them as equals rather than inferiors, has enabled us to make the progress in our field that I think most people familiar with the situation will readily agree has been made.

Unless some way is found pretty quickly to improve the situation, I fear we are going to lose prestige and influence rapidly. . . .

On December 8, 1947, extraordinary sessions of the Greek parliament and cabinet approved a decree prohibiting strikes and providing for the court-martial of offenders and possible death sentences for strike leaders. At one blow, the Greek government had undercut the patient work of the labor division of the American Aid Mission. Golden and Strachan considered resigning in protest, but decided instead to make a fight for the repeal of the law. When efforts to secure a protest to the Greek government from the mission and American embassy failed, Golden wrote to AFL president Green and CIO president Murray to urge that they register their disapproval.* Green and Murray did so, backing up their statements with a visit to Secretary of State George C. Marshall. Such a move against workers was intolerable, they said, in a country receiving extensive aid from the United States. As a consequence of their protest, two cables were dispatched to Athens, "Considering all features, including vigorous reaction of American labor, we feel strong representations warranted to achieve substantial modification." The second declared: "We have heard Golden considering resigning over anti-strike law issue. His resignation at the time would be serious blow to AMAG prestige and future effectiveness. This particularly true in light of great confidence U.S. labor and industry have in Golden. Urge him strongly to remain at his post in order help assure essential American objectives in Greece."

On December 10, 1947, Golden wrote a long letter to Thomas H. Holland, Acting Chief of the Department of State's Division of International Labor, Health and Social Affairs, giving the background to the sudden introduction of the antistrike legislation:

DEAR TOM:

The developments here during the past week have no doubt been officially reported to the department, but I thought you

* Matthew Woll of the AFL fired off a protest immediately upon hearing of the antistrike legislation to Premier Sophoulis and to Clinton Golden and a message of support to John Patsantzis.

would be interested in an informal report about them. I have therefore undertaken to record as briefly as possible, the developments from about October 14 up to and including December 10, 1947 in so far as they are related to our efforts to assist the Greek Confederation of Labor in freeing itself from the extensive control of the government and the influence of political leaders.

We were making steady and very satisfactory progress until Makris refused to cooperate with his colleagues in the GSEE. He has caused a great deal of confusion, ill-will and hysteria as a result of his apparent determination to secure more immediate concessions for his particular followers. . . .

At this time I do not know what the reaction abroad has been to the anti strike legislation enacted on December 7th. It certainly put an end to the strike preparations here in Athens and appears to have pretty well deflated Makris and his ambitions. The executives of the twenty-seven unions involved have all handed in their resignations. They were duly elected (not appointed) officers. Twenty three of them could be classified as national reformists and the remaining four as moderate socialists. I am unable at present to predict who will be elected in their places. The communists are evidently attempting to capitalize on the situation and are trying to rally support for their candidates. My comments and observations follow:

When the first tripartite national wage policy committee was appointed following Prime Minister Sophoulis' speech on October 14, 1947, difficulty was experienced in securing agreement among the members to be selected to represent the Confederation on the Committee. Due to the factional differences within the Secretariat it was at first proposed that all five members of the Secretariat serve. This was objected to on the grounds that it made the Committee too large and unwieldy. Finally, Patsantzis and Kalomiros were selected to serve.

It became evident from the beginning that Makris was opposed to participation by representatives of the Confederation in the work of this committee. The Unions of Bank and Public Utility Employees who follow the lead of Makris and are affiliated with the Athens Labor Centre of which he is president, refused to permit this committee to deal with the wages and salaries of their members. This had the effect of limiting the work of the committee to establishing minimum rates for the workers in private enterprise only.

When the committee reached agreement on the establishment of minimum wage of 11,000 drachma daily for unskilled, adult common labor, with no increases in prices of manufactured goods or services rendered, Makris nearly upset the agreement by his insistence on a minimum wage of 13,000 drachma, regardless of the effect such a higher minimum might have upon the price situation. Only after much heated argument and the firm position taken by the Minister of Labor, Protopapadakis, did Makris relent and seemingly agree to go along. This was October 20.

The Committee had agreed and publicly announced that it would have its final recommendations for the minimum wages for various categories higher than those of common labor completed not later than November 5. In the meantime, Makris announced that a general strike in the Athens-Piraeus area for a higher scale of minimum wages would be called on November 5. The government, alarmed by this threat and evidently influenced by the return a few days earlier of Tsaldaris from the United States, invoked the Civil Mobilization Industrial Conscription Act already on the statue books and applied it over the protests of Protopapadakis, to the public utility employees but excepted from its coverage, the bank and tramway employees.

Had Makris been permitted to carry out his threat of a

general strike, it is unlikely that there would have been much of a response because of the generally favorable worker reaction and public approval of the collective agreements that were concluded on November 5. However, the Civil Mobilization Act was imposed and only the bank and tramway employees went on strike for a 24 hour period. In the meantime, according to news reports, Makris had a conference with Tsaldaris who evidently advised him that if his followers did *not* go on strike "their problems would receive special consideration." By this act or statement, Makris was rescued by Tsaldaris from an untenable leadership position and Tsaldaris' reported remark about "special consideration" was interpreted by Makris and his supporters as being an assurance that they would receive *better treatment* by the government than the private enterprise employees had received under the terms of the new collective agreements.

On November 11, in company with Simpson and Hampton, the American and British labor attaches, I visited Tsaldaris to point out the dangers to the whole economy's recovery program if Makris and his uncooperative followers were to be given *special consideration* by the government and this meant specifically if they were to be granted higher wage adjustments than those provided for in the collective agreements. I pointed out that this was in effect, rewarding Makris for the position he had taken and would not only largely nullify the good reactions to the collective agreements by encouraging further political factionalism in the Confederation but would cause the private enterprise employees and the civil servants to demand equal treatment by further raises to bring their wages and salaries into line with the higher levels that might be established by any such methods. Tsaldaris denounced Makris as an "ambitious, irresponsible seeker of power." He said that because of his ambitions and lust for power he had been unwilling to appoint him Minister of Labor but had instead, appointed Protopapadakis because the latter was a "sensible" person with engineering training. Tsaldaris was advised that Makris was evidently intent upon bringing about a repudiation of the collective agreements and this in turn, would cause a very unfavorable international reaction that might influence the possibility of further aid to Greece. Tsaldaris said he was going to have a conference with Makris and if he persisted in his announced course he "would arrest him" although [as] a member of Parliament he was immune from arrest.

While we were in conference with the Minister, but quite unknown to us, Protopapadakis had summoned Patsantzis, Makris and others to his office and persuaded Makris, to reverse his position and agree to approval of the collective agreements at a meeting to be held shortly after, of the Confederation of Labor Executive. It later developed that the meeting was held with Makris absent and the remaining 13 members of the Executive in attendence, unanimously approved the agreement.

The next step then was to find a means of dealing with the wage and salary demands of the Banks and Public Utility Unions (some 27 in number). By action of a committee of Ministers having responsibilities in this field, another tripartite committee was appointed with two labor representatives, one from the Bank employees and the other from the Public Utilities Unions, as members. This committee began its sessions on November 22. After several sessions, some of which lasted from 5:30 P.M. to as late as 5 A.M. and presided over by the Minister of Labor, it became clearly evident that the workers were intent on getting not less than the application of the collective agreement conversion factors applied to their wage and salary schedule, but in addition thereto, a flat increase of 30%. Granting of any such proposals would have meant not only a completely "out of line" increase of wages and salaries, but also a considerable increase in fares and tariffs. Even the application of the conversion factors alone would have given wage and salary increases ranging from 20% to 64%. Granting of their demand for a flat 30% additional would have meant total increases ranging from 70% to 150% for the Utility Company employees. This in turn would have resulted in an increase in fares and tariffs ranging from 40% to 80%.

Unable to reach a common agreement, the committee members with the Union members not participating, reported to the competent Ministers responsible for their appointment, that they could not agree but recommended that the Collective agreement conversion factors be applied to the wages and salaries of the Utility employees. The bank employees situation had been separated from consideration of the entire situation because of its pecularities and the government had been formally requested by the Committee to find some means of making a "provisional" adjustment pending review of the entire banking and currency situation.

At this point, Makris and his followers again threatened a strike, to be effective on December 8. On December 5, the Minister's Economic Policy Committee met and drafted a proposed "decision" authorizing the application of the collective agreement conversion factors and directing the experts of the competent ministries to further augment this on the basis of "increased quantitative and qualitative output" but with the smallest possible increase in rates and tariffs to result therefrom. A copy of this proposed decision was delivered to me about 10:30 A.M. on December 5. Geoffrey May, Special Assistant to the Chief of AMAG, called me at once on the phone and asked for advice, inasmuch as he was going to meet with the same ministers at 11 A.M. the same day. I briefly reviewed the whole matter and pointed out that as worded, the proposed "decision" would permit paying *up to* at least 30% above the minimums established in the free enterprise collective agreements. He said he could see this and it could not be permitted without incurring a great risk of inflationary effect. He hurriedly left, with Charles Coombs, of the Mission's Public Finance Division, for the meeting of the Ministers Economic Policy Committee.

On Saturday, December 6 (the day following) the regular weekly meeting of the Division chiefs with Governor Griswold [Dwight P. Griswold, former Republican governor of Nebraska, chief of the American Mission for Aid to Greece] was held. I reported on the entire situation and indicated my concern about the effect of the proposed "decision." Griswold remarked that there had been a meeting of the Ministers "yesterday" (Friday, the fifth) and they had agreed to "hold the line on wages." No other comment was made and reports of other division chiefs were given.

Just before the meeting recessed, my secretary called me out to say that the Minister of Labor was most anxious to talk to me at once. I immediately went to my office and found our liaison man, John Litsas, with the Minister of Labor, waiting for me with the Minister's car to take me to his office. This was at 12:30 P.M.

Upon arrival at his office, the Minister summoned his associates Pavlakis and Malatestos, and with Litsas and I present, he asked whether I had participated in the meeting with the Ministers on Friday at which time it was decided to call an extraordinary or emergency session of Parliament for the purpose of enacting "no strike legislation." I advised him I had *not* attended the meeting but knew about a meeting and then told him of the receipt of the proposed "decision," etc. He replied that he had not been informed of the meeting and had only heard of it at 11:00 P.M. the night before (December 4th). He was greatly exercised because he had not been advised of the meeting or consulted about its purpose and stated there was no need for any such additional legislation because there was already on the statutes the Compulsory Mobilization and a Compulsory Arbitration Acts that could be invoked and delay any contemplated strike for 40 days pending the arbitration decision and that such a decision would then remove any "moral justification and support" for strike.

He asked how I felt about it and I told him I agreed that it would be most unwise to enact such legislation under the circumstances; that it would be interpreted as indicating panic and hysteria on the part of the government and would play into the hands of the communist and anti-government propagandists in Greece and abroad by giving support to their repeated charges of denial of elementary freedoms and civil liberties to the Greeks and finally would nullify much of the favorable opinion that the collective agreements had developed in the democratic countries.

The Minister then stated that according to Greek parliamentary custom and procedure, the Ministers would meet in advance of the emergency session of Parliament called for 5 P.M., on Saturday the 7th, prepare the proposed legislation and then appear before Parliament where it would be subjected to limited debate and then enacted at the same session. Under the circumstances, he felt that in as much as he had not been called into consultation with his colleagues, their action amounted to lack of confidence in him and about the only course open to him was to submit his resignation. I urged him not to do this, but instead, to go to the meeting of Ministers and point out the dangers of the course they had charted and if he felt it necessary, to quote what I had said about it. He finally agreed that he owed a duty to his country and he would follow this course. He stated, however, that he had no hopes of convincing his associates that the legislation should not be introduced but he thought it might be possible to persuade them to limit its application only to essential public utilities and services such as hospitals etc., and this only on an emergency and temporary basis. He pointed out that no attempt had been made to utilize the existing laws, and in his opinion the Ministers had been remiss in their duties in not preparing to make use of existing laws and facilities in as much as they were fully aware of the possibility of Makris calling a strike. I offered, in the event he thought it would be helpful, to appear either before the Ministers or Parliament, or both, to support him in his efforts to prevent such legislation. He thanked me warmly for my support. I left him at 1:30 P.M. and came directly to my home.

We were invited to a neighbor's apartment at 11 P.M. There I found the Minister of Supply, Zahmis and his wife. Through an English speaking friend, he advised me that Protopapadakis had proceeded as he had stated he would before the Ministers; he had told them of his talk with me earlier in the day; that Tsaldaris had stated that the "Americans" had been consulted about the proposed legislation and indicated their approval; that debate was still going on in Parliament on the measure; that there were still some 25 speakers to be heard. He (Zahmis) left at midnight to return to the session. Zahmis stated that he feared the government had become panic stricken partly as a result of what was occurring in France and partly because of the fear of similar developments in Greece if a strike should occur.

Parliament continued in session until 6 A.M., on the 7th, enacting the anti-strike legislation and providing for severe penalties for either workers or employers who conspired to halt production for any reason. I have not seen a translation of the law but from what I can gather, it sounds like what we would call a "no-strike-no-lockout-law."

During Sunday the 7th, I heard from friendly English

speaking Greeks that Sophoulis had come out in support of the legislation on the ground that it was necessary to safeguard against alleged plans of the communists to extend the strike and develop a revolutionary situation similar to that which it is thought they are trying to develop in France.

On Monday, December 8th, I met Geoffrey May at my office immediately upon arrival. He stated that no mention of any such contemplated legislation had been made during the meeting he and Charles Coombs had had with Tsaldaris on the 5th. Because of the widespread practice of paying strikers for the time lost while on strike, that is prevalent here, May had suggested that this practice should be discontinued in the event the bank and tramway employees went on strike as threatened on the 8th. If a public announcement to this effect was made prior to the 8th it was thought it might have some deterring effect on them.

May and I discussed briefly what might be done to indicate that AMAG had no part in, or knowledge of, this legislation until it had been introduced, but we came to no immediate conclusions. About 10 A.M., May, A. L. Moffat, Smith Simpson who had come in to discuss the situation, and I left for the Embassy for a conference with Keeley and his staff.

There it was agreed that a statement should be prepared for Tsaldaris to issue designed to take the sharp edge off reports of the legislation and to assure that it would be limited in application to those industries and services that were essential to public security, health and safety and would not be used to interfere with social progress. Copy of the statement as agreed upon, is attached.

May and Minor of the Embassy staff went to see Tsaldaris at 11:30 A.M., who readily agreed to use the statement in a press conference later in the day. A translation of the statement given out by him to the press is also attached.

Since the Embassy report to you of the 9th indicating that the legislation was initiated either by Tsaldaris or Sophoulis, I have learned from confidential but reliable sources that actually it was Minister of Finance, Helmis who proposed it. The reasons given are interesting.

Our public finance people have been pressing Helmis to operate within budget limitations. In making up the budget, no provision was made for the payment of the customary Xmas bonus of an extra month's pay for civil servants. The payment of such a bonus is deeply rooted in Greek custom as is the payment of a half month at Easter. When the collective agreements for private industry were signed, the responsibility for paying these bonuses was assumed by the employers.

Altho Helmis had an observer present during the collective agreement negotiations, no protest against a continuation of the practice was made by him. After the agreements were signed, Helmis did protest, but too late of course. As Christmas approached, Helmis was hard put to meet the problem of paying the bonus to the civil servants and at the same time was running a deficit of some sort in the army budget. He therefore developed the idea of paying the civil servants a flat 100,000 drachma or about one-fourth of the regular bonus, requiring the private employers to pay their employees *two weeks* instead of one month's bonus and then have the latter turn in the two weeks *not paid to the employees plus equal amount* out of their treasuries, to the Ministry of Finance as a sort of special tax to help meet his budgetary deficits!

Helmis feared that if this was attempted, it would result in strikes. Therefore he proposed the anti-strike legislation to Tsaldaris. Tsaldaris felt they had to enlist the support of Sophoulis so the threat of a revolutionary situation growing out of a possible strike of the public utility and bank employees was raised and Sophoulis then agreed to support the legislation.

There will no doubt be other explanations offered but from what I have seen of Helmis and his operations, this does not seem too fantastic to me. At any rate, I hope this rather long recital of developments will be of some interest and use to you in evaluating the situation here. . . .

Golden's correspondence with Meyer Bernstein, Joseph Scanlon and others fills in the picture in more personal detail.

Golden included copies of his letter to Holland, a copy of the antistrike law and a draft of a statement by Tsaldaris with the first letter below.

December 12, 1947

DEAR MEYER:

This will probably reach you too late to be of much use to Phil in composing a statement. Thus far or six days later, the reaction among the workers here is not too bad. Some political capital is being made by the most vocal but least influential political opposition. Makris is threatening a strike of the printers as a challenge to the law. Whether this will actually come off I do not know. In the meantime the process of negotiating new agreements seems to continue. The Minister of Labor showed me two that had been filed with him this morning that were negotiated between the parties without any governmental or other intervention whatever.

Some or perhaps the most of the Greek political leaders seem to have a great capacity for doing the wrong thing at the right moment. It must be a streak of orientalism in their method of reasoning. . . .

Clinton S. Golden

December 14, 1947

To: JOSEPH SCANLON

DEAR JOE:

Things were going along almost too well here I guess as far as my work was concerned. We were way ahead of the other divisions in concrete achievements. The collective agreement idea was taking hold fine in spite of some problems with an unscruplous leader by the name of Makris who is a member of Parliament and president of the Athens Labor Center. He threatened to call a strike of the bank and public utility unions in order to get 30% more than anyone else was able to. So last Saturday without a word of warning to either I or the Minister of Labor, an emergency session of Parliament was called and a drastic "no-strike–no-lockout" law was passed after an all night session providing the death penalty to both employers or Union leaders who initiated any work stoppages. It was wholly unnecessary and entirely uncalled for. However it does not seem to have thus far affected the improving morale of the workers here. Both they and most of the employers are pretty indignant about it.

The civil war situation is getting worse and I suspect the Greeks are pretty jumpy. They were greatly upset by the news of what the commies were up to in France and apparently thought something of the same sort was being planned for here. I am more concerned about the interpretations that will be placed upon this fool act, by the papers in other countries. It seems to me they provided the commies with a lot of propaganda material which they can use to prove their contentions that this is a "monarcho-fascist" government. If there had been a boat leaving last Monday I should have been tempted to make my departure. But I have cooled off and will try to keep going. But it is awful discouraging to encounter such a wholly unexpected and unnecessary performance . . .

December 16, 1947
Personal

To: David A. Morse
Under Secretary
Department of Labor

Dear Dave:

Howard pressed me for some sort of "constructive suggestions." [John Howard, AMAG chief council, met with Golden on the 16th.] Without having had time to think through the problem, I advised him that if the law cannot be repealed, then it should at least be amended by striking out the death sentence provision. Next the Prime Minister ought to call in the GSEE officers and frankly admit the legislation was a mistake. Then he might propose to them that the law would not [be] invoked in any dispute until after a majority recommendation from a tripartite review committee. The committee to consist of equal representation of workers, employers and public members. I am not at all certain that this is a workable scheme. It might be of some value in trying to regain the confidence of the workers in the government. The present government is probably the best Greece has had since the liberation but that is not saying much. In many respects the Minister of Labor is the most competent member but I know that he intends to resign shortly from his post.

I am certain that my usefulness here is ended and no matter what the government decides to do, I feel that I should leave. There is no way in which I can rationalize their fool acts. I have made no mention of this to anyone other than Griswold in my memo, John Howard, to whom it was referred and Geoffrey May, the governor's assistant. . . .

Clinton S. Golden

December 26, 1947

To: DAVID A. MORSE

DEAR DAVE:

. . . You will recall that the anti-strike law or "resolution" as it is called here, was enacted by Parliament during the night of December 6th. On Monday, the 8th, Abbot Moffat, Geoffrey May, John Howard and I went to the Embassy to discuss the matter with Karl Rankin, the new Charge d'Affaires who had just arrived a few days previously. Simpson was of course with us and was considerably agitated about this measure. He felt that we should at once formally request the measure be repealed.

I felt, in view of a very earnest discussion I had had early the preceding Saturday afternoon with the Minister of Labor, Protopapadakis, that this was simply out of the question unless we were prepared to risk having the government fall. Under the circumstances, it then seemed best to take some immediate action directed toward softening the blow or taking the sharp edge off the measure. With this in mind, a statement was prepared for submission to Tsaldaris together with the suggestion that he make it public at a press conference, later in the day. I have previously sent you a copy of our draft of the statement and a translation of the statement he actually issued. The latter was not as explicit as we had suggested. I think it had some limited reassuring effect on the workers here in Athens, but apparently this was not true out in the provinces.

Evidently most people were so stunned by the suddenness of this action of the government that they did not fully realize the implications for a few days, thereafter. We had been endeavoring to get authorization for a wage adjustment for the metal working and repair mechanics in Salonika and Northern Greece that would be in line with the adjustments provided for in the collective agreements. Because some half dozen of these mechanics were employed in municipal operations such